GROUNDS FOR GOLF

ST. MARTIN'S PRESS ❧ NEW YORK

The History and Fundamentals of Golf Course Design

THOMAS DUNNE BOOKS

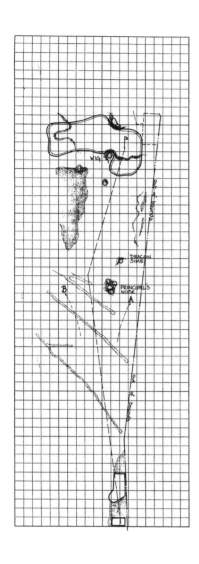

Grounds for Golf

GEOFF SHACKELFORD

THOMAS DUNNE BOOKS.
An imprint of St. Martin's Press.

GROUNDS FOR GOLF. Copyright © 2003 by Geoff Shackelford. All rights reserved. Printed in the United States
of America. No part of this book may be used or repro-
duced in any manner whatsoever without written per-
mission except in the case of brief quotations embodied
in critical articles or reviews. For information, address St.
Martin's Press, 175 Fifth Avenue, New York, N.Y. 10010.

www.stmartins.com

Library of Congress Cataloging-in-Publication Data

Shackelford, Geoff.
   Grounds for golf : the history and fundamentals of golf course design / Geoff
Shackelford.—1st ed.
      p. cm.
   ISBN 0-312-27808-X
   1. Golf courses—Design and construction—History. 2. Golf architects—History. I. Title.
GV975.S53 2003
796.352'06'8—dc21   2002034749

10 9 8 7 6 5 4 3

To Diane and Lynn Shackelford, who encouraged my interest in golf course design. And to George C. Thomas Jr. and Billy Bell for creating architecture that inspired further study into this fascinating art form.

Contents

Hole	Name	Par	Page	Handicap
Practice Tee	Introduction	xiii		
First	What Is Golf Architecture?	4	1	7
Second	The Spirit of St. Andrews	4	14	13
Third	Schools of Design	4	29	5
Fourth	Constantly Evolving	3	46	15
Fifth	Comic Relief	3	59	17
Sixth	Temptation	4	73	11
Seventh	The Great Holes	5	87	9
Eighth	Classic Designs	5	111	3
Ninth	The Architect	4	145	1
Out		**36**		
Tenth	Mind Games	5	172	4
Eleventh	Training and Daydreaming	4	186	8
Twelfth	Design Talk	4	200	12
Thirteenth	Understanding Maintenance	4	211	2
Fourteenth	Rustic Canyon	5	230	6
Fifteenth	Armchair Design	3	250	16
Sixteenth	Random Thoughts	4	258	18
Seventeenth	The Future	3	274	14
Eighteenth	Appendix and Acknowledgments	4	285	10
In		**36**		
Total		**72**		
Nineteenth	Index		293	

I believe in reverencing anything in the life of man which has the testimony of the ages as being unexcelled, whether it be literature, paintings, poetry, tombs—even a golf hole.

—C. B. MACDONALD

PRACTICE TEE

Introduction

Every golfer worthy of the name should have some acquaintance with the principles of golf course design, not only for the betterment of his game, but for his own selfish enjoyment. —*Bobby Jones*

Most golfers remember the 1996 Masters for Greg Norman's heart-breaking collapse on the back nine, resulting in the evaporation of a seven-stroke lead to eventual champion Nick Faldo. However, anyone with a passion for beauty, drama, the human spirit and the art of golf architecture witnessed the greatest gathering of these elements the modern game has seen.

The 1990s' two best players arrived at the final leg of Amen Corner, Augusta National's glorious short par-5 thirteenth. Faldo placed his drive in the fairway's center, while Norman hit a long but slightly way-ward ball that finished amidst the pine needles. When both players arrived at their ball, each talked to their caddies for several minutes, changed their club selection more than once and considered their options. All against the backdrop of blooming azaleas, towering pines, the shadowed fairway and millions of golf fans.

Watching Faldo switch clubs, television viewers assumed that he was debating whether to go for the green in two or lay up short of the creek. It turned out he had no concerns about reaching the green, but instead was trying to select the proper club, the right shape of shot, and the wisest line of play. Faldo was also waiting for Norman to play. The Australian had the honor and his shot might alter Faldo's approach.

Norman's predicament was even more remarkable. His ball sat on pine needles, the green within reach, and the lie acceptable enough that only a player of his caliber could believe that the shot to the green might be pulled off. His supposedly insurmountable lead spent, Norman wanted an eagle three to reinvigorate his game, even though a birdie four would have been serviceable. Norman grabbed the club needed to reach the green, but thanks to an aggressive CBS sound technician, viewers heard Norman's seasoned caddie, Tony Navarro, openly disagree with the selection. Norman's heart and soul probably told him that Navarro was right, but the temptation to play for the eagle three and send the crowd into a tizzy was just as compelling. Ultimately Navarro convinced Norman that a lay-up would still provide a chance at four, and more importantly, would likely eliminate a bogey six.

Defending Masters champion Ben Crenshaw was in Butler Cabin announcing for CBS. After those compelling moments between Faldo, Norman and Augusta's thirteenth had concluded, Crenshaw said: "I just can't get over the brilliance of this hole. Every year it just absolutely wrings you out with these decisions."

When it was over, both players made birdie but not until after they were teased, tortured and tempted by all of the options at hand. The architecture of Augusta's thirteenth conspired with the pressure of the Masters to provide the ultimate strategic battle.

It was golf architecture's finest hour. Every facet of the Augusta National design created tempting possibilities contrasted with prudent but less attractive alternatives. Surely the players encountered memories of past glories and failures. The drama was heightened by the tightly cut, sloping fairway lie for Faldo and the rustic clumps of pine needles that Norman faced. The angle, sizing and shaping of the green design added to the view the players faced. The fact there was so little water in the creek created one more thought: that if you hit it in there, you might still have a fighting chance to recover from one of the sandbars.

These are the elements of interesting golf course design. They are the features that make the grounds for golf so fascinating to study, discuss and savor. Golf architecture is the most interactive art form alive. Not only does golf course design reflect the simple, classic themes that all timeless art depends on, but course design is also vital to study if the golfer hopes to improve his or her game. As Bobby Jones said, knowing something about golf course design is important for every golfer's "own selfish enjoyment."

The world is a progressively realized community of interpretation.
—*Josiah Royce, late nineteenth-century philosopher*

Contrary to what they would like you to think, golf architects are not intense academicians holding superior intellect that only they and a few elite critics can relate to. Instead, like any successful artist, they base their work on sound principles and classic themes. If they employ talented people and display patience as they construct courses, their designs will display ingenuity and popularity with golfers over many years.

The variety of courses and design styles draw people to golf. Enthusiasts travel the world in search of fresh new layouts. Well-designed courses allow fine players to separate themselves from the rest of us. Yet, only a small percentage of the millions of golfers and fans of the game have been shown how interesting course design analysis and discussion can be.

Genuine appreciation and passion for any art begins when you pick up some bit of insight that opens your eyes in unimaginable ways. Knowing just a little something about what goes into creating a work of art, a building or an innovative product adds to our lives and encourages us to explore hobbies. Enjoying any art form is not a matter of who can bewilder us with the most intellectual nonsense about angles and lines and the neo-nonexistential sensibilities of the architect. The joy of golf design includes appreciating the beauty of an artfully designed hole, while having an eye to take in what the architect has presented. You learn to weed out the noise and use your analysis to outsmart your opponent. And most of the time, the toughest opponent is the design and how your mind processes its features.

Golf architecture thrives on the same fundamental elements of painting, music, baseball—basically any time-honored art form. Yet golf courses are much more interactive. Only in golf course design can we step back and find ourselves stimulated by the beauty of the painting—say the par-3 island green seventeenth at TPC Sawgrass—while also having the opportunity to leap inside the art to battle the artist, Pete Dye.

Golf architecture does not require an understanding of complex technical theories, scientific formulas or agronomy to be enjoyed. This may explain why anyone who has ever touched a golf club is an unofficial armchair architect. But other than some hard-to-find classics on the subject, few books have reached out to the layman who wants to learn the basics of course design while exploring the characters in the design profession, the lighter side of golf course design and the ways to use architecture to your playing advantage.

All you need is a passion for the game and an understanding of the basics and you'll be on your way. With just a little information you will begin to see any golf course in a new light. You will learn to spot the architect's deceptive ploys and even use them to your advantage. You will soon develop a constructively critical eye that allows you to see through a less than stellar design effort, while helping you gain a new appreciation for a course with lasting character.

Like developing a taste for fine wine, once you start you'll never be able to get enough of golf architecture. Studying the art of design also serves as a wonderful distraction for those who tend to obsess about their swing mechanics and find themselves watching late night reruns of *Golf Academy Live.*

In the vein of old-style course routing and design, in which architects followed the contours of the land, this book hopes to introduce you to the subject by heading down its own distinct path.

During the first few "holes," also known as chapters in most books, we'll start with the basics by asking, "What is a golf course?" Then we will take a fresh look at the home of golf, St. Andrews, and maybe even get to the bottom of that mysterious-looking Scottish links. How can such a peculiar ninety acres of bumps, roads and blind bunkers serve as the model for what a great course should aspire to be?

After warming up on these two relatively simple holes, you will be ready to tackle the various "schools" of design. This will help us break down each of the different eras and approaches to golf architecture. Developing an eye to identify the characteristics of each school will help you understand what an architect was trying to accomplish and how to read through some of their design ploys. Continuing with the schools, our next hole will follow up with a focus on the evolution of course design, allowing us to take a pain-free look at the history of golf architecture and its surprising influences.

Holes Five and Six describe two of the simplest and most important concepts that fuel sound course design in any era: the art of injecting comedy into golf architecture and the presentation of tempting shots. We all have encountered moments we should laugh at, and times when we should ignore our temptation to go for the green. Learning to spot these characteristics in design will make you a better player.

As the front nine works its way back to the clubhouse, you'll confront a couple of lengthy back-to-back par-5s. The first of our three-shotters looks at the greatest holes the game has ever known, followed by a study of four courses that are consistently labeled "great." Holes Seven and Eight will provide plenty of space to air it out, so feel free to take a breather in between each famous hole or classic course as you go.

The front nine finishes with a primer on what it means to be a golf architect and the different types of designers the profession has seen over the years. This is important not only in understanding what it takes to be a golf architect, but also why I admire the four talented architects featured. You've probably played a few of their courses or yearn to experience one of their designs some day. So besides appreciating their genius, you will know a little something about how to approach their courses or how to spot a genuine pontificator next time you attend a cocktail party full of armchair architects.

Our routing leaves behind those longer, challenging holes set amidst the pines and heads out to the shorter, quirkier holes that wind their way through sandy dunes. This is where you can improve your game and express your eye for design.

The Tenth Hole looks at the mind games architects tend to play, and offers ways to help you control those often annoying on-course thoughts. This is followed by an explanation of how you can sharpen your critical eye and maybe even imagine how you would redesign poor features. After all, Jack Nicklaus used to pass time between shots by wondering how he would redesign a hole. So design daydreaming can't be all that bad for your game, right?

Before we turn you loose as a designer, the Twelfth Hole will look at the delicate issue of making sure you are aware of certain terms. In particular, the focus here is on course design terminology, the bizarre names of modern layouts and other linguistic issues related to architecture. We follow that up with a pain-free glimpse at understanding maintenance that should improve your course management skills.

The Fourteenth Hole looks at a golf course project that was my first legitimate shot at learning about architecture both in the planning stages and "in the field." Hopefully you'll enjoy some of the stories and insights into the method of designing and building a modern day course.

Now that you have been armed with the history of design and the issues facing the architect both stylistically and technically, it will be your turn to experiment with what you've learned on paper. In the Fifteenth Hole, a few fictional hole sites are presented along with hints on how to best take advantage of them if you decided to try your own renditions.

Our final holes take a turn away from the dunes and back toward the clubhouse by posing random thoughts about the state of golf design and whether the art is serving the game as well as it should. Some minor preaching about various design styles, the influence of technology and the future of golf may occur. Finally, our last hole offers lists, sources and information on how to further your interest in golf architecture.

It is safe to say that no game in the whole realm of sport has been so mis-written and unwritten as golf. This is very strange, for probably there is no other game that is so canvassed and discussed by its followers. The reason may possibly be found in the fact that golfers are a most conservative class

of people, and that they follow wonderfully the line of thought laid down for
them by others. This at its best is uninteresting; at its worst most pernicious.
— *P. A. Vaille,* The Soul of Golf, *1912*

Regardless of your design philosophy or how this book influences your views, developing an eye for golf architecture will make you a wiser player. Better yet, it will heighten your appetite and love for the game. And if nothing else, a little more insight into design will make you, as Bobby Jones said, a golfer worthy of the name.

THE FIRST HOLE

What Is Golf Architecture?
The Fundamentals of Course Design

*A pleasurable golf course is not necessarily one that appeals at first sight,
but rather one that grows on the player like good music, good painting, or
good anything else. I also venture to suggest that a pleasurable course is
synonymous with a good one. No course can give lasting pleasure unless it
is a good test of golf. I also submit that no course can be really first rate
unless it appeals to all classes of players.*

—*Alister MacKenzie, golf architect*

If you fused the words of master architect Tom Simpson and golfing
great Bobby Jones, you might assume that golf courses are "infallible
tribunals" where we become the "dogged victims of inexorable fate."

Not exactly the most inviting or enchanting words to describe the
fascinating, sometimes magical landscapes where golf is played. Yet
Simpson and Jones did not intend to put golf courses in a negative
light. Nor were they complaining about the peculiar disasters that take
place on the links. They accepted that minor catastrophes came with
the territory and even celebrated the role of "inexorable fate." As with
many golfers, they learned that the most memorable on-course
moments are created by design elements, which only fueled their
desire to discover the fascinating complexities of golf architecture.

Golfers have always been attracted to the romance, humor and tragedy found on a golf course. Whether aware of it or not, they appreciate an architect's ability to create thought-provoking situations that foster dramatic moments. The most successful players accept that bizarre, sometimes unjust events take place on the golf course. They also know that golf courses are the most beautiful, enchanting and awe-inspiring venues in all of sport.

> *In golf we see in its profoundest aspect that profound problem of the relation of mind to matter. Nowhere in the sum-total of the activities of life is this puzzle presented to us in acuter shape than on the links.*
> —*Arnold Haultain*, The Mystery of Golf

Non-golfers often question why people pursue this sport with such passion. Is it, as most of them believe, merely to exercise or do business in a beautiful setting with friendly competition? Or is it "to shoot the lowest score," as one particularly self-important fellow recently insisted while disputing all other possibilities?

After all, golf may be the most difficult of recreational pursuits. And it certainly has become one of the most expensive. Yet like another demanding and expensive pastime, skiing, golf seems to addict participants despite a long list of potentially discouraging factors.

Skiing and golf share the same appealing qualities: the variety, beauty and character of their venues.

In skiing, no two runs are alike. The thrill of experiencing the obstacles of a new mountain creates genuine passion and vigorous discussion among ski buffs. The different types of runs provoke fervent debate over the merits of various mountains, and the strategic challenge of overcoming a tough run poses similar questions that other sports ask of their competitors. Skiers spend vast amounts of money on equipment and travel just to arrive at arctic, hard-to-reach locations. To non-skiers, their perseverance often seems silly no matter how crisp the mountain air may be.

The same peculiar passion applies to golf. Despite the cost and the effort required to play, golfers still find themselves addicted to the game. The variety of venues, and the interesting golfing situations they foster, encourages this devotion. How else can you explain the popularity of such a difficult, time-consuming sport?

No two golf courses are alike (although some rather unimaginative architects infringe on this notion from time to time!). Nearly every golf course has at least one hole worthy of discussion. And more than any ski run or other venues for sport, golf courses take on an individual character in the eyes of every player. The opportunity to experience new courses or to latch on to one that enamors your senses separates golf from all sports, including skiing.

Do people travel the world in search of fresh new bowling alleys? Or drive cross-country to experience newly resurfaced tennis courts?

The only other time sports and architecture are as closely inter-twined is in baseball. Fans of our national pastime love to study the quirky features of different ballparks. They passionately discuss the merits of various stadiums and how their home team should be built around the style of baseball their ballpark promotes. Still, you can only experience the baseball stadium as a spectator looking in. Your partici-pation is limited to standing in line for beer and a hot dog, catching the occasional foul ball or debating how a hitter can take advantage of the outfield dimensions. With a golf course, you can be both an interested observer and a fully engaged participant.

Some might argue that fishing and hunting provide a similar, but more exhilarating, experience than golf. Golf always has attracted those who swear by the merits of fishing and hunting, but few of us have ever fully understood why. Perhaps it's the golf courses them-selves. They provide the uncertain thrills and opportunities for success that hunting provides. Yet golf does it in a controlled environment, with an intricately conceived design that requires physical precision and mental control. A round of golf will always lead to a result of some sort, albeit usually not the result we hoped for. Nonetheless there is the chance to come away with something from every round of golf. And unlike hunting or fishing, when you hit a few great shots or post your first round under 90 or simply enjoyed the artistry of a beautiful design, you've done it without having killed a harmless animal.

Foxhunting: the unspeakable in full pursuit of the uneatable.

—*Oscar Wilde*

When you visit a museum and study a Claude Monet painting, it is just you and a security guard and fifteen other tourists trying to enjoy the painting. But say you get that rare moment alone with a masterpiece and you understand what the artist was trying to portray, there is still something that you are unable to experience. You cannot step into the garden Monet used for his painting and smell the flowers.

With a golf course you can enjoy the garden from afar and recount memories of playing the course years after you've left the grounds, because you were able to step into the landscape and experience its architecture. You were given the opportunity to tackle what the designer presented and study the design in different lights and varying conditions.

For the interactive side of golf course design to work the architect has to put forth hazards and greens that stir your mind to envision interesting shots. Or the designer must give the shrewd player a chance to outsmart his opponent by knowing, as Kenny Rogers wrote, "when to hold 'em and when to fold 'em." This is the tempting side of course design, also known as strategy. And no matter what the sport is, whether it's football, baseball, basketball, cricket or auto racing, the strategic side is what keeps us fascinated after we've come to appreciate the role of power and physical prowess.

In golf architecture, the player also gets to discuss the design with their peers. Before playing it, you can read something about how the layout was created. If you are lucky enough to have reliable golfing friends, then you can contest an affable match over this work of art. Afterwards, you can share a laugh over how you handled the do-or-die situations that fostered memorable, exciting on-course scenarios.

Some view a golf course as a piece of landscape architecture where creating a beautiful, mystical walk is the sole job of the architect. Any feature seemingly "unfair" or thought-provoking indicates design malpractice in the eyes of some. However, creating a beautiful environment, or better yet, preserving the existing one in an interesting way for golf, is just one of many design tasks.

Others view the work of a golf course designer as some sort of a highly technical confluence of behind-the-scenes associates working to create something so intricate that ten master's degrees and a truckload of blueprints are needed to understand the design. Thus, most golfers ignore their instinctual desire to learn about the design side of golf, and instead, focus on their swing mechanics and score. And we all know how dangerous that can be.

> *Excessive golfing dwarfs the intellect. Nor is this to be wondered at when*
> *we consider that the more fatuously vacant the mind is, the better for*
> *play. . . . Next to the idiotic, the dull unimaginative mind is the best for*
> *golf.* —Sir Walter Simpson, The Art of Golf, *1887*

Early Scottish golfers enjoyed the game for different reasons than most golfers do today. The Scots absorbed the nuances of their local golf course and enjoyed a friendly match. Swing analysis and posting scores came a distant second, if they were ever factors at all. Sure they worked to improve their games, but the spirit of earlier golfers allowed them to enjoy all facets of the game without ever taking their misfortunes too seriously.

The climate of early golf prompted players to debate other aspects besides the swing. Perhaps they did not have driving ranges where such swing surgery could take place on a daily basis. Or maybe the old golf publications provided a lighter take on course design and lore, elements of the game that are rarely covered in print today.

The modern game places an emphasis on handicaps, score and stifling swing mechanics. We all fight the urge to overdose on technicalities, as evidenced by the overwhelming popularity of Harvey Penick's simple, sweet instruction books.

The natural tendency of most golfers is to paralyze the mind with swing thoughts to overcome the architecture, as opposed to a "big picture" approach that places less pressure on the swing by emphasizing a more complete course management approach. Instead of visualizing shots and various scenarios for attacking the hole, the golfer envisions his left arm staying straight or keeping his swing "on plane" to overcome the challenges presented by the architect.

In short, a well-designed golf course is actually a simple thing to understand. With a little time and effort, the course will reveal its secrets if you are willing to listen.

In defense of modern golfers, many courses fail to provide enough opportunities for "strategic" decisions that ultimately affect the outcome of matches. This lack of strategy explains why some golfers become obsessed with older courses that reward thinking and local knowledge. And why some just never warm up to newer courses built to only be aesthetically pleasing. There is something special found in the "classic" courses built before the Great Depression. They were constructed slowly and carefully, with their features often shaped by hand. The architects worked diligently to conceive holes that would hold up over time. And their willingness to let the land dictate the golf created interesting playing situations.

Even the most apathetic designer will throw in a few interesting architectural touches, if nothing else by accident. Thus, understanding the elements of golf course design not only makes it enjoyable to analyze courses, but also can help your game. Studying golf courses also helps distract those who overanalyze the swing. More importantly, knowing a little something about design helps refine your management of a course, improves your ability to control negative thoughts and even helps you decide how to play shots based on the maintenance style of a course.

A good golf course makes you want to play so badly you hardly have time to change your shoes. —Ben Crenshaw, golfer and architect

Have you ever wondered what compels diehard golfers to travel the country and seek out new places to play, even if the courses are in remote lands? Or have you ever considered what causes them to bore you with the risk-reward intricacies of the latest Flynn and Toomey classic they just played?

The addiction usually starts after experiencing golf architecture that is unique. A golf course created by passionate architects with a genuine love for the game will always find a way to excite players. Certain layouts inspire golfers to discuss their design characteristics like a timeless novel or an exceptional film. Just as you are likely to track down the books of certain authors, the music of certain composers or wine of certain vintages, the more you learn about what goes into designing a course, the more likely you are to seek out the work of certain architects.

The fascination that some have with golf architecture has little to do with, as some believe, being able to say you played Pine Valley or Cypress Point. Yes, there are those folks in golf who do play these courses just to say they did and God bless them for finding enjoyment in being able to talk about their latest trip for the sake of letting you know they are well-connected and among our nation's social elite.

No golfer has ever been forced to say to himself with tears, "there are no more links to conquer." —*John Low,* Concerning Golf, *1903*

Before delving into some of the interesting design principles and courses, it is helpful to break a golf course down in basic terms. You may be surprised to learn as you read this book that the more you can simplify design elements, the better your chances are of managing your game, no matter your ability. Sure, architects throw in their share of subtle and intricate touches that require numerous rounds to figure out, but most golf architecture is simple. Here are the key elements that drive golf course design.

Routing

It is impossible in considering types of holes for a course to suggest any positive sequence of alignment, for each layout should be designed to fit the particular ground on which it lies . . . —*William Flynn, golf architect*

Routing describes the sequencing of the holes. It is the infrastructure to any golf course. Routing is the architect's way of creating variety and a mixture of looks. It is also how the architect initially takes advantage of the canvas he is given and is the most important step in the design process.

Some architects approach the routing like a writer who systematically takes a traditional three-act storytelling structure and applies it to any idea, regardless of characters who might add new dimensions to the story. In golf, the features of the ground are similar to unique characters, and the best architects work those fascinating characters in, even if it forces them to drift from what is perceived as a "normal" or "traditional" routing of a course.

Traditional to some people means that the architect has his trademark way of designing regardless of unique site features. Perhaps the architect likes to end his designs with a par-5, a par-3 and a long par-4, thus, the routing is driven by that principle. Or maybe the architect has to have both nines return to the clubhouse, or more commonly in modern design, he has been ordered to reach 7,000 yards from the back tees so the course is deemed one of "championship" quality. Such prerequisites affect how he routes the course and, ultimately, the character of the design. Often, quirks and nuances have to be ignored to achieve "traditional" expectations.

Such standards might explain why some courses feel forced, just as a film would seem dull because the screenwriter was paid to reach a set number of pages instead of simply telling a story at the best possible pace. And we all have seen the effect on a sports team when a coach is forced to insert a high-paid player because his stats and legacy are dramatic, when we all sense there is another player on the bench who does "the little things" that help the team win. The team ultimately suffers.

The best routings show hints that an architect decided to take a few chances, to use the features that others might not have thought of using. Something about the way the designer fits the sequence of holes together feels good, as if you don't quite know what to expect from hole to hole, but you can't wait to see what is next. And like a great album of music, the routing builds until you reach the climactic finish.

Par

That simple number, 4, is part of what fools many players. Par-4 theoretically means a tee shot, an approach, and two putts; therefore "reaching in regulation" requires being on the green with your second shot. That's what par-4 signifies to the golfer who isn't thinking.

—Robert Brown, The Way of Golf

Par may have more influence on a golfer's mental well-being than any trick an architect could produce. Coping with this sensitive issue comes later in The Tenth Hole, Mind Games. First, however, there is the question of what exactly par is and why it is so perplexing.

Several golf writers took the art of describing and analyzing the game to another level. Bernard Darwin, Herbert Warren Wind, Henry Longhurst, Peter Dobereiner, Dan Jenkins and Charles Price all managed to bring a unique perspective to golf. Price's account of par is still the best description ever presented on this mysterious topic:

> What is par? What does the word stand for? Those may seem curious questions to ask, for par is one of the very first words we come upon when we learn to speak in the vocabulary peculiar to golf.
>
> But what is par, exactly? You can be above it, below it, up to it, under it, or over it. But nobody ever got next to par. You can shoot it, break it, save it, waste it, make it, add or subtract it. On the other hand, you can't mend it, spend it, or undo it, and nobody ever multiplies or divides par. Tell somebody on the golf course you are under par and he will envy you. Tell somebody off the golf course you are under par and he will feel sorry for you. Is it any wonder that golf is the game where the lowest score is the best score?
>
> Although there are a lot of things you can do with par, there are also a lot of things you can't do with it, among which is understand it. You need only try to explain the word to someone who doesn't play golf to find yourself stumbling over thoughts you had long taken for granted. It's not unlike trying to explain sex to a ten-year-old. You don't know where to begin. And once you have begun you wish you knew how to stop.
>
> Par comes from the Latin of the same spelling, meaning "one that is equal." With that in mind, try explaining to a non-golfer that a five on one hole is just as good as a four on another, or a three on still another.
>
> Worse still, try to explain that par for a hole is determined primarily

by its length. That's why the one-hundred-twenty-yard seventh hole at Pebble Beach is only a par-three. Then why is the two-hundred-twenty-yard fifth hole at Pine Valley also a par-three? It should be pointed out, though, that the configuration of the ground can play a part in determining par. If a hole goes downhill, for example, it will play shorter and easier. If it goes uphill, it will play longer and harder. The one-hundred-twenty-yard seventh hole at Pebble Beach, to illustrate, goes downhill, whereas the two-hundred-twenty-yard fifth at Pine Valley goes uphill. That's why they are both par threes. You understand?

Par for each hole is determined by a length and severity nobody pays any attention to. By adding these pars together, you arrive at a par for the course that is actually meaningless. The real, honest-to-God par is the course's numerical rating, which more often than not works out to be some score that is patently impossible to play; nobody ever played a course in 75.6 for example. To add insult to injury, all these falsehoods are printed on a scorecard that you are supposed to regard as gospel. If you don't believe so, make a mistake on one during a tournament and see what happens.

There is no easy answer to what par is, and as Price explains so beautifully, it is meaningless and yet all-powerful in determining how golfers manage or view a hole.

Length

The merit of any hole is not judged by its length but rather by its interest and its variety as elective play is apparent. It isn't how far but how good!
—A. W. Tillinghast, golf architect

Similar to par, length is overrated in golf architecture. Just as the size of a meal indicates little about the quality of the food, the mandate to reach 7,000 yards strips some of the most interesting short holes from an architect's repertoire. To attain what are considered normal or standard lengths, architects are forced to ignore interesting natural holes and simply plow through features to reach certain distances. The result is no different than if a baseball manager stocked his lineup with long-ball hitters. There would be no one around to set the table, to get on base and distract the pitcher. You need variety in all pursuits, and golf course design is no different.

Long holes do pose interesting challenges and are part of the designer's palette. But length and the actual yardage of a hole are mere components of design. As architect C. B. Macdonald wrote, "No real lover of golf with artistic understanding would undertake to measure the quality or fascination of a golf hole by a yard-stick, any more than a critic of poetry would attempt to measure the supreme sentiment expressed in a poem by the same method. One can understand the meter, but one cannot measure the soul expressed. It is absolutely inconceivable."

Strategy

If the average golfer considers the points of strategy which have been worked out in advance for a properly designed hole, he will undoubtedly improve his game in his play of such a problem.
—George C. Thomas Jr., golf architect

Strategy is the element of thought in golf. It is the designer's way of asking the player to figure out the best way to the hole, and then allowing that player room to take their chosen route. If the architect has done his job, the avenue to the hole that leads to a lower scoring possibility should be more dangerous than the longer, safer route. Otherwise, without having to take a risk, there is little decision-making required and, thus, no strategy.

Strategy is the soul of any great activity. In golf, strategy has more possibilities than in most other sports. Some of golf's strategic interest, as in baseball, has to do with amount of time you have to consider your options. In auto racing or basketball, strategic decisions are split-second matters and thus less interesting for players and fans. Whereas in golf, you have time between the tee shot and approaching your ball, or while waiting for the group in front to clear the green before deciding whether to play over the water and at the hole.

Also, design strategy is dictated by other elements such as your opponent, the weather, the condition of the course or something as simple as your mood. Having some consciousness of design strategy and the risks involved with certain decisions will immediately make you a wiser player. But the basis for interesting strategic situations comes from the foundation laid by the architect.

Hazards

Most golfers have an entirely erroneous view in regard to the real object of hazards. The majority of them simply look upon hazards as a means of punishing a bad shot, when their real object is to make the game interesting. —*Alister MacKenzie, golf architect*

While the land is the architect's canvas, hazards are his paints. Bunkers, water, "waste" areas, ground contours, trees, boundaries and all other assorted golf course features foster interesting designs. The manner in which the architect uses his hazards determines how the design is both perceived and enjoyed.

Many golfers view any hazard in the direct line of play as unfair, but for the architect to eliminate such hazards is a recipe for dull design. Wise golfers are able to acknowledge the hazards before them, then do their best to maneuver around or over the hazards. The less-than-wise golfer curses the architect when they hit their shot into a hazard. But if the obstacle is visible and room to play around the hazard is provided, whose fault is it that a ball ended up in trouble?

The look and placement of hazards determines the architect's style. Some designers like their hazards clean and simple, while others try to make them fit the natural landscape. Some architects only place hazards to the sides of play to catch wayward shots, while some subscribe to the strategic school of thought by placing hazards in locations that force the golfer to maneuver their way around the course. And some architects place their designs around the existing natural features like trees or old stone walls, even if the use of such features seems peculiar at first sight.

Greens

. . . greens to a golf course are what the face is to a portrait.
—C. B. Macdonald, golf architect

The putting surface is the final tool the architect has to inject each hole with individuality. Both the green and hazard placement have to work together or else the hole will not function.

Greens are like fingerprints in that no two are alike, and interesting green design will always provide golf architects the opportunity for original design ideas. Size, shape and contouring have limitless possibilities, though at times the modern architect has found himself restricted by the emphasis on small, fast greens. The slicker the surfaces are going to get, the less opportunity the designer has to create interesting contour because no one has the time or desire to play a course with unputtable greens. Also, fewer hole locations are possible when small greens reach certain speeds, forcing a domino effect that leads to less interesting golf. Many of the best strategic holes are dictated by fascinating "pin placement" possibilities, so when these areas are lost due to green speeds and the strategy no longer works, the design becomes less interesting.

What is more engaging than to see how golf infuriates some big brute who can thrash anybody, ride bucking horses, shoot deer on the run and birds on the wing! What is so delectable as to see him in a nervous tremor as he stands on the tee, glaring fiercely at that still, white, little ball! How the game torments the adventurous soul . . .
—H. N. Wethered and Tom Simpson,
The Architectural Side of Golf, *1927*

The aforementioned elements produce the basics that every golfer sees when assessing the character of a golf course. Refining your awareness of design, particularly the style of the architecture, can also make a difference in the outcome of a round or match. And perhaps, enjoying architectural features will ease just some of the torment that golf inflicts on the adventurous soul.

The Second Hole

The Spirit of St. Andrews

Why the Old Course Is Still the Most Enduring Design of All

St. Andrews? I feel like I'm back visiting an old grandmother. She's crotchety and eccentric but also elegant. Anyone who doesn't fall in love with her has no imagination.
—*Tony Lema, 1964 British Open winner at St. Andrews*

To further understand how architecture became such an important part of the game, discussion must turn to St. Andrews, Scotland, where the first authentic course began to evolve over five hundred years ago.

Not only is it remarkable that the Old Course is still around, but it remains the world's most relevant design classroom. St. Andrews continues to host the British Open every five years and remains the course all budding architects or aficionados must study. No other sport can claim such a tie to its past, and how many forms of architecture have an easily accessible, several-hundred-year-old model to study at all times?

. . . golf at its best is a perpetual adventure, that it consists in investing not in gilt-edged securities but in comparatively speculative stock; that it ought to be a risky business.
—*Bernard Darwin, author*

The Old Course at St. Andrews elicits a response from every golfer upon first sight. Many are enamored with the bumpy linksland and the

"Grey Auld Toon" looming ominously over the eighteenth hole. Some, usually American tourists fresh from experiencing links golf for the first time, often question what all the Old Course hype is about. And some first-time visitors are like Sam Snead, who refused to believe it was even a golf course while on the train ride into town.

The grass was all scroggly and the greens looked like they weren't maintained, and the bunkers looked like they had never been raked. And I asked the gentleman sitting across from me, 'What old abandoned golf course is that?' And the gentleman took off his hat and stood up with a horrified look on his face and said, "I'll have you know that's the Royal and Ancient Golf Club of St. Andrews!"

—Sam Snead, after seeing the Old Course on his way to play the 1946 British Open

Snead went on to win the British Open a week later, and like so many others, became an admirer of the Old Course. Although he couldn't resist one more wry observation: "Until you play it, St. Andrews looks like the sort of real estate you couldn't give away."

What is so appealing about this ninety acres of quirky contours, waterways called burns, double greens, celebrity bunkers and road holes? How does the first golf course in the world continue to be held up as the best model for golf course design, despite having no significant elevation change or trees? Is it nostalgia that keeps the Old Course in the British Open rotation and atop the list of favorites among architecture die hards? Or does it remain golf's ultimate natural experience and the world's most enjoyable and complete test of golf?

Every golf course in the world owes something to the Old Course for, either by accident or design, it embodies every feature and architectural trick.

—Peter Dobereiner, author

The Old Course did not have an original designer arrive for a groundbreaking photo session, wave his arms, pose for a few staged shots with the owner, declare it the best work of his career, and then head off to the next project.

Instead, the holes evolved naturally over several hundred years with only an occasional assistance from man. The game was played at St. Andrews as early as 1362 and evolved into a recreational pastime during the mid to late 1400s when Dutch sailors would dock offshore, then use crudely crafted sticks to belt pebbles as they made the trek into town amidst the heather, whins and dunes. Counting their "strokes" as they went, scores became too hard to keep track of, so they cut holes at several points along their course, allowing them to keep a hole-by-hole tally on the way in and out of town.

Besides the Dutch sailors, the St. Andrews townspeople also took to the game. Competitive matches and even wagers were made; however it was all done rather quietly since golf was not officially recognized until a royal ban forbidding the sport was lifted in 1552. Naturally, the Scots do not prefer to hear this version of the Old Course's evolution because credit is given to the Dutch sailors. So should you be invited for a wee nip at the Royal and Ancient clubhouse, you'd be wise not to bring up the Dutch sailor story.

From the outset, St. Andrews was a twenty-two-hole course, starting up the hill behind the fabled Royal and Ancient clubhouse site and meandering down into the seaside flats amidst narrow corridors lined by dense gorse and rolling linksland. The course was soon viewed as too narrow and unsafe. It was also taking too long to play and maintenance became impossible because players were crowding the same gorse lined "trails" going out and back in. So the first major change took place in 1764 when the St. Andrews links was shortened to eighteen holes, a total which became the standard for most future golf courses.

By the mid-1800s St. Andrews began to take on the look we see today. Many of the putting surfaces were expanded to "double greens" in 1832, creating enough space to comfortably fit two holes per green. This way, players would not have to fight over the same hole on the shared putting surfaces. In 1848, local clubmaker and course "overseer" Allan Robertson created the famed "Road hole" green along with the most significant fairway and green expansion efforts yet. This work, along with the creation of a ten-hole course that later became part of Carnoustie, made Robertson the world's first golf course architect.

Thanks in part to another twenty-five pound investment in course improvements, the winter of 1856–57 saw even more upgrades to the links at St. Andrews. Greenkeeper Robertson used the financial windfall from the Royal and Ancient Golf Club to remove gorse and heather. The loss of heavy shrubbery revealed even more of those tempestuous contours that amaze any St. Andrews visitor, whether they are a novice golfer or a seasoned student of course design.

Robertson also rebuilt some of the bunker edges that failed due to weather and heavy play. Most of all, he devoted his energy to creating smoother putting surfaces. The rough greens had been so shaggy that it was impossible to detect where fairway began and ended. Improving the greens increased play and solidified the popularity of golf at St. Andrews. And soon, throughout Scotland.

It is also believed that some of the Old Course's 112 bunkers formed naturally when sheep would burrow into the dunes for protection during inclement weather. Architect and writer Robert Hunter stated that some of the Old Course bunkers may have been formed by collections of divots in areas that were once popular resting places for tee shots. Over time, the wind and elements whipped them into sand pits.

The unique bunker evolution, coupled with the porous soil and the rabbit-mown fescue turf, created firm conditions that define "links-style" golf. However the rabbits were later removed as part of the grounds crew after numerous battles within the township over what to do with the lovable bunnies. Ultimately, the rabbits multiplied too rapidly and interfered with the golf.

Old Tom is the most remote point to which we can carry back out genealogical inquiries into the golfing style, so that we may virtually accept him as the common golfing ancestor who has stamped the features of his style most distinctly on his descendants. —Horace Hutchison, author

Six years after Robertson's death in 1859, protégé Old Tom Morris took on the job of "Custodian of the Links." This marked Old Tom's triumphant return to St. Andrews after spending twelve years at Scotland's "other" significant links, Prestwick.

Morris had left his hometown in 1850 after a split with Robertson.

Both were making a fine living creating "featheries," those bean bag–like balls that were hand-stitched together and filled with feathers. Their flight patterns were rarely consistent but making featheries proved to be a lucrative business for Robertson. However, one day at St. Andrews, Old Tom was playing the back nine and he ran out of featheries. His curiosity got the best of him, and he played the new cutting edge gutta percha ball on his way in. Supposedly, Old Tom had picked up several guttas in the gorse while he was searching for his own featherie. But it was a no-no for a featherie maker to show any interest in the new, easier to manufacture gutta.

Guess who happened to be playing the front nine that day, and, as is so easily the case at St. Andrews with the nines running parallel, ran into Old Tom playing the inward nine with a gutta percha ball? You guessed it: Old Tom's friend and business partner, Allan Robertson.

Needless to say the two argued over the issue. Robertson could not fathom the idea of playing the gutta both from a financial standpoint, as well as the effect he felt it would have on golf courses. Old Tom believed the gutta made golf more enjoyable by rewarding sound ball striking more consistently than the unpredictable featherie. The gutta incident caused their partnership to end and Old Tom eventually left town in 1850 for the twelve-year stint at Prestwick. He molded that fine links into the course we know today while also refining his own game and his knowledge of green-keeping. He also started designing other courses on the side and managed to pick up British Open titles in 1864 and 1867.

Old Tom Morris, photograph taken by A. W. Tillinghast in 1898. (RALPH W. MILLER GOLF LIBRARY)

When Old Tom Morris returned to St. Andrews in 1864, he made several improvements to the

Old Course, ensuring his impact would be just as significant as Robertson's. However, even as popular and shrewd as he was, Old Tom dealt with some dicey political flare-ups in spite of his title as the "Custodian of the Links." By 1878, Old Tom had been scolded by the "Links" committee for taking too much initiative in creating two new greens, including the world famous eighteenth with its sunken "Valley of Sin" guarding the left front side.

However, not since a small pot bunker was covered over in 1949 has the Old Course design been significantly altered. Substantial length was added in the late 1990s on virtually every hole to ensure that the playing strategy remained undiminished in the face of improved technology and stronger players. The course and its bunkers are much more "groomed" these days and a bit more sterile than in the past thanks to the capabilities of modern machinery. Meanwhile players like Jack Nicklaus fear that equipment has finally rendered the course obsolete for the British Open, but no one is talking about changing it. Not yet anyway.

The fascinating green contours at St. Andrews. (LYNN SHACKELFORD)

The eighteenth green at St. Andrews with the "Valley of Sin" in front. The surrounding village looms like an old movie set. (GEOFF SHACKELFORD)

For most golfers, the spirit and subtlety of the Old Course remains virtually unchanged. Decision-making and the local knowledge required to master the course will always maintain its design integrity. Then again, if 350-yard drives become the norm, the only decisions for players will be whether to drive certain greens or lay up a few yards short. It would be a tragedy should the Old Course find itself rendered uninteresting after so many years of setting a brilliant example of strategic architecture interesting for all to play.

Still you ask, how does a peculiar-looking layout with 112 randomly placed bunkers, shared fairways, seven double greens and numerous blind shots reward championship-caliber golf? Is the successful player at St. Andrews merely the least unlucky golfer who knows the course best? And how is it fun or fair to the average player who cannot see where he is going and who is unable to carry many of the bunkers that would allow him to reach greens in regulation?

Commentators frequently remark that luck or "rub of the green" plays an especially significant role at St. Andrews. I disagree. If a "good straight drive up the middle" finds a "nasty hidden little pot bunker," then clearly the drive shouldn't have been aimed toward the middle of the fairway. This puzzles some people, but golf would surely be a monotonous game if the center of the fairway was always the optimum line, and at St. Andrews it usually isn't. I believe one of the Old Course's greatest qualities is its capacity to sift good shots from those that have been poorly conceived.
—Nick Faldo, British Open champion at St. Andrews

The Old Course requires boundless creativity, local insights and adapting to the ever-changing wind if the player hopes to be successful. However, no matter how bizarre the conditions get, the option to attack each hole from multiple angles makes St. Andrews fun for all golfers. As Alister MacKenzie once wrote, an old man who can barely advance his ball is still able to maneuver his way around, while the course still punishes the sloppy long hitter for careless play. It's no different than the old, weak-armed major league pitcher who can still "hit his spots" and strike out hitters while a wild, hard-throwing young gun scratches his head in Triple-A ball wondering why he's not in the big leagues.

The width of the Old Course and the bunker placement makes a round at St. Andrews a constant decision-making test for the elite player. No other layout requires as much thought or shotmaking skill, a distinctive and tricky combination that is prevalent in very few modern golf courses. But that combination of rewarding sound thought and only the most precise execution explains why the greatest champions in the game revere the Old Course.

Adapting to the constantly changing conditions and cruel bounces has always been the biggest obstacle to success at St. Andrews. Either the player accepts the difficulties or he does not. As five-time British Open winner Tom Watson says of the Old Course, "You've got to relish the challenge rather than fight the challenge."

The ability to relish the challenge separates certain players from the rest. The great ones delight in overcoming the trouble, while others are irritated by those dilemmas.

The notion of relishing what is presented before us on any golf course separates every golfer's best rounds or moments of glory from the days when things turned ugly. We all know of those rare days where our mind is not deterred by obstacles, where we relish the challenge. And we have all experienced many more days when the simplest of things seem to get in our way.

The list of Old Course Open champions reveals that most of golf's great champions have been up to the task of sorting out the bad breaks and the difficult decisions. Jack Nicklaus has two Open victories at St. Andrews and says it is his favorite place in the golfing world. Bobby Jones, who won the 1926 British Open and the 1930 British Amateur there, said he would choose to play the Old Course every day if limited to only one. Jones later patterned Augusta National's design concept on the complexities of the Old Course.

Unlike many of his fellow modern professionals, Tiger Woods developed a fascination with the Old Course after just a few rounds. Woods cites St. Andrews's room for shotmaking creativity and the need for adapting to changing conditions as an ideal test of golf. He relishes the challenges presented, which is probably why he won the 2000 British Open Championship there.

The Old Course wasn't planned, it evolved. So you're not matching wits against some architect. It's nature you're taking on there, and that's what's fascinating about it.
—Peter Thomson, five-time British Open champion

Tiger and observers such as Peter Thomson have referred to the genius of the St. Andrews design, and like so many wonders of the world, it is the work of Mother Nature. Timeless course designs utilize natural features above all else, with the Old Course presenting *the* ultimate case study in naturalness. Sure, the Old Course evolved with man's help, but the architects who have designed classic courses understand that over time, natural features create interesting golf and the most original sequences of holes. And no matter how quirky some natural features may seem, golfers accept those oddities because they were there long before golf was introduced to the site.

If such odd features were placed there by an architect, it becomes a different story.

Consider how the Old Course "rolls with the punches" and earns its distinctive qualities from a totally original and not particularly text-book sequencing of holes. The opener starts immediately below the two-hundred-year-old clubhouse and provides an excellent starter because it plays to one of the widest fairways in golf, with out of bounds down the right side and only a road named "Granny Clark's Wynd" bisecting play. The large first green is perched on the bank of "Swilcan Burn," and this is the only time water comes into play at St. Andrews. There is out-of-bounds down the right side that keeps long players honest, but otherwise, plenty of room lets you get started relatively pain free.

In terms of model architecture, things get peculiar after the starter. Not many architects could get away with designing six straight holes heading northwest, as numbers two through seven do. Even more unconventional is that those six holes have numerous blind bunkers,

PLAN OF THE LINKS

THE OLD COURSE

The "out and back" routing of the Old Course at St. Andrews. (GIL HANSE)

out-of-bounds to the right on each and quirky contours in the landing areas. Yet each hole has its own subtle strategy and character.

After the relatively normal forced carry par-3 eighth, two drivable par-4s at numbers nine and ten await. They are at the farthest point from the clubhouse and each can be driven depending on the wind. The much-copied par-3 eleventh then crosses, yes, crosses back over the par-4 seventh fairway where the two holes share a green perched above the Eden River Bay. From there in, holes twelve through seventeen play in a virtual straight line toward the southeast direction. And like the front nine, each has out-of-bounds down the right side.

At the 461-yard par-4 seventeenth, the players face many temptations and potential disasters on the infamous "Road" hole, where the tee shot must carry a wooden shed and play to a slender green perched precariously above an old road. The course makes a final left turn with the 354-yard, bunkerless and wide open par-4 eighteenth. As a finishing hole on any other course it would be a letdown. However, playing against the backdrop of medieval buildings to a green guarded by the "Valley of Sin," the "Home" hole may be the greatest stage in all of golf.

The "High" hole, the par-3 eleventh on the Old Course. Though it looks rather simple, the "High" or "Eden" has been used as the basis for many modern par-3 designs, including the fourth at Augusta National. (LYNN SHACKELFORD)

Yet, first-time golfers still come away feeling uncomfortable praising the course or even acknowledging they would want to play it again. Much of their disappointment comes from modern architecture's ability to create a "wow" factor the first time we play a course, with very little in the way of subtle features that make repeat rounds just as exciting as your first round. Thus it's difficult to absorb the complexities of St. Andrews the first, second or even tenth time around.

> *I do not get cross anymore when young golfers claim they detest the place. I just feel sorry they are so ignorant and unappreciative of what they have inherited—but I am sure most of these, as they grow older, learn to understand that golf is a dull game when every hole plays the same way every day. At St. Andrews you never know what to expect.*
> *—Henry Cotton, three-time British Open champion*

Ed Furgol said there was nothing wrong with St. Andrews "that one-hundred bulldozers couldn't put right. The Old Course needs a dry clean and press."

American Tour professional Scott Hoch called it the "worst piece of mess I've ever seen."

As Henry Cotton and others point out, however, the unexpected is where St. Andrews refuses to give in to the predictability of contemporary design or reveal itself to antagonistic golfers such as Furgol and Hoch. Again, it is the unpredictability and irregularity of the place that champions not only learn to adapt to, but come to adore. Such volatility in the day-to-day possibilities rewards their talent to adapt and to create heroic shots. This also makes playing the course repeatedly an exciting *adventure* each time out. And isn't a sense of adventure what we all hope for in our courses?

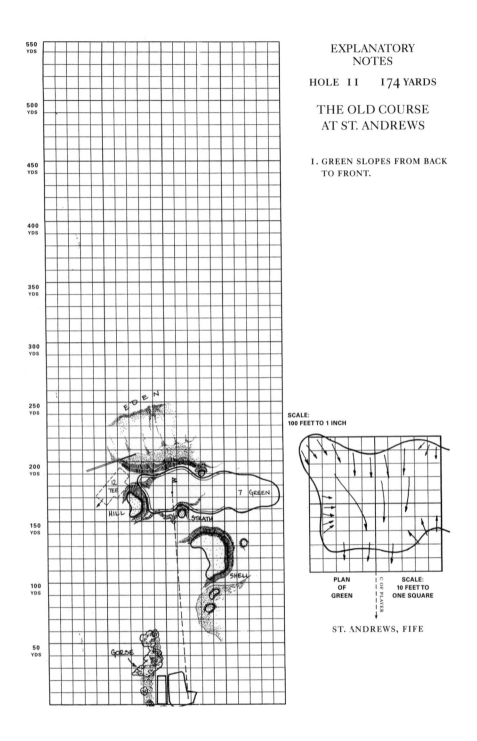

Rendering of the par-3 eleventh on the Old Course at St. Andrews. (GIL HANSE)

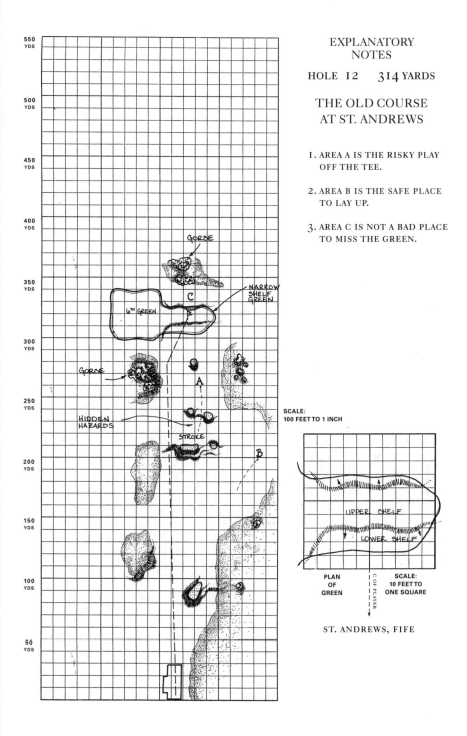

EXPLANATORY
NOTES

HOLE 12   314 YARDS

THE OLD COURSE
AT ST. ANDREWS

1. AREA A IS THE RISKY PLAY
   OFF THE TEE.

2. AREA B IS THE SAFE PLACE
   TO LAY UP.

3. AREA C IS NOT A BAD PLACE
   TO MISS THE GREEN.

GORSE

NARROW
SHELF
GREEN

C

6TH GREEN

GORSE

HIDDEN
HAZARDS

A

STROKE

B

SCALE:
100 FEET TO 1 INCH

UPPER SHELF

LOWER SHELF

PLAN
OF
GREEN

C OF PLAYER

SCALE:
10 FEET TO
ONE SQUARE

ST. ANDREWS, FIFE

Rendering of the par-4 twelfth on the Old Course. (GIL HANSE)

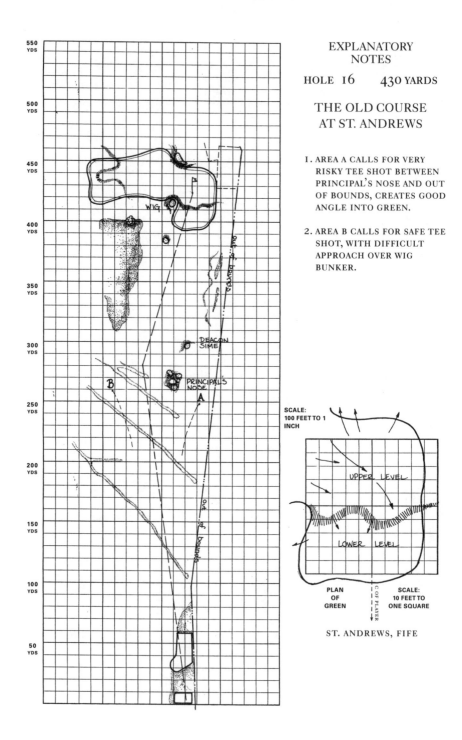

EXPLANATORY
NOTES

HOLE 16   430 YARDS

THE OLD COURSE
AT ST. ANDREWS

1. AREA A CALLS FOR VERY
RISKY TEE SHOT BETWEEN
PRINCIPAL'S NOSE AND OUT
OF BOUNDS, CREATES GOOD
ANGLE INTO GREEN.

2. AREA B CALLS FOR SAFE TEE
SHOT, WITH DIFFICULT
APPROACH OVER WIG
BUNKER.

SCALE:
100 FEET TO 1
INCH

UPPER LEVEL

LOWER LEVEL

PLAN
OF
GREEN

C OF PLAYER

SCALE:
10 FEET TO
ONE SQUARE

ST. ANDREWS, FIFE

Rendering of the par-4 sixteenth on the Old Course. (GIL HANSE)

The Third Hole

Schools of Design

Different Approaches to Golf Architecture

A golf course is something as mysterious as St. Andrews, as majestic as Pine Valley, as ferocious as Oakmont, as subtle as Hoylake, as commonplace as Happy Knoll.   —*Charles Price*, Golfer at Large, *1982*

Institutions devoted to the training of golf architects have never existed, thus the phrase "schools of design" can be misleading. Like the various movements in art, music, architecture and sports, golf course design has witnessed distinctive stylistic eras influenced by a range of elements, from cultural calamities to basic changes in the way golf is played. The Great Depression, World Wars, shifts in maintenance practices, economic booms and the popularity of professional golf have all influenced how architects design.

If you are a fan of our national pastime you know that baseball stadium design has known a variety styles, all influenced by the era those ballparks were constructed in. The early, often quirky parks were built on low budgets and incorporated existing site features into the outfield boundaries. These were the ultimate *natural* ballparks.

Then there was the post-war school of larger, cleaner parks such as Dodger Stadium, which maintains a certain straightforward charm today. However, many of its features influenced the 1970s boom of "multipurpose" artificial surface stadiums where designers made a great effort to eliminate the defining quirks of the older parks and never shied away from exposing plenty of concrete. Worse, the fan's ability to see and enjoy the game was forgotten in the design process.

Today, we are witnessing somewhat of a "retro" movement in stadium design, though the results have varied in capturing the character of the classic parks. The two greatest success stories are Camden Yards in Baltimore and Pac Bell Park in San Francisco. In each case the parks successfully incorporate existing features, lending immediate character. Camden has the old railway building in right field, Pac Bell the San Francisco Bay within easy reach of a Barry Bonds home run.

Just like with a modern golf course, forcing these oddities instead of incorporating existing features will ultimately fail to lend genuine character. That is why so many of the new ballparks have never quite matched the character and passion felt for a Crosley Field in Cincinnati or a Polo Grounds in New York.

> *Give me daytime ball at Wrigley Field. And let me have one of those classical old venues at* 6,300 *yard where they didn't move any earth around and where they didn't have to build in ungainly water hazards. I want a baseball diamond with real grass, and a golf course with greens the character of Ebbets Field.*
>
> —*Bradley Klein,* Rough Meditations, *1997*

Why is it necessary and of interest to know something about the schools of golf course design? For starters, a basic understanding of the different approaches provides a historical perspective that will add to your interest in golf design. Knowing the schools will enrich your understanding of what has motivated architects to design holes the way they did. More importantly, a general awareness of the design school you are dealing with will help you plan and manage your game better. The most overlooked fundamental to successful course management is the ability to detect and sort out simple design ploys, particularly if those ploys were masterminded by the most cunning architect of all, Mother Nature.

The Natural School

*I believe the real reason St. Andrews's Old Course is infinitely superior to
anything else is owing to the fact that it was constructed when no one knew
anything about the subject at all . . . what a pity it is that the natural
advantages of many seaside courses have been neutralized by bad
designing and construction work.*   *—Alister MacKenzie, golf architect*

For many golfers, the ultimate school of design was based on the
least amount of effort and interference from man. The driving force
behind the earliest design school was established on a simple notion:
complete naturalness. So natural are some holes, that in many cases
this school gave birth to great holes by accident. Like the old ballparks,
they were not trying to conform to any steadfast rules, so holes were
built on whatever land was available, with whatever hazards were
already present.

The "natural" school evolved during the mid-seventeenth century
at St. Andrews and at its immediate Scottish descendants, places such
as Prestwick, Crail and other early Scottish links. These layouts sub-
scribed to few formulas. There was no set par that Old Tom Morris
searched for when he was paid one pound to lay out a course, and he
did not pursue a predetermined yardage goal or even a set number of
holes. Prestwick was a twelve-hole course for some time and St.
Andrews a twenty-two-hole affair. These layouts were created by
selecting sites that seemed logical for golf (and useless for farming
because the sea had rendered the soil infertile). Once the routing was
settled on by Old Tom or Willie Park or Allan Robertson, areas for play
were cleared of their native shrubbery. This process exposed contours
and sand pits where spongy, rabbit-mown turf was established to create instant links golf.

When the lure of these early seaside courses became apparent,
other Scottish towns wanted similar grounds for golf, with only site-
driven deviations from the basic situations found at St. Andrews. Eighteen holes eventually became commonplace and total par was
narrowed to range from 69 to 73. However many other towns with less
accommodating sites settled for total pars in the mid-sixties. The land

dictated the golf and no one seemed to mind as long as they could play the sport.

Whether intentional or not, the early "designers" were bona fide minimalists. They worked around what nature left behind. They never considered making major changes to the ground in order to accommodate golf. Instead, the golf worked around all features, even man-made elements such as walls, roads and ruins, just like the golf did at St. Andrews.

Until 1948, there was nothing to separate the eighteenth fairway on the Old Course from the town of St. Andrews, meaning those old town shops were "in-bounds." Recovery shots were frequently played from the doorsteps of the various stores and hotels lining the famous "Home" hole. Though unusual, such natural and unencumbered play added to the charm of early golf. The freedom for recovery shots and absence of boundaries lent an adventurous spirit to the game, which explains why the Scots took to golf with such passion.

As Old Tom Morris curtailed his design activities around the turn of the twentieth century, a new wave of golf professionals came along and took on the more complicated role of "player-architect." Unlike Old Tom, who had absorbed the quirky charms of the Old Course and who did not believe in leaving his handprint on the landscapes of Scotland, this new wave of professional golfers sought to influence the land they were asked to design on. They sought to make the game "fair" by eliminating dunes that obstructed views or by refusing to incorporate unique elements such as roads, walls or boundary fences. They also sought to place hazards where they saw fit, instead of using existing natural pits or sand blowouts.

New designs started showing up on inland terrains where the canvas contained fewer interesting features than on linksland. Architects began to fancy themselves as innovators. Their inland design efforts marked a major shift to the first man-made attempts at inflicting penalties on the golfer.

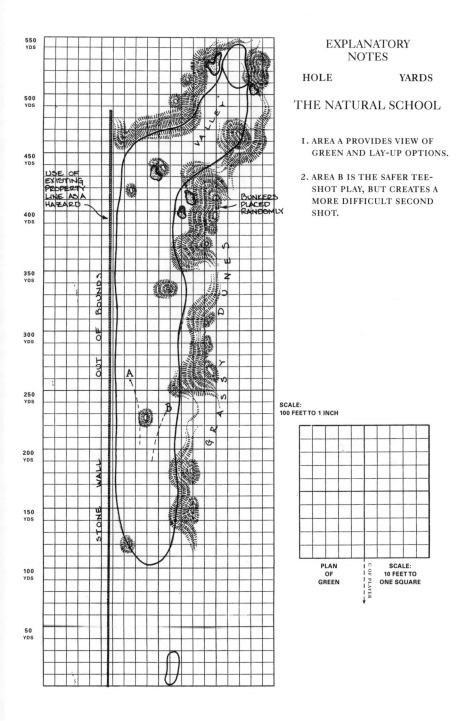

EXPLANATORY
NOTES

HOLE   YARDS

THE NATURAL SCHOOL

1. AREA A PROVIDES VIEW OF
   GREEN AND LAY-UP OPTIONS.

2. AREA B IS THE SAFER TEE-
   SHOT PLAY, BUT CREATES A
   MORE DIFFICULT SECOND
   SHOT.

SCALE:
100 FEET TO 1 INCH

PLAN | SCALE:
OF | 10 FEET TO
GREEN | ONE SQUARE

C OF PLAYER

USE OF EXISTING PROPERTY LINE AS A HAZARD

BUNKERS PLACED RANDOMLY

VALLEY

GRASSY DUNES

OUT OF BOUNDS

STONE WALL

A

B

550 YDS
500 YDS
450 YDS
400 YDS
350 YDS
300 YDS
250 YDS
200 YDS
150 YDS
100 YDS
50 YDS

Rendering of a par-5, the "natural" school of design. (GIL HANSE)

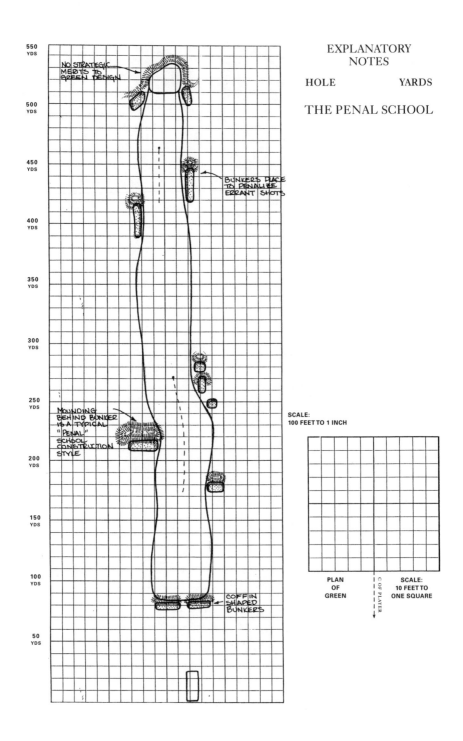

Rendering of a par-5, the "penal" school of design. (GIL HANSE)

The Penal School

There are some hazards, though, that cannot really be correctly described as entirely fair in their character. . . . With all deference to the opinions of others who have made a study of the game, my opinion is that due care should be exercised in seeing that each hole is placed well clear of obstacles, and the hazards should only be calculated to catch and punish a player who, after playing a bad or a faulty stroke, deserves to meet such a fate.
—*J. H. Taylor, professional golfer*

The primary goal of "penal" school architects was to shift hazards away from the centerlines of holes, and place them to the sides of fairways so that the straight player would be rewarded. Bunkers, they reasoned, had to be plainly visible and out of the way of straight hitters. Many of the architects driving this shift in design reasoned that the uncertain nature of links golf needed to be minimized if the sport was to grow in the new century. The designers of this novel wave of "fair" courses declared that their ideas were less primitive and more refined than the previous generation.

Besides stripping the natural and sometimes unpredictable sporting elements out of golf, these early touring professionals also introduced a "novel" approach to the artistry and appearance of courses: geometric design. Inspired by the Victorian tastes of the era, coffin-shaped bunkers, triangular mounds, defined sets of bunkers and other geometric features became "the new thing" in golf as early as the 1870s. These geometric and penal design themes prospered around the turn of the century and until World War I, when all construction halted.

When Scottish and English golf professionals moved to the United States during golf's early twentieth-century expansion, they brought the same geometric and penal principles to new design in America. Eventually, golfers grew tired of the penal nature of the courses and their unnatural appearance.

Viewing the monstrosities created on many modern golf courses which are a travesty on Nature, no golfer can but shudder for the soul of golf. It would

seem that in this striving after 'novelty and innovation,' many builders of golf courses believe they are elevating the game. But what a sad contemplation! The very soul of golf shrieks!
—*C. B. Macdonald, on early American "penal" designs*

The soul of golf shrieked upon first glimpse of some of these penal courses, so much so that they inspired men like Macdonald, H.S. Colt, Alister MacKenzie and Donald Ross to quickly usher in the most popular design school, the strategic.

The Strategic School

There is no necessity for artificial barriers. Play does not have to be systematically controlled. An opposite principle is involved. This principle is freedom. And by freedom we compel the golfer to control himself, that is to say, his instincts. If he judges his skill is great enough, he will of his own accord go for a strategic hazard to gain an advantage just as the tennis player will go for the sidelines of the court. —*Max Behr, golf architect*

Besides the penal school's lack of desire to retain any sense of naturalness, the absence of interesting *thought* required to play these penal courses did not sit well with a group of golfers who had developed their games studying the natural school layouts. Each of these fine golfers had experienced the Old Course at St. Andrews and absorbed its ability to charm longtime players after numerous rounds. They sought to figure out how the Old Course retained its repeat playing interest and realized that St. Andrews consistently charmed golfers because it was *different* every day. These fine players and students of design became conscious of St. Andrews's ability to reward the calculating, patient golfer who could also carry out a variety of shots. It became apparent that the Old Course was the ultimate *strategic* design, with its architectural character worth emulating on all designs.

The demand on both cerebral and physical skill became the goal of strategic design school architects, and as a philosophy, it differed radically from the penal mentality that attempted to emphasize only down-the-middle ball striking. The mental side of penal design tends

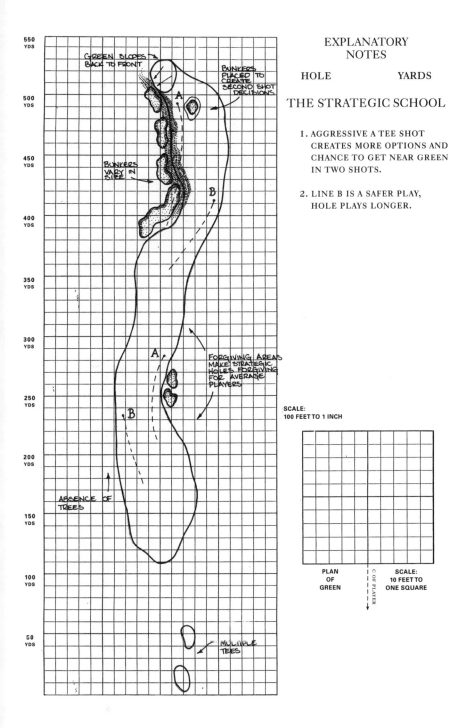

HOLE   YARDS

THE STRATEGIC SCHOOL

1. AGGRESSIVE A TEE SHOT
   CREATES MORE OPTIONS AND
   CHANCE TO GET NEAR GREEN
   IN TWO SHOTS.

2. LINE B IS A SAFER PLAY,
   HOLE PLAYS LONGER.

550 YDS
500 YDS
450 YDS
400 YDS
350 YDS
300 YDS
250 YDS
200 YDS
150 YDS
100 YDS
50 YDS

GREEN SLOPES BACK TO FRONT

BUNKERS PLACED TO CREATE SECOND SHOT DECISIONS

A

BUNKERS VARY IN SIZE

B

A

FORGIVING AREAS MAKE STRATEGIC HOLES FORGIVING FOR AVERAGE PLAYERS

B

ABSENCE OF TREES

MULTIPLE TEES

SCALE:
100 FEET TO 1 INCH

PLAN		SCALE:
OF	C OF PLAYER	10 FEET TO
GREEN		ONE SQUARE

Rendering of a par-5, the "strategic" school of design. (GIL HANSE)

to reward those who can endure the most torture, with little or no opportunity to outsmart the architect. (We see this kind of torture test annually in the U.S. Open, where the player who can hold up the best to physical torment and pressure wins, not always the best strategist, shotmaker and most complete golfer.)

In the strategic school of thought the architect's goal is to present options for the player to debate, ultimately rewarding the more daring play carried out with skill. The penalties in strategic design are more subtle for the less courageous or poorly planned attack, which is why strategic designs are more fun and playable for golfers of all levels.

The subtle penalty on a strategic hole might mean that a safe tee shot played short of a bunker leads to a longer way to the cup or perhaps leaves the player an obstructed view of the flag. By contrast, the penal school hopes to not leave room for such subtle or interesting possibilities. Either the player hits the ball straight to achieve success, or does not and pays a price.

Two English architects spearheaded the strategic school of thought during the early twentieth century: H.S. Colt and Alister MacKenzie. In America, Chicago native Charles Blair Macdonald and Scottish golf professional Donald Ross shifted the American game to this strategic approach during the post-World War I years. All four of these pioneering designers influenced other aspiring architects, spreading the strategic school with an emphasis on natural-looking designs that provoked thought and, ultimately, proved the most fun to play over time. Their design efforts inspired the careers of architects A.W. Tillinghast, Seth Raynor, George Thomas, William Flynn, Perry Maxwell, William Langford, Tom Simpson, Stanley Thompson, Willie Watson and many others.

When 1920s golfers realized the joys of playing a natural looking, strategically designed course, the architects were given more freedom to take the strategic possibilities to new levels. And as golfers saw the genuine beauty that stemmed from golf courses constructed with an emphasis on naturalness versus the crude geometric style, the strategic school thrived until the Great Depression all but ended the Bobby Jones–inspired golf boom.

Though strategy has remained a component of some design, it

reached its zenith from 1910 to 1937. Robert Trent Jones and a few other architects then arrived and introduced a new perspective based on old ideas and a few new ones.

The Heroic School

Saw a course you'd really like, Trent. On the first tee you drop the ball over your shoulder. —*Jimmy Demaret, three-time Masters champion*

Robert Trent Jones became the first architect to set out with the goal of making golf design a lifelong career. During the mid-1930s he laid out his own curriculum at Cornell, became acquainted with architects such as Alister MacKenzie and ultimately studied under Canadian master designer Stanley Thompson. Trent Jones spent several years with Thompson before starting his own firm in the late 1930s. However, business was slow until the end of World War II when a new course boom occurred during the 1940s and '50s. A marketing specialist who fostered the term "signature design," Trent Jones sought ways to separate himself from the architects of the previous generation, while still making it clear he believed in certain timeless design principles that they practiced.

So instead of calling himself a member of the strategic school, Jones created the concept of the "heroic" hole, which combined the best principles of strategic design with the dramatic hazards found in the penal school. In other words, he believed in holes that required dramatic, heart-stopping decisions with grave consequences for miscues. The concept was exciting in the way it utilized the basics of strategy, and was enough of a shift from the previous generation to help Jones's career by making him appear to be a novel, fresh designer. However, Jones only built a handful of truly heroic holes, and they are among the world's most talked about and popular to play. Unfortunately, the majority of the holes he designed fall much closer to the penal school.

Architect Dick Wilson, a protégé of Shinnecock Hills designer William Flynn, was another prolific architect from the 1960s and '70s who created designs similar to the work of Jones. He also successfully

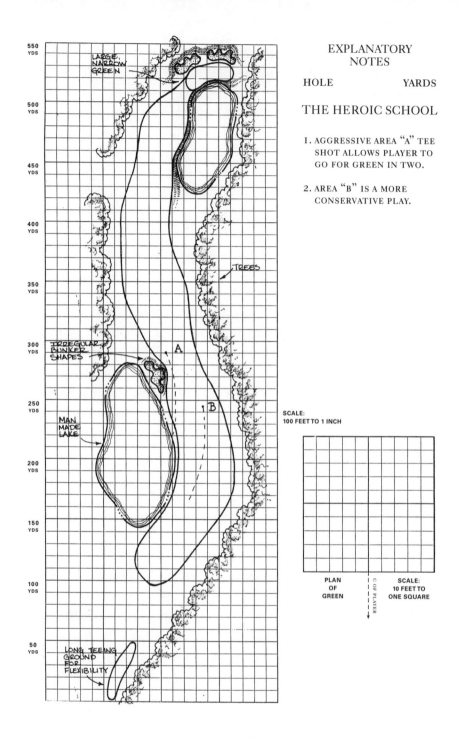

Rendering of a par-5, the "heroic" school of design. (GIL HANSE)

blended the penal and strategic schools. Both designers used large, flashy bunkers with cloverleaf shapes. Neither architect was afraid to create man-made lakes, something rarely done to that point in golf architecture.

The Freeway School

Freeway design is more concerned about visual balance and symmetry than strategy. . . . Although a freeway hole is more equitable to all golfers than either the heroic or penal designs, it is also very unimaginative, requires little thought to play, and is not very inspiring of great golf.
—*Michael Hurdzan, golf architect*

This school was labeled by Dr. Hurdzan in his book, *Golf Course Architecture*. It describes many of the lifeless designs created from the late 1950s to the early 1980s. Even as the sport celebrated a time with arguably the strongest group of players competing at once (Palmer, Nicklaus, Player, Trevino, Watson, Weiskopf, Miller, Floyd, Kite, Crenshaw, etc.), standards for course design slipped. There was little interest in the subject and few architects in any field were motivated to maintain past standards or elevate their profession to new levels. In other words, courses were constructed a bit like freeways, with no real thought given to character, just a concern for basic function.

Pete Dye came along during the freeway era, and alarmed some with his wild, linksland-inspired designs. To many, his work was extreme with its use of certain elements, but fans of all architecture are grateful to Dye for igniting a resurgence of thought-provoking and original architecture that later motivated a generation of contemporary architects such as Bill Coore and Tom Doak. Dye's work also renewed interest in the classic design of Scotland and the work of the certain early American architects that had long been unappreciated. In particular, three of Dye's favorites: Seth Raynor, Charles Banks and William Langford.

Dye's influence is difficult to classify in any particular design school, but instead will be appreciated for its singular influence in the face of the many forgettable "freeways." And as controversial as he was

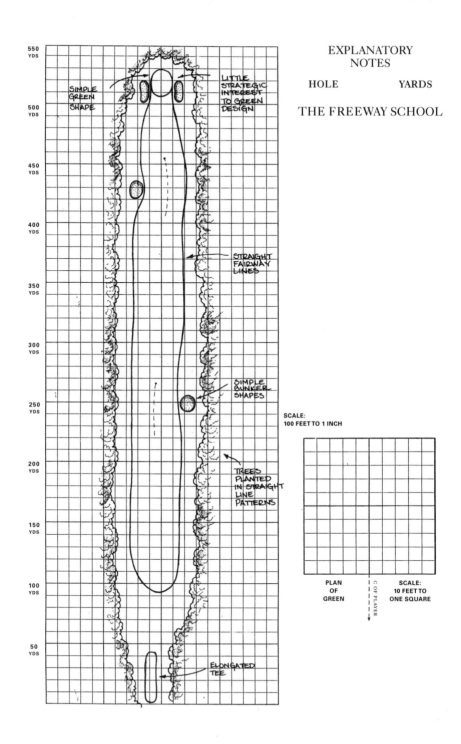

550
YDS

500
YDS

SIMPLE
GREEN
SHAPE

LITTLE
STRATEGIC
INTEREST
TO GREEN
DESIGN

450
YDS

400
YDS

STRAIGHT
FAIRWAY
LINES

350
YDS

300
YDS

250
YDS

SIMPLE
BUNKER
SHAPES

SCALE:
100 FEET TO 1 INCH

200
YDS

TREES
PLANTED
IN STRAIGHT
LINE
PATTERNS

150
YDS

100
YDS

PLAN
OF
GREEN

C OF PLAYER

SCALE:
10 FEET TO
ONE SQUARE

50
YDS

ELONGATED
TEE

Rendering of a par-5, the "freeway" school of design. (GIL HANSE)

42

at the height of his cutting-edge design work during the early 1980s, another movement was born to offer an alternative to Dye's quirky perspective.

The Framing School

Any time you design a course, you want to frame the hole. If you have a picture, and the frame doesn't work, then you get a new frame.
—Tom Fazio, golf architect

It took years before golfers understood that Pete Dye's work was a juiced-up version of the classic, traditional designs mixed with his own artistic flair. But many have never come to like his work or because it seemed too "quirky," too busy-looking or just too difficult.

The modern day Tour professional is not a big fan of Pete Dye, and in modern times, the touring pro has become a powerful voice in determining which courses are revered and which are hated. As big money and the needs of the PGA Tour pro have enveloped the game, their complaints that Dye's TPC at Sawgrass was too offbeat led to a wave of architects and famous players presenting themselves as semi-Dye imitators. These architects present similar aesthetic dramatics that Dye used (water, mounding, railroad ties), but with the notion of "playable, fair" designs. This meant that the tricky strategic dilemmas and any kind of hazard for overly ambitious shots were minimized or eliminated. Some architects eventually took the anti-Dye theme to a greater extreme, pushing hazards so far out of play that their only purpose was as a "framing" device instead of a strategic or even a penal tool.

A few top architects have become enormously popular in the post-Dye era by taking a landscape architecture approach to golf course design, emphasizing prettiness, simplicity and perfect visibility over strategy, naturalness and subtle character. Framing is the priority, the playing interest second.

The spending and design emphasis on framing compliments the current state of motion pictures. You have Hollywood turning out expensive "event" pictures that are comprised of numerous special

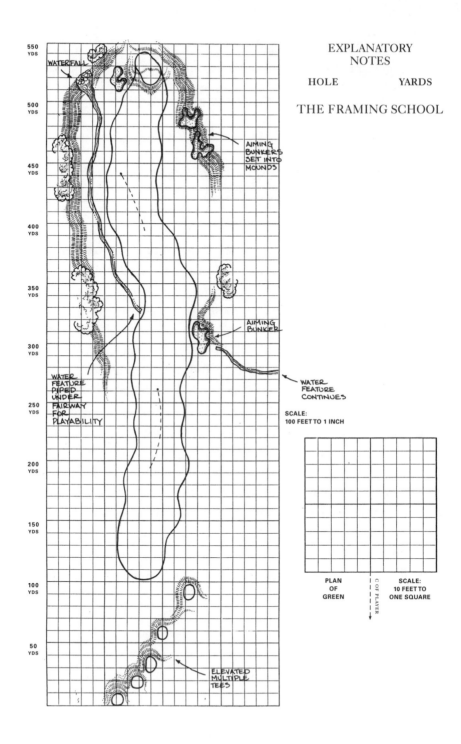

550 YDS

WATERFALL

500 YDS

450 YDS

AIMING BUNKERS SET INTO MOUNDS

400 YDS

350 YDS

AIMING BUNKER

300 YDS

WATER FEATURE PIPED UNDER FAIRWAY FOR PLAYABILITY

WATER FEATURE CONTINUES

250 YDS

SCALE: 100 FEET TO 1 INCH

200 YDS

150 YDS

100 YDS

PLAN OF GREEN

C OF PLAYER

SCALE: 10 FEET TO ONE SQUARE

50 YDS

ELEVATED MULTIPLE TEES

EXPLANATORY NOTES

HOLE   YARDS

THE FRAMING SCHOOL

Rendering of a par-5, the "framing" school of design. (GIL HANSE) effects and attractive actors to look at, but the scripts often lack a story or any emotion by the time they are filmed.

As the framing mentality spread, a certain breed of "independent" golf architect came along, mostly inspired by the Pete Dye method of building courses. These architects are commonly referred to as "minimalists," because they, like the "independent" filmmakers of recent years, refuse to give up on the use of strategy (golf's storyline).

The Next School

Golf architecture is a new art closely allied to that of the artist or sculptor, but also necessitating a scientific knowledge of many other subjects. The modern designer . . . is likely to achieve the most perfect results and make the fullest use of all the natural features by more up-to-date methods.
—Alister MacKenzie, 1934

As you will learn in the following chapter, economics and the state of the game dictate which school of thought emerges (or re-emerges) in the future. Will the golfing public's thirst for lower-cost, shorter, interesting and still playable designs ultimately become a popular facility to develop? Or will the desire for lavish, "instant gratification" courses that address major changes in technology fuel the next design wave? As litigation moves full steam ahead with seemingly every feature bearing some potential liability, will architects forget about interesting design and focus all of their attention on protecting golfers from the occasional wayward shot?

The future depends on the evolution of the sport and the climate surrounding the game, just as it has for the previous two hundred years.

The Fourth Hole

Constantly Evolving

How Design Has Been Influenced by Events Surrounding the Game

> *. . . it is necessary to point out certain mischievous tendencies that can influence the progress and spirit of the game . . .*
>
> —*Tom Simpson, golf architect*

To appreciate the architecture of all courses, you do not need to understand the complexities of drainage, irrigation, construction or agronomy. To better enjoy the game and sharpen your critical eye, you will want to realize the elements influencing why courses of various generations take on their unique style.

Events that have fostered the evolution of design trends often started with something as simple as a Dutch sailors looking for a diversion on their way into town. Subtle changes came when golf pros started selling their design services, with more significant shifts coming as the result of two world wars. Modern golf course design continues to reflect the trends of the society surrounding the game, with today's most pervasive design influence coming in the form of awards, rankings and marketing.

The Natural School

The difference between the golf courses of America and of Great Britain can best be expressed by the two words "artificial" and "natural": and that means a whole lot more than the mere presence or absence of the fabrication of man. —Bobby Jones, golf great

Why is it that the "founding fathers" in politics or other favored pastimes seem so wise, and proceeding generations always unable to live up to early standards? Is it nostalgia that blinds us, or is it fact?

Sure, the founding fathers of the United States were not able to foresee certain events, but they created a near-perfect system of government that has never been matched elsewhere. The Beatles still sound fresh compared to today's rock bands, while Mozart, Beethoven, Wagner, Schubert and Bach continue to inspire modern classical composers. So is it time and nostalgia that lends a timeless quality to so many art forms, or have we been blessed by shrewd innovators?

Golf's early designers were influenced by the Old Course at St. Andrews and little else. The makings of an amusing sport became apparent while the Dutch sailors were batting away at rocks on their way into the town of St. Andrews. The odd contours and the need to avoid natural obstacles made the game different from any other sport known to man. The early pioneers understood that the individual character of each property would make every layout a new and fresh place to play. Flattening out the features and laying down the same holes over and over again would have made golf a confusing, awkward version of cricket.

When early figures like Allan Robertson and Old Tom Morris were commissioned to create new golf courses outside of St. Andrews, whether by ingenuity or lack of manpower, they allowed the natural or existing features to influence the design. Without any predecessors to refer to, there were no "rules" for designing a course, so they simply placed holes around or on top of whatever existed.

This unrefined approach maintained the spirit of St. Andrews and the concept of using existing attributes to create memorable holes. Old Tom Morris recognized this simple notion and passed it along to the protégés who visited his golf shop. Many listened, but when money entered the picture and professional golfers began competing for design work, some of his counterparts felt they had to separate themselves from everyone else in some way, so the J. H. Taylors of the world developed radically different styles of design. They convinced themselves that change was necessary to bring justice to the game.

The Penal School

> *Players, not unnaturally, when so much is at stake, insist more and more on a rigid standard of equity. It would be unwise to underrate the fascinations of publicity or the importance of golf as a spectacle to entertain enthusiastic galleries; but at the same time it is necessary to point out certain mischievous tendencies that can influence the progress and spirit of the game, tendencies which, in the long run, by laying an undue insistence on apparent miscarriages of justice (for which the architect is usually held guilty) reduce the imaginative element of our courses to a lower level than they should rightly possess, and have the effect of diverting the poetry of golf into less desirable channels.*
>
> *—Tom Simpson, 1929*

When they began contesting tournaments for prize money, golf got its first taste of how pervasively the playing professional can influence the overall character of the game. Around the turn of the twentieth century golf magazines started recognizing competitive events and fine players. Many believed that those who played golf with skill could do no wrong, thus, famous players were commissioned to do many things, including new course design.

In some cases excellent players bring a fascinating, worldly perspective to architecture that others are unable to provide. But good golfers often tend to think of their own game while overemphasizing design attributes that they deem to be "fair." Fine players tend to discourage design features that require thought, usually at the expense of adventuresome golf for the majority.

You might think the situation would be different. The greatest players are those that can make tough decisions under pressure and follow through with skillful, creative shots that most of us are unable to manufacture. Those decisions and inventive shotmaking opportunities are created by interesting architecture, yet few players recognize this.

A similar distorted view of the playing professional's needs and the good of the game would evolve in baseball if you let hitters determine the size of the strike zone or the distance to the outfield fences. In the hitter's mind, eliminating the strike zone would be the fairest method of eliminating bad ball and strike calls. While we're at it, how about fences at around 175 feet from home plate? If you let pitchers dictate strike zone boundaries, we'd see few balls hit. Every pitch would be a strike. This is why pitchers and hitters aren't allowed to determine rules or design baseball parks.

Promoting "just" golf and absolute fairness, the early turn-of-the-twentieth-century designers were thinking of their on-course livelihood when placing hazards and greens. These player-architects placed an emphasis on rewarding those who hit their ball down the middle by eliminating features such as contours or bunkers in the line of play. Features that might actually ask the player to *think* of an alternative line to the hole, or shape a shot to open up a view of the green. Golf pros old and new believe holes should be black and white, as opposed to arbitrary fields of maneuver where the player has to constantly adapt to the elements.

Random unpredictability was found on the natural school layouts and revered by most when they discovered that a round of golf was a constant adventure amidst a natural setting. The early player-architects sought to reverse this style and introduce predictability and order to a game that was thriving on its randomness.

New driving distances and balls that flew higher with more consistent spin led a charge to create new courses that could defend themselves against this modern version of golf, and the penal school thrived in part because of this demand.

Less easy to understand from these penal school days was the passion which these early designers had for dismantling lovely natural landscapes and turning them into bizarre obstacle courses replete with coffin-shaped bunkers and chocolate-drop mounds. Perhaps it was a reflection of the Victorian age and the excess that came with it. Or maybe it was their heartfelt belief that courses should look man-made in order to demonstrate that golf was just an oversized version of chess. Unfortunately, the cerebral elements that make a chess match interesting were left out of most penal school designs.

The Strategic School

We want our golf courses to make us think. However much we may enjoy whaling the life out of the little white ball, we soon grow tired of playing a golf course that does not give us problems in strategy as well as skill.   *—Bobby Jones*

As Old Tom Morris grew older, wiser and more accommodating to visitors coming to see St. Andrews, he received many curious students hoping to discuss the art of course design and construction. Some were anxious to understand why they these "penal" school courses were offensive and why the Old Course at St. Andrews was adored by so many. These curious design aficionados knew there was a better way to design a golf course.

Old Tom helped budding architects like Donald Ross, A.W. Tillinghast and C.B. Macdonald understand why the Old Course and other links should be their model for post–World War I courses. Starting around 1905, the idea of a natural looking course that provoked decision-making began to reappear in new designs. A few courageous souls dared to defy the famous professional golfers. By the start of World War I, golfers experienced a group of new courses that reinvented the old-school ideas of thoughtful design, all in a natural, attractive way.

The strategic-school architects not only sought to separate themselves from the crude-looking penal-school designs by golf professionals, they also were feeding off of society's general desire for more "natural" and unpretentious art with softer edges. Impressionism was gaining in popularity (with certain people anyway). So was the Arts and Crafts movement that prided itself in handmade, wood-based architecture and furniture. It was the movement that preceded and influenced Frank Lloyd Wright, a cause motivated by its distaste for modern machinery and the disappearance of craftsmanship.

The "picturesque" school of landscape architecture, where landscapes were made to look natural, experienced a resurgence in England and the United States thanks to people like Frederick Law Olmsted. Formal gardens were rejected in favor of landscape design that appeared less "planned."

The society and times in which the strategic-school architects practiced their "new" ideas made for a perfect fit. This new spirit of adventure mirrored what the world was seeking in their lives. As the Roaring Twenties hit their peak, the desire for natural, spontaneous, adventuresome art found its way to golf course design. Several architects created more daring, sometimes incredible-looking and -playing golf holes. They did so by creating imitation sand dunes (Pebble Beach) or intricate sandy waste areas that appeared completely natural (Pine Valley). Contrary to many myths fostered by modern architects, the effort to create a subtle, natural-looking design often required earthmoving and expense. But it was carried out so beautifully that today's experts are unable to detect where man's hand was prevalent and where nature's work was kept intact.

Meanwhile, strategic-school architects were creating intricately thought-out holes that appeared as if their intricate challenges happened by accident. There were heated discussions in the major golf publications weighing the strategic versus the penal school. Even though the architects were fighting a tough battle with famous golf professionals who felt their need for fair design was vital, the merits of the strategic school gained popularity thanks in part to the writings and influence of British golfer Horace Hutchison, and then the great Bobby Jones.

When the Great Depression hit in October of 1929, new projects soon disappeared until the postwar years. Jones's Augusta National was one of the last major courses built during the strategic-school era, but in spite of its brilliance, the Depression prevented it from launching the strategic-design revolution that its architects, Jones and Alister MacKenzie, had hoped for.

The Heroic School

Every hole should be a hard par and an easy bogey.
—Robert Trent Jones Sr., golf architect

Robert Trent Jones and Dick Wilson led the post–World War II boom in design, and their style was based on architects before them, minus some of the desire for naturalness and strategy that architects like MacKenzie and Ross preached. Historians have never fully understood why just fifteen years after the most successful era in design, the game witnessed such a drift in style, or why architects worked so hard to erase the work of strategic-school architects, but the shift was dictated in part by advancements in construction machinery.

During the postwar years, the world saw a focused age of immense growth and reconstruction, with little time for artistic touches, in all forms of architecture. Efficiency and rapid construction fueled architecture, whether the design in question was a school, office building, garden or a golf course. There was little time to take in natural features that made a site interesting. The reduction of on-site time from architects also meant that design strategy took a back seat to what at times became an assembly-line approach to course construction.

Until the late sixties, the postwar generation separated itself from the excesses of the Roaring Twenties. Considering how trying and tragic times were from 1930 to 1945, one can certainly understand how society would drift from the ideals preached by the previous generation. However, the determination to head down a far different path, regardless of what principles seemed timeless, led to less interesting design work.

The influence of golfing greats Ben Hogan, Sam Snead and Byron Nelson should never be underestimated in how design was perceived. Their unprecedented ball-striking ability and the emergence of steel shafts throughout the game supported the prevailing belief that many courses were no longer able to prevent players from overwhelming the design. Players were shooting low winning scores on many courses from the 1920s, and thus, golfing administrators felt that the old courses needed to be updated and modernized to "defend" themselves. Unfortunately, many of the most intriguing and natural design features were eliminated in the name of creating tougher and less charismatic golf courses.

The Freeway School

"Championship course" is a catch-penny label used by resort developers and signifies only that the course in question is a dreary slog of over 7,000 yards for anyone foolish enough to play it off the back tees.
—Peter Dobereiner, golf writer

With no inspiration or demand from the public for higher architectural standards, the "freeway" design mentality picked up speed during the 1960s golf boom. Leaving golf with courses that had little or no architectural features of interest, freeway design continued until Pete Dye came along during the early eighties and proved to golfers that architecture needed a fresh perspective. As the sixties and early seventies were a time of unrest and uncertainty, architecture of all types was given little thought as an art form capable of uniting and enriching people's lives. Tour any college campus and look at the character of buildings constructed in the 1920s compared to those erected during the 1950s and '60s. The difference in craftsmanship and subtle character is astounding.

During the late 1960s, music became the focus of society's interests, as did photography. Meanwhile other art forms suffered creatively, including golf design. You could buy Rembrandts, Monets and van Goghs for low prices, while memberships at Ross and Tillinghast designs were virtually given away. An appreciation for and interest in the work of the "masters" did not drive art and architecture. Function was the primary purpose.

Golf also became big business for many Americans during the freeway-design era thanks in large part to the invention of the golf cart and the popularity of driving ranges. As more courses opened, golf professionals made a nice living renting carts, selling driving-range balls and giving lessons. Golf pros were doing so well that management companies later formed and took over many golf course operations during the eighties. The corporate-bottom-line desires of these companies gradually seeped into all aspects of the game, to the point where golf went from being a nice business for individuals and families to being *big* business for larger, less personal companies.

Golf architecture that dared to be different was looked down upon or considered an unnecessary added expense, even though courses with more exceptional designs were of higher value to both golfers and companies. Still, most believed bunkers, interesting greens and other design features slowed down play and prevented the maximizing of revenues. In many cases, cart paths were designed with more care than the courses themselves.

But some were looking to create courses that were a bit more dazzling. As offensive as the TPC at Sawgrass seemed to the professionals when it debuted in 1981, golfers embraced the eye-popping early eighties work of Pete Dye because he was able to create instant value in the form of green fees and real estate. Dye designs provoked discussion and soon turned all name architects into a commodity that was viewed as an integral part of developing a community or resort. Even though most golfers find Dye's work too difficult to play, his ability to build monstrous designs seemingly with the wink of an eye allows Dye to get away with features that would drive other less charismatic architects out of business.

As the economy boomed during the Reagan years, upscale resorts became even more popular than they were in the Roaring Twenties. To deal with the increasing competition, developers looked to "name" architects to help customers determine where to vacation. These developers were willing to pay handsomely for famous names regardless of their talent or willingness to devote time to a project.

Whom did they turn to? Big-name touring pros.

The freeway era also saw televised golf influencing maintenance and design more than ever. Architects created elements such as lakes or contrasting white sand that translated well to television and color print. The increase in the number of televised events along with color televisions led viewers to expect more man-made design features that added color and beauty to golf. Green grass and excessive length continued to be a fetish for golfers as they watched Jack Nicklaus and other greats smash drives longer than ever before on courses maintained like no one could have ever imagined.

The trend of flashy, sometimes garish "championship" courses flourished, even during a rough stretch in the post-Reagan economy. Maintenance standards continued to soar, placing golf course superintendents under extreme pressure to produce manicured layouts. The cost of higher maintenance standards was passed along to the golfers.

In spite of a mild recession, corporate America embraced golf by the early nineties as a means of entertainment and as a quality sport worth associating with. The infusion of cash led to another shift in architecture, an upscale offshoot of the "freeway" style. Golf course designers worked feverishly to outdo one another and the excesses of the eighties, largely in the name of marketing and attracting tournament golf.

The Framing School

We don't find too many memorable photographic scenes on some of the older, classic designs. Pinehurst #2, for example, is not dramatic in appearance because it was designed to be played, rather than photographed. —Tom Fazio, golf architect

Contemporary design from 1991–2001 found itself less influenced by golfers' desire for fun or affordable designs, and more by rankings, brand names and who could build the most expensive and lavish course that would bolster a cocktail party conversation. Some view the nineties as golf's version of Hollywood's summer-action-movie mindset.

With well-marketed summer movies, the thrills or laughs are exciting for filmgoers the first time around, but long-term interest is unlikely when the story is thin. The same goes for golf courses that are lavish in special effects, and light on strategy. They don't attract repeat interest, which in the golf business can be deadly. There were several examples, however, where architecture with lasting character became the focus of a project when the developer understood the long-term benefits of a sound, thoughtful design. Courses like Sand Hills, Pacific

Dunes and its neighboring Bandon Dunes figure to remain in the hearts and minds of golfers for years to come, thanks in large part to their well-crafted designs.

Even as the golfer has more information at his hands than ever before, golfers rely heavily on the stamp of a big-name architect who may have only visited a project twice and couldn't remember any of the holes if you interviewed him today. This is a far cry from the days when an architect would spend hours debating the placement of one bunker or questioning whether his green contours complimented the hole's strategic purpose.

The belief that PGA Tour professionals are more informed about true character in design may be the most interesting notion of all in modern golf. Their views are not as extreme as the turn-of-the-twentieth-century professionals who propelled the penal school into prominence, perhaps because most player-architects today only visit a project two or three times during construction, and even then, most of their time is spent posing for photographs.

Like his peers from the early twentieth century, the modern professional golfer's philosophy is often driven by how a design fits his game and whether the course seems fair. Some pros even state that if the course is conditioned nicely during a tournament and it is conveniently located in relation to their hotel, they love the place. If the pro deems something in the design to be wrong or not a comfortable fit with his game, look for the "unfair" word to come out of his mouth.

The final characteristic of the framing era that mystifies some is the lack of on-site construction supervision by the architect. Imagine Mozart signing off on a symphony and not making any changes during rehearsals? Or not even attending rehearsals and leaving the work to an apprentice!

It is one thing to put ideas down on paper, it is another to reflect on them and modify features in order to achieve the best results. Many of the great Renaissance painters created detailed drawings of their portraits or landscapes before they actually painted, and rarely do you find those drawings matching the paintings. The drawing was a means to start and inspire other ideas for the final product.

Today's big-name architects are well compensated for their work, yet they will turn out as many as twelve new courses a year while issuing quotes that say their latest work "is the best piece of property" they've "ever been given to work with." After a big opening-day ceremony that may only be the architect's third or fourth time on the site, he collects his pay and moves on to the next job with little care for how his finished product plays from day to day.

Unfortunately, as a complex art form that requires skill, time and creative use of technology, golf architecture has suffered with this overpriced assembly-line approach. As architects have become increasingly reliant on their computers to whip out plans that they rarely supervise during construction, we see fewer big-budget courses with the individual character that provides long-term playing interest. And we see few layouts that were fine-tuned as construction commenced so that playability functioned in an appealing way.

Making the framing school era even more confusing is the consistency with which many of the most famous architects claim they are designing in the style of the natural and strategic school architects, even citing the names of the architects in their brochures. Some are more than willing to declare that they are creating courses that are much better than the master architects ever did in the good old days. A few even state that we are in a new "Golden Age," yet too many courses that cost $125 to play aren't memorable by the time you are headed out the entrance road.

What drives this peculiar assembly-line approach to golf development? Rankings and marketing.

The reason for the survival of the award system is purely commercial.
—*Robert Henri, artist*

No influence in the history of golf course design has been more bizarre and nonsensical, yet as powerful, as the magazine rankings.

Depending on which magazine you read, each has their own method of judging courses. Bi-annually these are among the biggest-selling issues, so they carry enormous weight with golfers regardless of how much fidgeting goes on behind the editorial doors to temper the panelists' obsession with conditioning or friendliness of the course beverage-cart attendant. Like any other subjective list, people have very different views as to what makes a course special. Some believe very strongly that the difficulty of the course, as long as it is fair, is the ultimate. Others genuinely look at each course differently, research important facts about the design, and analyze whether the architect created something original that will be fun to play repeatedly. And a few panelists simply have no clue what they are looking at and probably were appointed to a panel because they carried a low handicap or host a talk show.

However, as weird as the rankings can be and as expensive as they have made golf course development, the various lists have brought a greater awareness of golf architecture. The late nineties and early twenty-first-century ranking obsession may ultimately be viewed as constructive for golf architecture because the lists raised awareness for golf's master architects and courses, many of which are now undergoing restorations inspired by a course's newfound respect for its tradition.

Nothing could be better for the health and fun of the game than for players to witness golf architecture's ability to bring amusement and joy to our lives, and as the twentieth century came to an end, the rankings were serving to recognize many worthy efforts. Which proves that even the most peculiar forms of evolution can have a positive influence on the ever-changing art of golf course design.

THE FIFTH HOLE

Comic Relief

Humor Is One of the Architect's Most Important Design Tools

*On the golf course, a man may be the dogged victim of inexorable fate, be
struck down by an appalling stroke of tragedy, become the hero of
unbelievable melodrama, or the clown in a side-splitting comedy.*
                                                        —*Bobby Jones*

Regardless of what design schools influenced the courses you play, a
majority of golfers would agree that if they are unable to remember
most of the holes after a round of golf, there is a good chance that the
designer did not inject much character into his effort. The ability to
recall each hole is just the start of understanding what makes certain
holes fun to play no matter how well (or poorly) we play golf.

Any architect can create a memorable hole by building waterfalls,
island greens or, as we've seen in recent times, even erecting faux-
ancient ruins. However, the genuinely memorable hole results from
subtle, carefully conceived design touches, the most prominent of
which are the focus of the next two chapters.

Great holes and courses have emerged from each era no matter
how much you may disagree with the design school's driving principles. Choose any well-known hole from the schools and each will share
certain traits: The holes display a sense of humor, or they tempt you to
try something risky. Or a combination of both.

The humor of golf is a divine comedy in the deeper sense. Like all sources of laughter it lies in contrast and paradox; in the thought of otherwise grave men gravely devoting hours and money to a technique which so often they, apparently alone, do not know they can never master. The solemnity of the eternal failure is vastly comic. The perpetualness of their hope is nobly humorous.
—R. C. Robertson-Glasgow

This chapter deals with the most misunderstood element on the architect's palette, the color known as comic relief. Humor is an under-appreciated aspect in all forms of architecture, whether it be a building or a golf course. Think back to your best on-course memories and likely they involve attempting a wildly creative shot. Or watching a friend trying to extricate themselves from some bizarre situation created by the architect. A predicament which, at the end of the day, you were able to laugh about.

People who hike mountain trails take home fond memories of seeing something surprising in nature, something that produced a chuckle. At a museum, the art that usually sticks with us is not necessarily the most powerful or famous painting but, instead, one that displayed individual character and perhaps even a sense of humor. Sometimes, this art is so individual that it is labeled quirky by some, fascinating by others and humorous by those who realize the artist was trying to warm our hearts.

A diehard fan attends a sporting event hoping to see something unusual, perhaps a triple play or speedy leadoff man attempting to steal home. But often the humorous moments stick with us even longer. A manager waddling out to argue a call, or the awkward-swinging pitcher getting the game-winning hit. These are the surprises that elicit a smile or even a warm chuckle. Comedy is vital to all pastimes, but particularly in golf where the difficulties of the game can so easily drive even single-digit handicap players to take up bowling.

During golf architecture's short lifetime, the enduring holes display the best strategic values and natural beauty, but with a twist. Usually, a comic twist, perhaps a quirky Robert Trent Jones–mastermined contour jutting out of the center of a green, a Pete Dye pot

The eighteenth green and bunker at Muirfield in Scotland. Even a stern, demanding, rather straightforward course like Muirfield has its touches of subtle humor. (GEOFF SHACKELFORD)

bunker right where you want to hit your drive, or maybe George Thomas's bunker smack dab in the center of a green.

Sometimes, maybe the comedy stems from a pile of boulders that fell off a truck during construction, say at a place like Sherwood Country Club. And just maybe an architect with a sense of humor like Jack Nicklaus decided to create an interesting hazard by keeping the rocks just where they fell, producing something unique on what might have been an otherwise forgettable hole.

Like many elements of modern life, golf architecture sometimes takes itself a bit too seriously. The humorous side gets lost when people overvalue the modern PGA Tour pro's mantra for good design: fairness. We see few courses where the architect took a risk to create a truly memorable hole, and others where the designer failed to utilize a natural feature that might add a touch of humor to the design. The primary result of this shift stems from one trend in particular: the shift from match play to stroke play as the main form of competition.

Sure, the average golfer still uses match play in their regular games, but the current structure of golf requires players to turn in every round in order to maintain a handicap. Why an eighteen-hole score is the best way to measure a handicap for a hole-by-hole format like match play, I'll never know. But it's the system and we all live by it to maintain a handicap.

The concept of turning in an eighteen-hole score has become so important to so many golfers, that the game and even its architecture is approached from a stroke play point of view. Design features must be conducive to scoring, meaning anything that could lead to a high score in match play becomes unfair in a stroke play situation. But sometimes those strange, seemingly unfair (but usually just misunderstood) design features are the most humorous. And in match play they rarely bother us because we get a fresh start on the next tee.

I loved match play. I would study a guy I was playing, just like Ted Williams studied pitchers. I'd look for a weak spot. —Sam Snead

Alister MacKenzie, the distinguished architect, philosopher and friend to all golfers, gave the most appealing explanation in favor of match versus stroke play. This appeared in his posthumously published masterpiece, *The Spirit of St. Andrews*:

I believe that one gets far more fun in playing a match for five or ten dollars . . . than you can ever get in taking your score. If your score is a good one, you will remember it, but if it is a bad one why make life a burden by doing so? In Scotland, on completing a round, no one ever asked you, "What is your score?" It is always, "Did you beat him?" or "Was it a tight match?"

At some clubs in England and in a small minority in America, the question is the same as it is in Scotland, but on many courses in England and most in America it is, "What is your score?" or "What did you shoot?" In Britain, the better the course the greater the match and the less the medal play.

It often seems to me that on a good course golfers get their fun in attempting the varied and thrilling shots that are required in trying to beat their opponents, but on an indifferent course the only excitement they get is their score. Surely there is far more fun in a contest against flesh and blood than against a card and pencil.

There are many of us who firmly believe that a contest between flesh and blood is the only true form of golf, and that too much attention to score play is detrimental to the real interest of the game. If too much attention were paid to the vitriolic outbursts of unsuccessful competitors in medal rounds, there would not be a first class hole left in golf.

It is always the hole that gives the most lasting pleasure and excitement, like the Road and Eden Holes at St. Andrews, which are most fiercely criticized. Golfers must have something to talk about, and they usually talk most about something they imagined spoilt their score. They rarely attribute their misfortune to the real cause, and that is that they have not played their shots quite well enough.

Fairness in golf architecture almost always tends to emphasize simple, dull and humorless design elements. To make a course "compatible" for stroke play, the riskiest and most interesting shots have to be left out of our modern courses. Risk and reward situations, the lifeblood of timeless design and true fun for all players, are sacrificed in the name of fairness. The architect's ability to put a fresh twist on an old design idea is often shelved because it might be received as strange or unjust even though the very same course that inspired the idea is ranked in the top twenty in the world!

Comic touches like a blind pot bunker behind a green or a fairway full of uneven lies are no longer considered distinctive design touches in the stroke play mindset. They are cruel and unusual. However, those same eccentric features become interesting in match play situations because no one cares about the eighteen-hole medal play total, just a hole-by-hole match score.

The "unfair" blind shot or the rocks in the center of play become a challenge to overcome. When one player uses the design feature to outsmart his opponent, there is sense of appreciation for both the player's intelligence and the interesting architecture. Those instances when a score of nine outlasts a ten end up being the focus of a hearty postround laugh even if the moment was not so funny on the course.

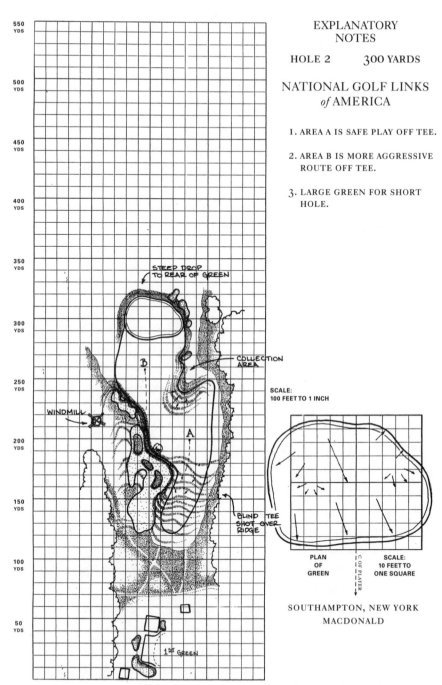

HOLE 2   300 YARDS

NATIONAL GOLF LINKS
of AMERICA

1. AREA A IS SAFE PLAY OFF TEE.

2. AREA B IS MORE AGGRESSIVE
   ROUTE OFF TEE.

3. LARGE GREEN FOR SHORT
   HOLE.

550 YDS

500 YDS

450 YDS

400 YDS

350 YDS

300 YDS

250 YDS

200 YDS

150 YDS

100 YDS

50 YDS

STEEP DROP
TO REAR OF GREEN

COLLECTION
AREA

B

WINDMILL

A

BLIND TEE
SHOT OVER
RIDGE

1ST GREEN

SCALE:
100 FEET TO 1 INCH

PLAN
OF
GREEN

C OF PLAYER

SCALE:
10 FEET TO
ONE SQUARE

SOUTHAMPTON, NEW YORK
MACDONALD

Rendering of the par-4 second at the National Golf Links of America. A hole with strategic and also disastrous possibilities if the player is careless. The short yardage combined with the unusual terrain makes this one of the most fascinating, bizarre and enjoyable holes in the world. (GIL HANSE)

When you come to think of it, that is the secret of most of the great holes all over the world. They all have some kind of a twist.

—C. B. Macdonald

The "master" golf architects were complex and sometimes intense thinkers. They analyzed the subject and could probably bore you with minutiae regarding the construction, strategy and maintenance of their courses. Fortunately, however, they brought a sense of humor to the job of golf course architect. Whether they were building a public course, a private club or the most basic municipal layout, they always managed to include humorous design twists.

The shift away from comic relief in modern design is a result of both changing expectations from golfers (particularly course ranking panelists) and also due in part to laziness by the architects, because architects rarely take advantage of the best and most humorous elements created by Mother Nature. After all, who can criticize a three-

The "Dell" hole at Lahinch in Ireland. The tee shot on the par-3 sixth is blind, playing to this narrow green set amidst towering grassy dunes. The tee is over the hill to the left. This hole requires a sense of humor to enjoy the first few times the player attempts to play it. (LYNN SHACKELFORD)

hundred-year-old oak bisecting the fairway, or a tiny green perched above a natural creek, when the design incorporated existing, *natural* features? If it's natural, golfers will embrace a feature even if it annoys their straight line to the hole or their view of the green. If the architect forces a feature or tries too hard to create a design quirk, our instinct is to reject such features.

Golf courses need to demonstrate a sense of humor in order to keep this most punishing of games fresh and enjoyable. It's rare to come across a 130-yard par-3 with an enormous green like the Short Hole at the National Golf Links. Or to play challenging par-4s under 300 yards where players of all levels are tempted to play at least one aggressive shot. And it's even more rare to see back-to-back par-3s like Alister MacKenzie built at Cypress Point to take advantage of the Pacific Ocean. And how dare a modern architect create a do-or-die 485-yard par-4 that probably should be a par-5, ala the Road hole at St. Andrews? After all, it might be unfair.

It is rare these days to stumble upon a green that is pitched gently from front to back or to find bunkers placed in the center of play instead of to the more predictable sides of the fairway. Architects claim they can't design witty features or even drift from the "classic" design features because they feel golfers and the developers won't accept a little humor thrown into design, even though comedy has been the linchpin of every great hole, no matter the school of design.

To some degree the architects or developers are correct in subscribing to the notion that pretty-but-bland holes are the safest route to go. I recently became mesmerized by the comments of one self-important golfer who stated emphatically that golf was not about having fun or about seeing new and interesting courses or about spending time with friends in the fresh air. No, he said, the purpose of playing golf was to shoot the lowest score possible. Those other things like friends, fresh air, a fun match or enjoying the natural surroundings, all were secondary elements. I'm afraid he's not alone in this belief.

A study of early golf architecture, golf writing and even instruction articles reveals a wonderful sense of humor throughout the years. From the days of Old Tom to the Golden Age years of Bobby Jones up to the renaissance years of Nelson, Hogan and Snead, players never lost sight of the fact that golf was a recreational pursuit that should never be taken too seriously. Even until the early eighties, professional golf and architecture still witnessed occasional moments of wonderful humor, and there was an overall feeling that golf was a sport of skill. But that's all golf was: a sport, not life or death.

Understanding the need for occasional design humor does not mean golf courses should turn into big, windmill-strewn versions of miniature golf. Instead, comedy in golf architecture should be used carefully, just like the masterful screenwriter or novelist knows when to break the tension of an otherwise serious story with a well-timed joke.

Architect George Thomas built two mounds in front of a green at Bel-Air, causing a member to name the hole "Mae West" after the buxom film star of their day. The mounded green not only called upon a skillful approach to the hole, but added a comedic touch amid a stretch of long, difficult holes. In 1927, Thomas also placed a bunker in the center of Riviera's sixth green, when such a notion was considered ridiculous, even in a free-swinging era that encouraged such light-hearted novelties. Thomas knew how to present comic relief touches that in no way overshadowed the courses in question but, instead, broke up a series of complicated, sometimes punishing holes.

Alister MacKenzie never shied away from a boomerang-shaped putting surface, a feature rarely tried today because a ball could end up on the wrong end of the boomerang and the player could actually be on the green and still not have a trouble-free two-putt opportunity. Heaven forbid a poorly placed shot should be punished by not having an easy two-putt! Of course, MacKenzie was so crafty, he usually contoured his greens so that even a player with a ball on the wrong side of the boomerang could recover with a little imagination and two well-executed putts.

Donald Ross's greens often contained tiny bumps or "pimples" that could alter the character of a hole completely, while also injecting strategy and a touch of eccentricity to his work. These "pimples" became more humorous when years later the greens were dug up, and crews found that the large pimples were created by burying a boulder and covering it with dirt!

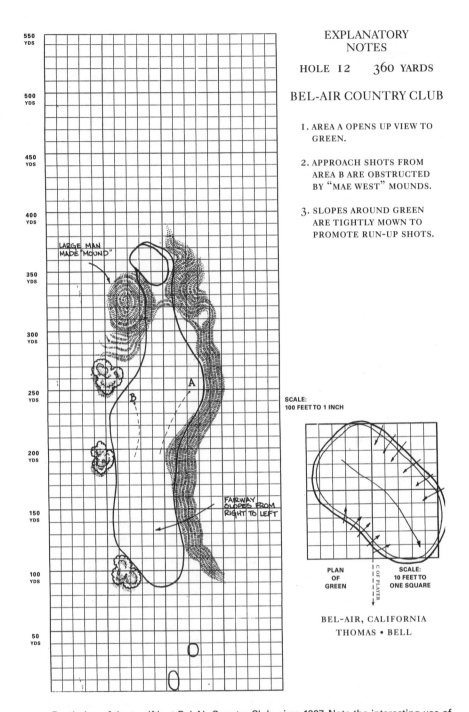

EXPLANATORY
NOTES

HOLE 12   360 YARDS

BEL-AIR COUNTRY CLUB

1. AREA A OPENS UP VIEW TO
   GREEN.

2. APPROACH SHOTS FROM
   AREA B ARE OBSTRUCTED
   BY "MAE WEST" MOUNDS.

3. SLOPES AROUND GREEN
   ARE TIGHTLY MOWN TO
   PROMOTE RUN-UP SHOTS.

SCALE:
100 FEET TO 1 INCH

PLAN
OF
GREEN

C OF PLAYER

SCALE:
10 FEET TO
ONE SQUARE

BEL-AIR, CALIFORNIA
THOMAS • BELL

Rendering of the twelfth at Bel-Air Country Club, circa 1927. Note the interesting use of the mounds as well as the strategic concept of rewarding a well-placed tee shot with a better view of the green. (GIL HANSE)

68

George Thomas's twelfth at Bel-Air not only provided interesting strategic problems, it also served as a welcome dose of comic relief amidst many long, difficult holes on Bel-Air's storied back nine.

The sixth green at Riviera by George Thomas, with a bunker in the center of the green. Golfers find this bunker either humorous or humorless depending on the outcome of their tee shot. (GEOFF SHACKELFORD)

The short par-4 sixth hole at University of Michigan's course was designed by Alister MacKenzie and Perry Maxwell. Some might quite call it quirky, others might say it's poor design while some think it's one of the world's great greens. The golfer cannot help but smile when they look at this green and ponder their approach shot, and the potential shots required if the approach is not carried out. (LYNN SHACKELFORD)

When carried out with a deft touch, eccentric design features not only work to make shotmaking more interesting, they lend a splash of memorability without overshadowing the overall course architecture. Even George Crump, the man responsible for what many consider the best course in the world, placed a huge pimplelike feature in the center of Pine Valley's eighteenth green. The bump was removed, perhaps because it was a bit over-the-top, but this bump might have been Crump's way of trying to bring a smile to your face after a punishing day at the wondrous but demanding Pine Valley.

A. W. Tillinghast, who wrote two witty novels and designed many classic "tests" of golf, repeatedly used comic relief touches throughout his designs. The creation of carry bunkers in the middle of par-5s, funky green contours and whimsical mounding all put a smile on your face when playing certain Tillinghast courses.

Move ahead to modern architecture and ask yourself, How many new courses do you experience a design-induced laugh on? How many make you say to yourself, "Now that took courage and a sense of humor to create. What a flair for design this architect has!"?

Sure, Donald Trump gave architect Jim Fazio a piece of property next to a Florida penitentiary where the prisoners have been known to bellow at Trump's female members as they play. Perhaps a funny thing for the club caddies to witness, but somehow I doubt that was a planned dose of comic relief architecture.

Early in his career, Jack Nicklaus displayed a great sense of humor at renowned designs like Desert Highlands, Muirfield Village and the Private Course at PGA West. Some of the jokes worked, some didn't, but he took chances and the courses were the subject of passionate discussion.

At the now infamous seventh at Sherwood Country Club, Nicklaus made the spontaneous in-the-field call to leave a few large rocks that had fallen off a truck onto the center of the fairway about 280 yards from the tee. A great player like David Duval still can't figure out how to avoid the rocks after several rounds at Sherwood, even though 25 yards of fairway awaits on all sides of the boulders. Not only do Duval

The seventh at Sherwood Country Club by Jack Nicklaus, viewed here from the green looking back toward the fairway. This infamous hole has very few admirers among the modern Tour professionals because of the rocks down the fairway center line. Many cry that it is unfair; but credit Nicklaus for having the comedic touch for making an otherwise ordinary hole quite memorable. (GEOFF SHACKELFORD)

and a few others players struggle with the rocks, they get downright upset about them!

After Mr. Nicklaus's early designs, however, it is rare to look for humor in a twenty-first-century Nicklaus design. He's known as a quick-witted man and an immensely creative individual with a vision for golf, so we can only hope that in his senior years the golfing climate will encourage Nicklaus to throw in more of these spontaneous, unusual touches. It helps too that Nicklaus was influenced by Pete Dye, perhaps the ultimate architect/comedian.

Bobby Jones is held up by many as the archetypal rule-abiding, demure, Southern golfing sportsman. Yet he had a wonderful sense of humor that the current Augusta National Golf Club regime, busy dismantling his dream course, would never appreciate.

When Jones designed Augusta National with Alister MacKenzie, he insisted on placing a blind pot bunker in the center of the eleventh fairway at roughly the spot where a good drive would finish. According to writer David Owen, who documented this story in the club's official history, Jones wanted the course "to have a hazard that could be avoided only with good luck or local knowledge—the sort of seemingly arbitrary booby trap that is plentiful on the Old Course."

During his initial round at Augusta National, Jones's father, Colonel Bob Jones, drove a tee ball into the little pot bunker. When he came upon his drive, the Colonel shouted, "What $*&%$#@!* fool put a $*&%$#@!* bunker right in the middle of the $*&%$#@!* fairway?"

Playing in the group, Bobby Jones replied, "I did."

Unfortunately the bunker was filled in several years later, but its humorous contribution to one round of golf probably gave Jones as much pleasure as any shot he ever hit. That is why design with a sense of humor is vital to everyone's enjoyment of golf.

The Sixth Hole

Temptation

Enjoyable Design Depends on the Architect's Ability to Entice, Lure and Tempt

The trouble with resisting temptation is that you may not get another chance. —*Edwin Chapin, minister and writer*

Fueling the role of comedy is a rather simple element that helps define the character of any timeless hole. Temptation.

Golf has a near-unanimous group of holes deemed "great." They come from different design schools, and evolved in unique ways. They are not great simply because they are hard to par, nor are they timeless only because they are pretty to look at. Instead, they are talked about and beloved by golfers of all levels because they provide options.

These classic holes consistently make the various magazine "lists," and in modern-day culture some have come to be known as the dreaded "signature hole." Despite the knowledge that there is this set of select holes seemingly above all criticism, the element propelling their greatness often goes unnoticed. Yes, great holes are physically difficult to conquer, but it's their ability to *tempt* the golfer with enticing options that separates the classics from ordinary designs.

The element of temptation is the driving force behind all of the most interesting features in golf architecture. The shots we enjoy hitting most are those that elicit internal deliberation, causing us to debate whether to try a risky shot versus the safer play. They make us wonder if the time is right to take a chance and to consider whether we will regret having taken the easy way out.

Whether it's the final round of the Masters or simply a decision to play directly at the flag during a late afternoon nine, tempting situations are the most memorable in golf and are the product of sound design.

Sometimes the tempting qualities of a hole pose obvious questions: Do I hit a driver or lay back with an iron off the tee? Maybe the fairway is just wide enough that you consider trying to hit the longest drive of your life, so that after all of these years a long tee ball will help you get home in two shots on a lengthy par-4 that has always eluded you.

Temptation in design is also created through subtlety. Perhaps the architect left an opening to a long par-4 green; an opening just wide enough to make us believe we should play a run-up shot onto the putting surface, even though the percentages say that a lay-up followed by a chip shot would prove more scorecard friendly. Or maybe temptation is created by short grass around the green.

With "tight lies," golfers constantly face a tricky chip-shot decision where we could lob the ball over a ledge, putting backspin on the shot to possibly knock the ball closer to the hole. If the area between the player and the hole consists of only long grass, there is no decision to make. Just pull out the sand wedge and hope you make a clean strike of the ball. But if the grass is cut closely, better-known in modern golf as a "chipping area," *options* exist.

One option is the temptation to play a deft bump-and-run shot that is somewhat at the mercy of the bounces the ball takes, but probably the best percentage play for avoiding disaster. Or the player can pull out a putter, the safest play of all, but a play that is less likely to allow us to land the ball so close that we leave ourselves a "gimme." Or, the highest risk but potentially most rewarding shot of all could still be played, the lob shot.

The tempting traits of famous holes are usually dramatic and obvious. The more questions we are forced us to ask of ourselves, the more tempting and fun it is to play. Better yet, the more time we are contemplating options translates to less time devoted to fretting over swing nuances, the pace of play or annoying playing partners.

The biggest temptation is . . . to settle for too little.
                                        —Thomas Merton, monk and poet

Temptation only works when there is a balance of risk and reward. Creating the proper balance separates the talented architects from those who do not fine-tune their work "in the field." Like any artistic endeavor, engineering details and elaborate computer-aided renderings impact design character and keep too many architects in their office instead of on-site supervising construction. This limits their ability to ensure that strategy works once the course is ready for play.

The "rush" to reach opening day explains why many layouts try to create dramatic holes, but ultimately fail to hold a player's interest with tempting choices during follow-up rounds. Also, the reluctance of architects and developers to subtly adjust their course a year or two after opening hurts many potentially strong designs, simply because there is a reluctance to admit the design is not quite functioning as well as it should.

The ultimate character of the course must be developed as the construction progresses.   *—William Flynn, golf architect*

The less frenetic pace of construction during the 1920s gave architects time to fine-tune the placement of hazards until they offered the ideal balance of risk and reward. This helps explain why many "classic" courses are still so compelling even as longer-flying golf balls threaten to limit intriguing decision-making scenarios.

To "balance" dangerous shots with a tempting "safe" play, the architect must provide wide enough fairways and large enough greens for the less aggressive player. The designer should offer safe playing areas for the cautious approach, while also creating riskier options that allow the courageous player to go for broke.

Many times the architect will present us with a shot that we may not be capable of playing. But when the safe play is simple and within easy reach, our natural instinct is to assume that the risky play may not be as hard as it looks and, thus, is worthy of our consideration. (What golfer has ever turned down the chance to pull off a miracle shot, even in the face of a safer play that might have led to a similar score or prevented disaster?)

Tempting and wider playing corridors suggest that the architect must have enough acreage to work with, and the understanding of a client who knows that courses like Augusta National were once interesting but still challenging because of their width. As the length of courses continues to expand and housing-surrounded layouts become routine, the modern architect is often handcuffed when trying to create fairways wide enough for tempting options (the acreage is devoted to length instead).

On many older courses, excessive numbers of trees have been planted in places that the old architects meant as tempting lay-up areas. While at other layouts, fairways are narrowed and surrounded with rough, undermining the tempting possibilities. One can only guess that the love for "defined" fairways is meant to mirror the way major championship courses are set up, but this approach ultimately grows tiresome to play and becomes a less interesting test of skill.

When tempting fairway space is lost we are left with only the difficult shot and few fascinating questions to ponder. Golf becomes a test of who obeys the design best, as opposed to who out-thinks and out-maneuvers. The shift toward "obedient," down-the-middle play and away from option-filled holes might explain why some golfers find modern courses too difficult, while the same complaints were not heard fifty years ago when talking about the very same course.

However, these factors are not an excuse for today's well-compensated architects to give up on the notion of temptation in design. There is no rational explanation as to why hazards are not better placed to promote risk versus reward golf. Or no good reason given why less penal but still subtle contours are rarely used to effect an overly ambitious shot.

Tempting design breeds the sporting spirit of golf. It is vital to the game's long-term interest and feeds our desire to play certain courses over and over again, even if the tempting features are subdued and simple. In fact, the subtler the better, because as architect A. W. Tillinghast said, we don't need to be subjected to "attacks of hysteria" on every tee.

Sure, it is exciting to have a few heart-stopping, do-or-die holes on every course. However, the timeless layouts present tempting situations on each hole without overwhelming our senses. Pine Valley and Bethpage State Park's Black Course get away with a certain relentless style because width is provided to play safe. Golfers also play these courses knowing they are going to see a certain kind of test unlike anything in the world. But for most classic designs, there is a simplicity to the features that yields the most lasting satisfaction. Maybe it's a carry bunker 215 yards down the right side, or a small green that gives us fits, but tempting design features do not have to be blatant to work in an interesting way.

Another factor that makes the creation of temptation difficult is the modern mindset of "protecting par." A hole will not tempt unless its problems can be conquered with a birdie or eagle from time to time. This concept is lost on many setting up courses in modern times who seek to prevent golfers from ever triumphing over famous holes. The desire to make sure the course can "defend itself" (i.e., not give up birdies), tends to override the importance of rewarding shrewd play.

To further understand the issue of temptation, golf's greatest and most tempting "corner" can help us understand that its lure and intrigue relies on a balance of tempting elements and the chance that a well-played shot will be rewarded.

It's the most tempting golf course in the world.
>   —*Jackie Burke, on Augusta National*

Writer Herbert Warren Wind labeled holes eleven, twelve and thirteen at Augusta National "Amen Corner." And even though the player should pray before dealing with this unpredictable set of holes and let out a big "Amen" when stepping onto the fourteenth tee, the outcome of most shots at this dreaded little corner is determined by how well the player resists temptation. Or in some cases, how successful the player was in recovering after caving in to temptation.

The wind combines with the firm, fast conditions to heighten the entire Amen Corner mystique, but the angles in which the greens sit next to hazards lead to tempting possibilities, no matter the conditions. The downhill, par-4 eleventh is not unlike many holes in golf. It's a

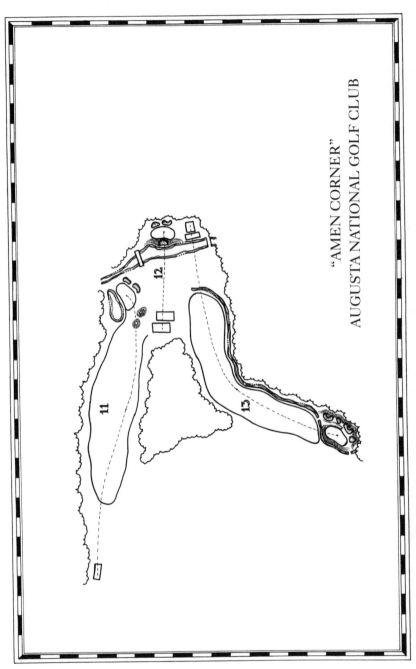

"AMEN CORNER"
AUGUSTA NATIONAL GOLF CLUB

Rendering of the most tempting sequence in golf, "Amen Corner" at Augusta National Golf Club. Depicted here are the eleventh green, the par-3 twelfth and the par-5 thirteenth. Named by writer Herbert Warren Wind, Amen Corner is legendary because of the tempting qualities of each shot and the resulting triumphs and disasters caused by the character of these interesting holes. (GIL HANSE) long two-shotter playing downhill. The green is guarded by a pond, with plenty of room to bail out to the right. But something about the width and downhill nature of the hole, the size of the green and its situation in the round makes it tempting for players to go at this flag even though such a play is rarely necessary. Perhaps it's because so much room is afforded to play safe that the aggressive shot looks enticing. But at key moments players seem to feel they are cheating themselves by bailing out right of the green.

How many times have we seen players come to the twelfth tee at Augusta during the final round of the Masters, and listened to the announcers talk about how "he needs to play to the center of the green and take his three." Every Masters contestant knows this is not a hole you take chances on, yet with a short iron in their hand, something always makes them want to leave their clubface open through impact just a split-second longer and play straight at the hole.

The twelfth green's slightly angled setting makes the far right hole a bit longer than the yardage to the center of the green, meaning the player intending to go at the center but instead playing at the hole is ultimately penalized for the slightest mishit or greedy play. If you can resist the temptation of going for the far right hole location, your chances of success are excellent. But so few are able to resist.

In my opinion this thirteenth hole is one of the finest holes for competitive play I have ever seen. The player is tempted to dare the creek on his tee shot by playing in close to the corner, because if he attains his position he has not only shortened the hole but obtained a more level lie for his second shot.
—Bobby Jones, on Augusta's 13th

The par-5 thirteenth hole at Augusta National used to be a paltry 465 yards from the member tees, 485 yards from the back tee. It has since been lengthened in the recent dismantling of the Jones-MacKenzie design, but it will hopefully continue to tease and torture great players more than any hole in the world. The design features are so well-balanced that golfers of all levels are tempted to try shots they might not normally consider.

A top player on his game believes a score of five is a letdown because birdie or even eagle is nearly always within reach. The design beguiles the player into cutting off that creek-and-pine-guarded corner with the hopes of shortening the hole and approaching the green from a flat lie. If the player is long and precise off the tee, this allows for a shorter club to be used to attack the putting surface. The green is perched dangerously behind a trickling creek. The rear of the green is guarded by several bunkers and a grass swale. Plenty of elements are entering into the equation, but each is just difficult enough to cause the player to question himself.

Everything admired about the thirteenth at Augusta National revolves around its ability to lure the player into playing shots they don't necessarily need to hit. Whether driven by past memories of success or the point the hole falls in the round or simply the short yardage on the scorecard, Augusta's thirteenth often gets the better of golfers. It baits them to go for the risky shot regardless of whether they need to or not. There have been times we've seen shrewd players lay up despite their desire or need to go for the green in two. Rarely do those players make worse than a par, and often they make a four.

But you say, where is the temptation for the average golfer who is unable to reach the green in two?

The entire left side of the hole flattens out before reaching the creek, whereas the center and right side of the fairway is severely sloped. The temptation lies in trying to lay up as close to the creek (and the flat lie) as possible, without going into the water hazard. Simple, subtle and probably not worth the risk to most players. But then again, who is comfortable hitting a short iron off a downhill, sidehill lie into a green guarded by water? Maybe it is worth the risk to lay up a little closer to the creek for the flatter lie and a better angle to the right side hole locations, right?

Not only are the questions caused by design fun to witness as a Masters spectator or television viewer, but we all encounter such tempting situations on the course from time to time. And if we decide to yield to temptation and play the bold shot, these are our best golfing memories, regardless of the outcome. Otherwise, as Oscar Wilde seemed to be saying of classic golf design, "The only way to get rid of temptation is to yield to it. Resist it, and your soul grows sick with longing for the things it has forbidden to itself."

The true hazard should draw the player towards it, should invite the golfer to come as near as he dare to the fire without burning his fingers. The man who can afford to take risks is the man who should gain the advantage. —*John Low*, Concerning Golf, *1903*

Although Jackie Burke was correct in stating that Augusta National is the "most tempting golf course in the world," temptation does not have to be limited to the home of the Masters. Temptation should not have to rely on creeks set amidst an array of azaleas and towering Georgia pines. It should play a role in the placement of every hazard built on every course in the world. Temptation should be considered in the design of every green complex.

Consider Exhibits A and B on the folowing pages. The hole in Exhibit A is the simplest of all strategic holes. A bunker is placed at the corner of the dogleg. The player who places their shot near or beyond the bunker shortens the hole and opens up a better view of the putting surface. Notice how the green opens subtly to the "bunkered" side of the fairway, thus rewarding the more courageous player.

Exhibit B shows that the player is not tempted by the bunker placement. But instead is merely asked to play down the center of the fairway minus the option of a riskier play that rewards with a payoff awaiting the heroic golfer. The hole in Exhibit B asks no questions, allows for no visualization of interesting shots and is devoid of daring features that tempt the player into something nervy.

Temptation is defined best by the architect posing interesting questions and the player figuring out how best to answer them. The beauty of tempting golf course design is obvious. Nearly always, the player has no one to blame but themselves for mistakes. But if he is successful, the player can bask in the glory of his success. Why? Because he overcame the most tempting questions the architect could pose. The player took a risk and was rewarded for intelligence, patience, courage and skill.

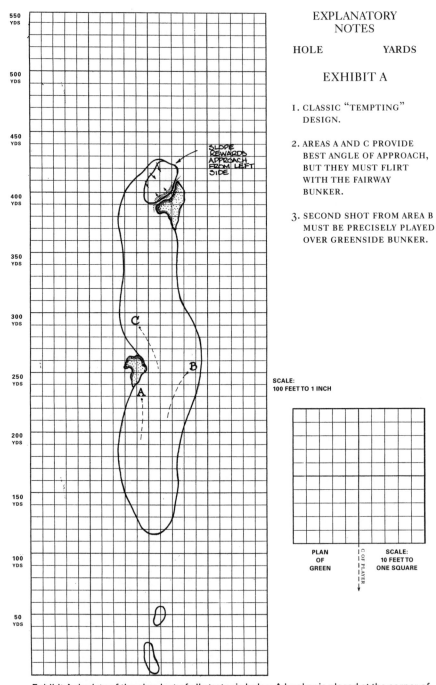

550
YDS

500
YDS

450
YDS

400
YDS

350
YDS

300
YDS

250
YDS

200
YDS

150
YDS

100
YDS

50
YDS

SLOPE
REWARDS
APPROACH
FROM LEFT
SIDE

C

B

A

EXPLANATORY
NOTES

HOLE   YARDS

EXHIBIT A

1. CLASSIC "TEMPTING"
DESIGN.

2. AREAS A AND C PROVIDE
BEST ANGLE OF APPROACH,
BUT THEY MUST FLIRT
WITH THE FAIRWAY
BUNKER.

3. SECOND SHOT FROM AREA B
MUST BE PRECISELY PLAYED
OVER GREENSIDE BUNKER.

SCALE:
100 FEET TO 1 INCH

PLAN   C OF   SCALE:
OF   PLAYER   10 FEET TO
GREEN   ONE SQUARE

Exhibit A depicts of the simplest of all strategic holes. A bunker is placed at the corner of the dogleg. The player who places their shot near it or beyond the bunker shortens the hole and opens up a better view of the putting surface. Notice how the green opens subtly to the "bunkered" side of the fairway, thus rewarding the more courageous player. The farther the player strays from the corner of the dogleg, the more the greenside bunker comes into play. (GIL HANSE)

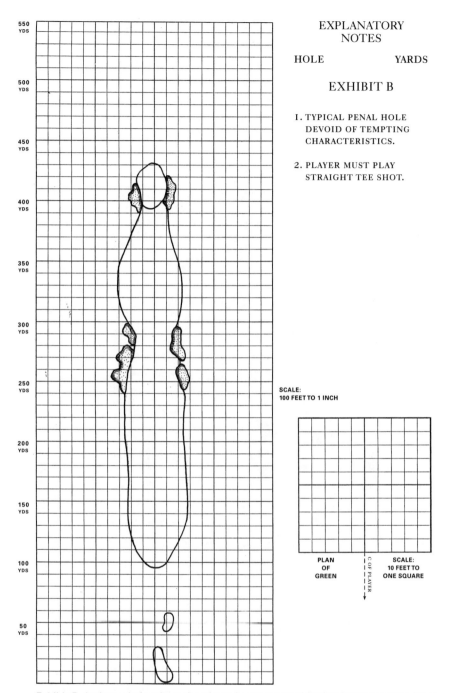

EXHIBIT B

1. TYPICAL PENAL HOLE
   DEVOID OF TEMPTING
   CHARACTERISTICS.

2. PLAYER MUST PLAY
   STRAIGHT TEE SHOT.

SCALE:
100 FEET TO 1 INCH

PLAN   SCALE:
OF   10 FEET TO
GREEN   ONE SQUARE

℄ OF PLAYER

550 YDS
500 YDS
450 YDS
400 YDS
350 YDS
300 YDS
250 YDS
200 YDS
150 YDS
100 YDS
50 YDS

Exhibit B depicts a hole where the player is not tempted by bunker placement. He is required to play down the center of the fairway. There is no option for a riskier play that rewards the heroic golfer. The hole in exhibit B asks no questions, allows for no visualization of interesting shots, with no daring features tempting the player into something nervy. (GIL HANSE)

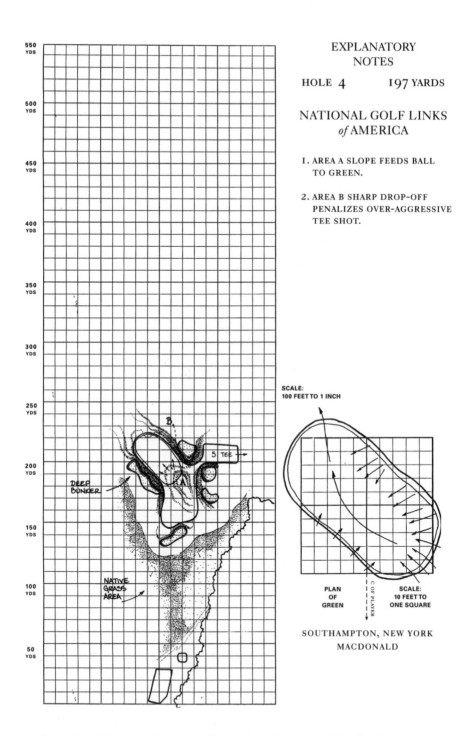

EXPLANATORY
NOTES

HOLE 4   197 YARDS

NATIONAL GOLF LINKS
of AMERICA

1. AREA A SLOPE FEEDS BALL
   TO GREEN.

2. AREA B SHARP DROP-OFF
   PENALIZES OVER-AGGRESSIVE
   TEE SHOT.

SCALE:
100 FEET TO 1 INCH

PLAN
OF
GREEN

C OF PLAYER

SCALE:
10 FEET TO
ONE SQUARE

SOUTHAMPTON, NEW YORK
MACDONALD

Rendering of the par-3 fourth, the Redan at the National Golf Links of America. (GIL HANSE).

What is a Redan?
The most tempting hole of all.

Said the North Berwick caddie to Mr. Macdonald when he was on the quest for ideal holes for the coming National Golf Links, "Here's the hole that makes a man think."   —*H. J. Whigham, author*

We frequently hear television commentators, architects and historians throw around the term "Redan" when describing various holes or characteristics of a given green site.

The well-designed Redan par-3 was the first model for tempting architecture and continues to serve as the best example of temptation. The original Redan par-3 can still be found at North Berwick's West Course in Scotland. Named after a particular fortress used in the Crimean War, North Berwick's 192-yard par-3 fifteenth hole is based on the simple theory of biting off as much of the hazard as you think you are capable. Sometimes, however, golfers are tempted into playing straight at the hole, which on most Redans is a mistake unless you hit a perfect shot. But haven't we all been tempted into hitting stupid shots, because somehow our mind magically recalls the "perfect" shots we've hit in our life? Or we just get that feeling that today is the day. And when it is our day and we can outduel the design, there is no better feeling in golf.

Charles Blair Macdonald, along with his associate and engineering specialist Seth Raynor, built versions of the Redan on each of their designs. Macdonald defined it this way:

> Take a narrow tableland, tilt it a little from right to left, dig a deep bunker on the front side, approach it diagonally, and you have the Redan. At North Berwick, of course, all these things were done in the beginning by nature. The only original thing that the greenkeeper did was to place the tee so that the shot had

to be played cornerwise, so to speak, instead of directly down the tableland.

The original Redan par-3 and the seventy or so offshoots in the United States present decisions for all golfers, all of the time. Thousands of green designs for par-4s and even par-5s have been based loosely on the Redan because it consistently tempts and taunts the player with decisions.

In most cases, the Redan presents an angled green that slopes slightly away from the player, with a bunker in front of the green and a nice bit of helping contour on the approach designed to give the golfer options in attacking the hole. The player who plays straight for the flagstick had better hit a high, precise shot. The less bold player can stay away from the fronting greenside bunker and run his shot into the green, using the contour to help kick the ball onto the surface. Then there are the options somewhere in between the boldest shot and the safe lay-up.

The Redan offers every level of golfer the chance to bite off as much as he wishes or as much as his game allows. The more direct line the player takes to the pin, the more precise the shot must be. As the player gets greedier, the stakes go up, and the penalties for failure become more severe. A well-conceived Redan offers the kind of temptation and reasoning that makes golf so addictive.

The Seventh Hole

The Great Holes

The Thirteenth at Augusta National, the Tenth at Riviera, the Road Hole at St. Andrews and the Sixteenth at Cypress Point

Just as close as he dare: That's golf, and that's a hazard of immortal importance! For golf at its best should be a contest of risks. The fine player should on his way 'round the links be just slipping past the bunkers, gaining every yard he can, conquering by the confidence of his own 'far and sure' play. —*John Low*, Concerning Golf, *1903*

Anyone interested in golf has discussed (or argued) with friends over what ingredients produce a "great" hole. Is greatness defined by a hole that is "tough but fair"? With some astounding visual effects thrown in? Or is it defined by the mysterious "shot values" term and some beautifully manicured grass?

Perhaps a great hole is a result of simply knowing it when you see it, like baseball scouts who have a gut feeling about a prospect. Instinct tells you that there are no specific elements contributing to the merits of the hole. Instead, the hole appeals to your senses and rewards your shots. It feels great to you and, at the end of the day, you just like the way it looks.

While all of those elements factor in to how we weigh the merits of a course, there is more to recognizing greatness than just a self-important, feel-good observation. Four general areas require your attention in studying golf holes, not only in determining their quality but in figuring out how to play them better.

When you consider the elements defining a timeless hole design, you may uncover which design features are essential to the merits of all holes you've come to enjoy playing. And you may see why other golf holes commonly held up as sacred actually have little of the character that leads to compelling golf.

All too often "difficulty" is held up as the most important indicator of a hole's worthiness. The tougher the hole, the better it must be. Sure, we all love a challenge. And a tempting design can boggle the mind to the point the golfer has no chance of pulling off a confident stroke. But the problems posed by a hole must be presented in a way that can be overcome by a combination of intelligence and skill, otherwise what is the point? Anyone can build holes that are physically impossible to play.

A hole that poses great physical difficulty does not require expertise to design. Anyone can place hazards in such a way that par is an impossible task. It is the talented architect who can present holes that are genuinely challenging yet reward skillful play. The four elements to keep in mind when analyzing a hole include the strategy, the green, the naturalness and artistry of construction, and finally the often misunderstood role of "playability."

> *It is important to emphasize the necessity for the golfer to use his head as much as his hands; or in other words, to make his mental agility match his physical ability.* —*H. N. Wethered and Tom Simpson,*
> The Architectural Side of Golf

Strategy. Like an old black and white film that may not have the modern touches of color and digital sound, the classics still hold their own on the fifth viewing thanks to a great story. And in golf design, the strategy is the "story" of each hole. Regardless of how beautiful or dramatic a hole may be, the basic strategy dictates how interesting a hole is the first time around while also making it compelling to play the fiftieth time.

To determine whether a hole is strategic or not, you can ask a simple question: Does it allow for all golfers, regardless of ability, to consider different playing options? Does one route to the hole tempt us more than another? Does it provide an equally tempting lay-up option? Most of all, does the player who decides on a plan and follows it with sound shotmaking find himself rewarded over an opponent who took a less aggressive avenue to the hole?

Options and the chance to play safe while still sneaking by a better but less wise player—that is your indication that strategy is present.

> *A putting green has features just like a human, or, at least, it should have to be worthy of the name. Of course there are many which are no more impressive than the vacant, cowlike expression of some people, but then again there are some with rugged profiles which loom head and shoulders above the common herd, and the moment we clap our eyes on one of these, impulsively we murmur, "Ah! There's a green for you!"*
>
> *—A. W. Tillinghast*

Green. The green complex is the climax to our story, the third act of the play, the coda to golf's eighteen-hole symphony. The structure of a green dictates the golfer's decisions as he plays the hole. The size, shaping of contours, the general slope and the overall memorability of key features play a role in making the strategy work. After all, if a player cannot recall the primary features of a green after one or two rounds, then planning an intelligent attack of the hole is nearly impossible (and not much fun).

An excellent green design contains character that is dictated by its setting and the naturalness of its contours. The approach—the thirty or so yards leading directly into the green—is as important as the putting surface itself and should be considered when judging the character of a green. The approach is also vital to consider when managing your way around a course. Few golfers take advantage of the approach even when it is clear the architect created this as an avenue to the hole.

> *All artificial hazards should be made to fit into the ground as if placed there by nature. To accomplish this is a great art. Indeed, when it is really*

done well, it is—I think it may truly be said—a fine art, worthy of the
hand of a gifted sculptor. —Robert Hunter, golf architect

Naturalness and Artistry of Construction. This is where the hugely popular talk of aesthetics plays a role, though probably in a different light than you might expect. The emphasis in modern design rests on who can create the biggest "wow" factor no matter how much money or environmental obliteration is necessary to create such an effect.

Consideration of actual playing strategy is often lost in a morass of visual accoutrements and signature holes that feature cascading water-falls, quarries, island greens and other dramatic features. It is always interesting to see how architects utilize these splashy elements. "Wow" elements certainly can be exciting to witness on first glance and look sensational in a glossy magazine photograph. But rarely do these superfluous touches make a hole fun to play more than once or twice, unless the features are used to create decision-making dilem-mas or the occasional heroic carry shot.

Meanwhile a modern-day appreciation is slowly developing for the courses which contain features so natural that they appear to have been "found." The more natural the layout is, the more it gives the player a feeling of battling nature and the more interesting the battle becomes. This notion of an ultra-natural style of design was the goal of master architects who practiced during the 1920s, and their vision for authenti-cally natural design is being appreciated once again now that many have experienced their fair share of man-made golf course features.

The creation of natural features requires artistry in the construc-tion of a course. We all can spot artistic and natural-looking holes by appreciating the *irregularity* of features and the gracefulness of con-tours. Any kind of straight, sharp-edged features are easily identified. These contrived looks are a product of shaping work carried out by large earthmoving equipment with little finishing handwork to soften the manufactured edges. Over time, hard and ungainly features become bland, even annoying, which is why the artistry of construc-tion is a subtle but important aspect of design analysis.

Unnatural-looking and -playing courses have the same effect on us that a musical performance would if the performer lip-synched to a recording. You've paid to hear the performer sing, even if their voice may not be as strong or they may occasionally forget a line, but at least the music is coming from them. If performed live, the song is sure to take on some spontaneous character that lends individuality to that particular rendition.

The same authenticity is found in the most popular and timeless golf courses. Some are constructed in a way that parallels genuine live performances, where you feel some spontaneity in the design ideas presented. Others feel like tape-recorded efforts that you've heard and seen before, carried out with little passion for nature.

> *There are few problems more difficult to solve than the problem of what exactly constitutes an ideal hole. The ideal hole is surely one that affords the greatest pleasure to the greatest number, gives the fullest advantage for accurate play, stimulates players to improve their game, and never becomes monotonous.* —Alister MacKenzie

Playability. We all have read the magazine blurb where the architect states that his design will be "challenging for the good player, but still playable for the average golfer." This is a noble intention and certainly the hope of all architects when building a course. But when we see these courses proclaiming their playability, we often learn that they tend either to be extremely difficult because the trouble has been placed to the sides of the holes or, because the architect tried so hard to not punish average golfers, to have few interesting features for most players to deal with. They are playable for all, but boring.

Playability should mean that a hole is fun for the average player and just as challenging for them to try outmaneuvering as it is for the excellent golfer. Most of all, playability must mean that there is a way to the hole for the average player who is patient and shrewd, but also the temptation to go for broke if he chooses.

At the same time, playability should mean that if the player wants to take the safe way home, that route must be somewhat easy and lack overtly penalizing elements. A well-designed hole does not make inflicting punishment its primary purpose. Instead, the best holes create inconveniences for those taking the safer route. Sometimes they make par nearly impossible to obtain, all because the green takes more shots to reach.

The main argument between advocates of the penal school designers and the strategic architects is over the placement of hazards. Penal architects like everything on the sides of play, rewarding only the straight shot and punishing only slightly wayward strokes. Strategic architects prefer fewer hazards, and when they do use a bunker, they place them in a variety of places because most golfers hit wayward shots. And if the course is well designed, the wayward shots will already receive a great deal of inconvenience by not having a reasonable angle of approach to the green.

Or in many cases the angle may be playable, but the mishit does not allow for a view of the green. This more subtle form of penalty makes the strategic courses more interesting for the skilled player, and less penal for the wild golfer. If greens are well conceived, as they are at Augusta National where the fairways were once extremely wide, the errant golfer will still find plenty of trouble because his wayward shots will be met with inconvenient angles of attack to the putting surface.

Playability is a key ingredient to making the four great hole examples featured here fun for golfers of all levels: Augusta's famed par-5 thirteenth, Riviera's short par-4 tenth, the Road hole at St. Andrews, and the heroic par-3 sixteenth at Cypress Point.

The Thirteenth at Augusta National Golf Club, Par 5, 485 Yards

Designed by Alister MacKenzie and Bobby Jones

> *Whenever I played the thirteenth or fifteenth hole at Augusta, [my dad] had a habit of kneeling down, cupping his hands and yelling, "Lay up, lay up!" He was just beside himself every time I got near the water.*
> —Ben Crenshaw

Strategy. The tee shot must deal with a creek guarding the left side, with a hard left turn 240 yards off the tee around pines and water. The wide fairway is sloped steeply toward the creek, but near the water's

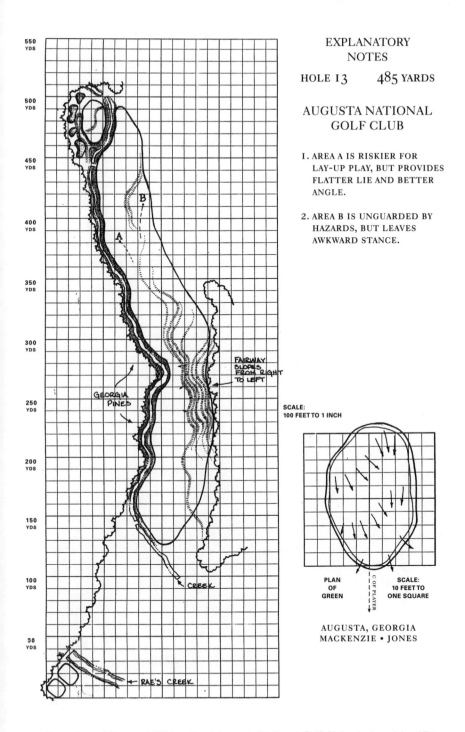

EXPLANATORY
NOTES

HOLE 13   485 YARDS

AUGUSTA NATIONAL
GOLF CLUB

1. AREA A IS RISKIER FOR
LAY-UP PLAY, BUT PROVIDES
FLATTER LIE AND BETTER
ANGLE.

2. AREA B IS UNGUARDED BY
HAZARDS, BUT LEAVES
AWKWARD STANCE.

SCALE:
100 FEET TO 1 INCH

550 YDS

500 YDS

450 YDS

400 YDS

350 YDS

300 YDS

250 YDS

200 YDS

150 YDS

100 YDS

50 YDS

FAIRWAY SLOPES FROM RIGHT TO LEFT

GEORGIA PINES

CREEK

RAE'S CREEK

PLAN OF GREEN

C OF PLAYER

SCALE:
10 FEET TO
ONE SQUARE

AUGUSTA, GEORGIA
MACKENZIE • JONES

Rendering of the par-5 thirteenth at Augusta National Golf Club, designed by Alister MacKenzie and Bobby Jones. (GIL HANSE)

93

edge the area flattens out. The closer the player hits their drive to the creek, the shorter this dogleg left plays and the better the player's chance is of drawing a less severe stance. What lends the strategic fun to this hole is the notion that a safe play off the tee and an even safer lay-up shot will still give most golfers a short shot that could set up a birdie putt, and at worst, a par. Yet, if your swing is feeling sharp, eagles and birdies are well within reach with a price to pay should you fail to execute your shots.

Green. This putting surface has been tinkered with extensively over the years, but the natural features of this hole are so sound that even the tinkering could not harm it. At times the changes have threatened to eliminate the "temptation" factor. A deep swale was added by Jack Nicklaus's design associates around the rear of this green in 1983, but has been softened since the initial change was not well received.

The green design is fairly close to Alister MacKenzie's original in size and shape, especially since a long-lost far back right hole location was restored in 1999. The beauty of this green is that it sets up with a strong slope from back to front. This tilt convinces many players going for the green in two that they have a chance of holding the putting sur-

The approach to Augusta's thirteenth. (LYNN SHACKELFORD)

face. But the tilt also lets golfers know that if they lay up, there will be a reasonable chance of hitting a short iron close to the hole locations nearest the creek. This information adds yet another dimension to the decision-making adventures here.

The day-to-day hole location dictates different second and third shot options, and calls on the player to consider numerous possibilities as to which angle is the best one to attack the flagstick. This day-to-day variety is the mark of a masterfully designed green and why Bobby Jones said he loved links golf.

Naturalness and Artistry of Construction. We've all watched the Masters and know that it is difficult to find a more idyllic setting for golf. The afternoon shadows, pines and azaleas are breathtaking. But setting the scenery aside, consider how the hole sits on the landscape. By all accounts, the creek and the tilt of the fairway were "found" by architects Alister MacKenzie and Bobby Jones. They left these features alone. Construction photos show that some fairway grading work took place to presumably modify what they found and perhaps soften a few of the slopes or deal with drainage issues. However it is difficult to tell when watching on television or viewing the hole in person that the contours are anything but natural. This kind of undetectable shaping indicates that they disguised the man-made work by creating just enough irregularity. Jones's and MacKenzie's original design also featured less ostentatious bunkering behind the green than you see today. They were subtle, "river" bunkers that blended in as if they were old swales that fed the creek and were merely filled with sand.

Playability. This is a difficult hole for the average Augusta member because of the severe slope of the fairway. Most golfers struggle with sidehill lies, not because we are physically incapable but because we forget to account for their effects in preshot planning.

On Augusta's thirteenth, the crafty player has a wide fairway to play to along with generous lay-up areas. The green tilt will hold a decent approach shot, making it a very playable hole for all golfers. And thanks to the strategic elements at hand, the short hitter who strikes solid, well-placed shots can easily sneak up on the less intelligent, perhaps over-anxious golfer. One can only imagine how many thousands of times a short hitter has quietly scored better than the player who caved to temptation and unsuccessfully tried to reach the green in two shots.

All of these elements beg the question, why aren't there more holes designed like the thirteenth at Augusta National? After all, short par-5s with creeks and tall trees are features frequently found and used by architects. Is there something about the slope of the fairway, the sharp bend of the hole or the mystique of "Amen Corner" that makes this hole so great? Or is it shrewd planning by the architects, who saw wonderful natural features and only modified them slightly for golf?

A decision by the architects made near the end of construction is one that in today's world of "championship" standards and 480-yard par-4s might not occur. In old magazine articles, the thirteenth was cited as a long par-4 until as late as a few months before the course opened. MacKenzie and Jones obviously recognized the beauty of a short, tempting par-5 over a less interesting long two-shotter. With that simple change during construction, the tempting factors discussed above became infinitely more interesting, fun and dramatic for golfers of all skill levels.

The Tenth at Riviera Country Club, Par 4, 311 Yards

Designed by George Thomas and Billy Bell

> *This is a shameless little harlot that just sits there at the end of the bar in her mesh stockings and miniskirt and winks at you.*
>
> —Jim Murray, writer

Having watched many of the world's best players tackle this hole in competition along with witnessing regular golfers attempt to play it, there is little doubt that Jack Nicklaus was correct in stating Riviera's tenth presents more options than any short hole in the world. The only mystery is why this two-shotter is not used as a model for architects when trying to come up with unique short par-4 designs.

Strategy. Nicklaus has repeatedly stated that there are a number of options here, yet if you study his rounds at Riviera he almost always

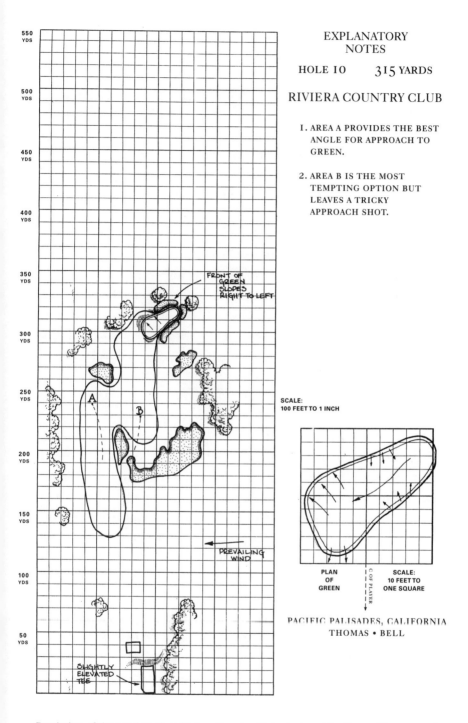

EXPLANATORY
NOTES

HOLE 10   315 YARDS

RIVIERA COUNTRY CLUB

1. AREA A PROVIDES THE BEST
   ANGLE FOR APPROACH TO
   GREEN.

2. AREA B IS THE MOST
   TEMPTING OPTION BUT
   LEAVES A TRICKY
   APPROACH SHOT.

SCALE:
100 FEET TO 1 INCH

PLAN   SCALE:
OF   10 FEET TO
GREEN   ONE SQUARE

PACIFIC PALISADES, CALIFORNIA
THOMAS • BELL

Rendering of the par-4 tenth at Riviera Country Club, designed by George Thomas and Billy Bell. (GIL HANSE) played the tenth the same way no matter where the flagstick was located and no matter where he stood in competition. The only time he altered his game plan was if the hole played downwind, in one of Southern California's nasty Santa Ana winds. With a gust to his back, Nicklaus could drive the green with as little as a 3-wood. But few have the patience and strength of mind to stick to their game plan like Nicklaus or Tiger Woods, and that is where this hole ultimately gets the best of most golfers.

Anyone can stand on Riviera's tenth tee and see that the green is really only about 285 yards away if you take the straight line to the green. No matter how good or bad your game is, the shortest way is naturally the best avenue to success, right?

Unfortunately, as those who play straight toward the hole soon find out, the green does not open up from the right (the short, straight angle). I have seen golfers who have played the course hundreds of times stubbornly take this shorter route even knowing what lies ahead, yet they wonder why they can never improve on their normal round in the low 90s!

The wise play is down the left side, away from the green, where plenty of width is provided and where the best angle of approach will present itself. There is also a riskier option in between the fairway bunkers. As far as difficulty goes, this option falls somewhere between the safest play left, and the short way home down the right. This "middle" ground route to the putting surface leaves a shorter wedge shot to a long, slender green and proves tempting. The approach is a scary shot if you are not confident with your wedge game, but birdie is well within reach and par is a rather simple matter if you play your cards right (or in this case, *left*) off the tee. If you are careless, the deep bunkers surrounding the green mean an almost certain bogey and oftentimes an even worse score.

Green. If the green opening was angled just a bit more to the right, the strategy would not work and the hole would be receptive to poorly planned tee shots. If the green opening angled more to the left, the temptation for long hitters to drive close to the green would not exist. It would also be too difficult for the average player who can, in the current scheme of the hole, hold his own with the long hitter who either is careless or not very deft with a wedge in their hand (and we all know those long hitters who hate the delicacy of wedge play).

There is nothing intricate in the contouring found on this green. It is a long, bowling pin–shaped surface that tilts from right to left, away from the players who hit their tee shot down the right side. The first third of the green features a subtle left-side tier that falls off to a chipping area, while the remainder of the green is surrounded by sand. The simplicity of the green design makes it that much more frustrating when you register bogey or worse here. There are no quirky contours to blame and few bad bounces you can receive. Either you hit a good shot or you find serious trouble, which on a hole of such short length is essential to creating drama.

Naturalness and Artistry of Construction. The Riviera site contained many interesting natural features, but the location for the tenth hole was less than ideal. The terrain was flat and almost as wide as it was

View from above the par-4 tenth at Riviera. (GEOFF SHACKELFORD)

long. Yet, George Thomas created the most interesting strategic short par-4 that he or perhaps any other architect has ever built, and a two-shot affair that is unanimously adored by famous golfers, architects and everyday players.

So with such a fine hole, albeit on flat land and in an awkward setting, this would seem to deflate the theory that a golf hole must have elevation change or heroic natural features to be interesting and dramatic.

The deep bunkering here has evolved to its current state due to excessive play over the years. Still, the enormous carry bunker off the tee is imposing and it finds a way to lure players to carry it and land on the less appealing right side. Something about the thrill of defying the bunker and its gently raised face suckers wise doctors, lawyers and Hollywood super agents to carry it, when in fact players with experience and local knowledge know that they should avoid going down the right side. The entire hole is beautifully constructed because its scale is large and fits the wide-open situation. The tenth looks dramatic despite not having any ocean or natural hazards to enhance its beauty.

Playability. Admiration for Riviera's tenth comes from the consistency with which it rewards the patient tactician while penalizing the careless, greedy golfer who looks to jumpstart his or her round after tallying their score on the front nine. Thanks to the options presented by George Thomas, the worst golfers in the world can make par here while playing in the same group as the best players in the world, who can register bogey just as quickly.

The Road Hole, Seventeenth on the Old Course at St. Andrews, Par 4, 465 Yards

Designed by Mother Nature, green complex by Allan Robertson

It is the worst hole in golf. —*J. H. Taylor*

You tee off over a wood building, trying to avoid slicing out-of-bounds into a hotel that Henry Longhurst once said looked like a "chest with all the drawers pulled out." Then you try to land a long iron or fairway wood approach onto a green that sometimes doesn't hold a short wedge shot. If your approach fails and your ball goes over, it may ricochet off a road and finish against an old stone wall.

That's just the beginning of the 461-yard Road hole.

Amidst all of this wackiness is the most dramatic, tempting and original long par-4 in golf. Many are critical of it, but usually they fail to understand that the Road hole is not the product of a wickedly cruel architect's desire to punish golfers, but instead, the result of evolution and adjusting golf to a unique setting. The hole is actually "natural" even though man-made obstacles play a role in determining your fate. But fate is ultimately decided by how well you plan your attack and sort out the various scenarios the hole presents. And then, it's a matter of how well you execute your shots.

Strategy. The tee shot plays over a wooden shed that used to be a railway station during the early twentieth century. If you played the hole prior to the mid-1960s you aimed at the small "d" in "D. Anderson," who advertised his golf shop on the side of the building. Today, depending on your ability and selected route to the hole, you choose a letter from the "Old Course Hotel and Spa" lettering. Out-of-bounds runs down the right side where the hotel sits, so the farther right the player aims off the tee, the more risk he or she enters into the equation. However, the fairway's right side is the optimum place to land your drive even though you can't see this area. The farther left you play off the tee—the route most of us take—the longer the approach shot is to the green and the more likely we are to be playing the hole as a three-shot affair (in most cases, the wisest approach).

The Road hole was a par-5 until the Links Management Committee decided to lower it to a par-4 in advance of the 1964 Open Championship. Most players are like Jack Nicklaus, feeling that the hole is a par-4$^1/_2$. Thus, they manage it like they do Augusta's thirteenth: one shot at a time but always tempted to go for the aggressive shot that gets you to the green, and yet aware that a five is not the worst score in the world.

The options allow players to plan their strategy with a clear mind, basing their route of attack on the weather, their standing in the round

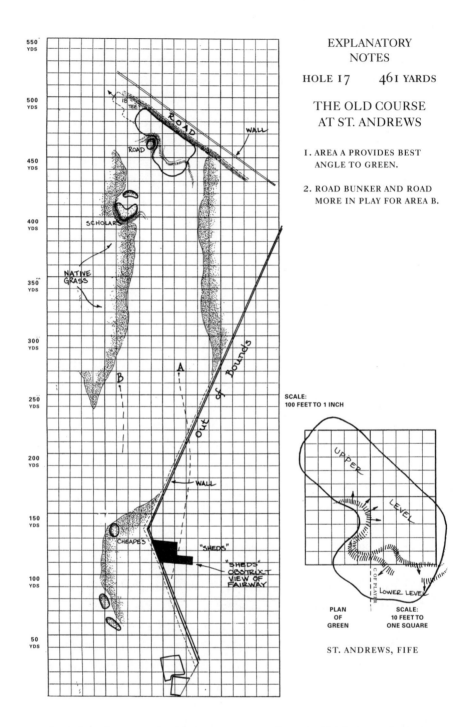

550
YDS

500
YDS

450
YDS

400
YDS

350
YDS

300
YDS

250
YDS

200
YDS

150
YDS

100
YDS

50
YDS

18
TEE

ROAD

ROAD

WALL

SCHOLAR

NATIVE
GRASS

A

B

Out of Bounds

WALL

CHEAPES

"SHEDS"

"SHEDS"
OBSTRUCT
VIEW OF
FAIRWAY

EXPLANATORY
NOTES

HOLE 17   461 YARDS

THE OLD COURSE
AT ST. ANDREWS

1. AREA A PROVIDES BEST
   ANGLE TO GREEN.

2. ROAD BUNKER AND ROAD
   MORE IN PLAY FOR AREA B.

SCALE:
100 FEET TO 1 INCH

UPPER

LEVEL

C OF PLAYER

LOWER LEVEL

PLAN   SCALE:
OF   10 FEET TO
GREEN   ONE SQUARE

ST. ANDREWS, FIFE

Rendering of the par-4 Road hole, the seventeenth on the Old Course at St. Andrews,
designed by Mother Nature and Allan Robertson. (GIL HANSE)

and the day's hole location (*if* you remembered to check the tin cup's locale when playing the first hole). Some golfers have no trouble with the options and ever-changing possibilities, others struggle with on-the-spot planning.

After dealing with the choices for the tee shot, numerous dilemmas await for the second. Trying to make a 4 or even a 3 out of desperation will almost certainly court disaster, bringing the hazards in the front and rear of the green into play.

Green. The putting surface is a 45-yard long, horizontally angled green perched above the fairway. With a crowned effect and the deep "Road" bunker guarding the left third of this upper shelf, no putting surface is more terrifying or difficult for such a long hole. The green is perched with a road to the immediate rear, meaning any shot barely bounding over the putting surface will hit the path and lead you to trouble. But the character and beauty of this green should be the focus, not the penal nature of the hazards.

Even though the green is crowned it affords a generous opening with a sharp tier to confront if you hope to make it to the top level.

View of the second shot to the Road hole. (GEOFF SHACKELFORD)

The road and back edge of the green on St. Andrews' seventeenth. (GEOFF SHACKELFORD)

Thanks to its wide opening and space to play safe around the green, many tempting choices present themselves. Even the golfer who places a long tee shot down the right side and is left with an iron to the green should consider laying up. This play avoids bringing all of the elements near the green into play, even if this means accepting that you will likely take a bogey five.

Likewise, the pressure of a match or the simple desperation to take a stroke off your normal score, or even your desire to play aggressively, all pose elements that may tempt the golfer into an unwise play. The Road has the strangest and yet greatest of all greens because it manages to create so many options, but only rewards the most precise shots.

Naturalness and Artistry of Construction. Unlike the thirteenth at Augusta, there has never been any confusion over golfers ignoring the Road's strategic elements in favor of its overwhelming beauty. Yes, it is a strange-looking tee shot and it is obnoxious to see a high-rise hotel towering over the fairway, reminding golfers that St. Andrews needed stricter building laws in the late 1960s. However, if you look away from the hotel you will see the medieval town and the Royal and Ancient Clubhouse sitting to the left. The wide-open, rolling contours of the home hole are in full view. It is the most beautiful and daunting setting in golf. If a Hollywood production designer created a set similar to St. Andrews, golfers would not take it seriously.

The Road hole's subtle ground contours are striking but rarely noticed because of all the other distracting hazards. And even though most of these bumps and hollows were created by nature, the green was a product of Allan Robertson's imagination. The sharp tier and the Road bunker were created by Robertson and remain one of the great architectural inventions in golf. There is plenty of room around both the tier and fronting bunker to lay-up. This leaves a fascinating pitch shot or options few could imagine. Bobby Jones even played his approach well left of the green, near the eighteenth tee, depending on certain conditions and hole locations.

Playability. This is the most difficult of the four holes featured because the green is severe and requires incredible precision. Again, however, the short hitter who is accurate and who quietly plods their way to the hole can nearly always make a five or six here. And a score of five or six is often good enough to match your opponents, including the best players in the world. (Some of golf's greatest have said they would gladly take a five here every time around.)

There is plenty of room to play safe off the tee, to lay up on the approach, even enough width on the upper tier of the green to play a safe chip shot, take your two putts and stroll over to the eighteenth tee. Yet each safe choice also manages to get diverted by a more tantalizing one that is within reach if the player pulls off a precise shot. That constant choice between a safe outlet and a bolder option makes this hole dramatic, regardless of what par is and regardless of how peculiar the Road Hole may seem.

The Sixteenth at Cypress Point Club, Par 3, 233 Yards

Designed by Alister MacKenzie, Robert Hunter and Marion Hollins

> *The desirability or otherwise of having water hazards depends largely on their spectacular character and beauty. The amazing thrill of driving successfully over the ocean at the sixteenth hole at Cypress Point more than*

compensates for the loss of a dozen balls. Even absolute dubs succumb to
this thrill.   —*Alister MacKenzie*

The par-3 sixteenth at Cypress Point plays over the Pacific Ocean with the wind blowing in off the sea. It is easily the most famous and awe-inspiring hole in golf. It is also nearly impossible for most golfers to birdie, much less make par on. However, the temptation to play over the Pacific toward the green, even with a safe left-hand bailout, provides the genuine excitement found in this hole and others with a similar "forced carry" design. The room to play safe is also why, despite its extreme difficulty, the sixteenth eludes criticism.

The temptation is so great on Cypress Point's sixteenth that its architect, Alister MacKenzie, deemed this shot "the Lindbergh Thrill" after the idol of his era, Charles Lindbergh. (Lindbergh became the first to fly solo across the Atlantic in 1927, the same year MacKenzie and Robert Hunter were in the final planning stages of Cypress Point.)

The possibility of launching a shot over an enormous hazard with the reward of landing safely on the other side may be the ultimate thrill in golf. Many golfers get the chance to try such a shot on golf courses with par-3s playing over water. It just happens that Cypress Point's is over the Pacific Ocean. To attempt a shot over such a natural chasm and to carry it off is an experience that the golfers lucky enough to play there remember throughout their golfing life. And they are known to share details of the shot with friends, the same friends who go on to commiserate with *their* friends about how golfers have it in their heads that everyone else cares about such stories! But they will never understand because they never experience the thrill of succumbing to the temptation of an intimidating hole, and overcoming its obstacles to pull off the occasional "miracle" shot.

Alister MacKenzie was initially against the idea of the hole playing as a par-3. He openly stated that a one-shotter would be too penal and would lack the strategic interest to be enjoyed over time. But the visionary behind Cypress Point, Marion Hollins, proved to MacKenzie that the green could be reached with one swing. MacKenzie saw that with a large area of bailout fairway to the left, originally planned to be

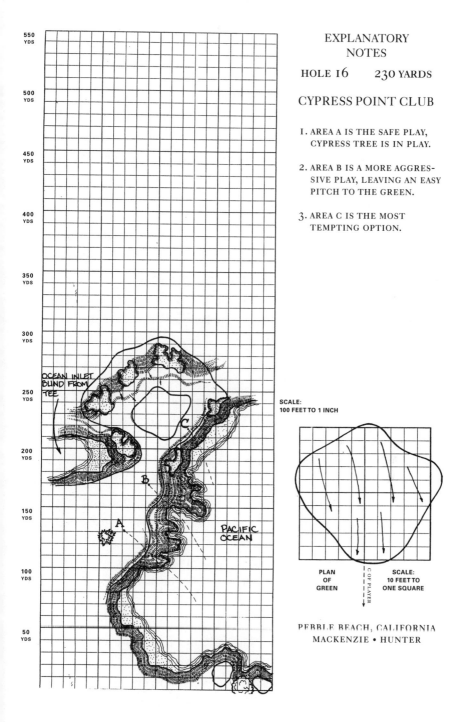

EXPLANATORY
NOTES

HOLE 16   230 YARDS

CYPRESS POINT CLUB

1. AREA A IS THE SAFE PLAY,
   CYPRESS TREE IS IN PLAY.

2. AREA B IS A MORE AGGRES-
   SIVE PLAY, LEAVING AN EASY
   PITCH TO THE GREEN.

3. AREA C IS THE MOST
   TEMPTING OPTION.

550 YDS
500 YDS
450 YDS
400 YDS
350 YDS
300 YDS
250 YDS
200 YDS
150 YDS
100 YDS
50 YDS

OCEAN INLET
BLIND FROM
TEE

C

B

A

PACIFIC
OCEAN

SCALE:
100 FEET TO 1 INCH

PLAN
OF
GREEN

C OF PLAYER

SCALE:
10 FEET TO
ONE SQUARE

PEBBLE BEACH, CALIFORNIA
MACKENZIE • HUNTER

Rendering of the par-3 sixteenth at Cypress Point Club, designed by Alister MacKenzie
and Robert Hunter. (GIL HANSE)

the fairway of a par-4, wise players would have the option for the safe play. Knowing the shot was within reason, this made the "Lindbergh Thrill" enticing and possible.

Who can *resist* the temptation of going for the sixteenth green or any hazard-guarded green that we think is within our reach? Only a few golfers have the willpower to resist, because as Mark Twain said, "There are several good protections against temptations, but the surest is cowardice."

Strategy. One misconception about the sixteenth at Cypress Point is that it is the ultimate "all or nothing" shot. It does become a do-or-die shot when the player decides to go straight at the green, which is what most of us would do with our one chance at this hole or other par-3s with similar carries over water. But here, plenty of room is afforded for the golfer to lay up safely. And the closer the golfer gets to the green with their tee shot, the tighter the lay-up area gets but the better their chances of making par become.

The best strategy? Play it as a par-4 as MacKenzie initially planned. A drive and a pitch. The worst you'll normally make is a four and that's often good enough to win the hole outright. Or if it's a leisurely round, four is enough to keep your dignity intact. Then again, who cares about dignity if you only get one crack at the greatest par-3 in the world or other similar dramatic holes? It's too tempting to simply lay up.

Green. MacKenzie was a master when it came to building greens full of interesting character, yet after Marion Hollins convinced him to make this a par-3 instead of a two-shotter, MacKenzie and Hunter wisely kept the green simple and receptive to long shots. Anyone who reaches it safely should not have to work too hard once they are putting on this large, flat surface.

Naturalness and Artistry of Construction. Again, there isn't much to say with regard to naturalness. The hole incorporated every existing feature: the leaning cypress trees in the lay-up area, the protective bank to the rear of the green where bunkers were cut and the natural edges of the ocean. The architects fit the hole to the land. Anything else would have been foolish.

Playability. This is probably the least "playable" of the four greats

A rear view of the sixteenth green at Cypress Point. Note the large, flat nature of the green, just one more feature that entices players to go straight at the green. (GEOFF SHACKELFORD)

featured here, not because of physical impossibilities but because the sixteenth imposes such intense fear in all golfers. The forced carry required to lay up is still difficult because the landing area is obscured and imposing when the wind is up, but it's much easier than it looks. Most golfers could handle this hole without much trouble, assuming they erase doubts that invariably appear at the worst time possible: the long, quiet walk from the fifteenth green to the sixteenth tee.

Alister MacKenzie worried about this hole playing as a reasonable par-3 because he was a strong believer in creating holes that allowed the weaker golfer with a wise game plan to catch up to the more physically gifted, but careless, player. In essence, that's what the great holes

Alister MacKenzie addresses a tee shot on the par-3 sixteenth at Cypress Point. (RAY MARCH)

are all about: rewarding mental skill as much as you reward physical skill. If a hole is designed to have an intelligent purpose and it is constructed with care, it should give lasting pleasure to golfers for years to come—just as the sixteenth at Cypress Point and the other great holes always have, and always will.

THE EIGHTH HOLE

Classic Designs

Pine Valley, Pebble Beach, the National Golf Links of America and Bethpage Black

A good golf course is like good music or good anything else: it is not necessarily a course which appeals the first time one plays it, but one which grows on the player the more frequently he visits it. —*Alister MacKenzie*

The notion of aspiring to present both a work of art and an entertaining motion picture is the goal of most filmmakers. The motion pictures that fall short of our expectations are those where the desire to make a thoughtful, artistic statement lost sight of satisfying the audience's desire to be entertained. Or there are the movies that seemingly try to pull out every trick imaginable to entertain us, only to forget that authentic satisfaction comes from provocative storytelling.

Many golf courses entertain on their initial go around, particularly with the modern day emphasis on "instant gratification" design. But these layouts fail to pique our interest on repeat visits because the initial thrills feel cheap on further review.

Then there are other courses making bold design and artistic statements. Places that architecture aficionados rave about for their cutting-edge use of angular cross-bunkering schemes and their neo-classical sensibility.

But when it comes to basic design function with simple, tempting situations, these "cutting-edge" courses are often not fun to play because the architect tried so hard to create something bold and original that he lost sight of what should be the ultimate goal: to create eighteen fun holes for playing golf.

There are designs that manage to pull off the most difficult of all tasks: serving as both artistic masterpieces worthy of study, while also entertaining golfers day in and day out. They are the greatest courses in the world.

> *I'd rather be able to appreciate things I cannot have than to have things I am not able to appreciate.* —*Elbert Hubbard, philosopher*

Many of the major golf publications have discouraged discussion and analysis of the classic courses in recent years for fear their readers will feel left out. After all, many of the classics are impossible-to-access private clubs. Certainly this notion of only talking about public-access golf is an understandable way for the magazines to do business, since many golfers will never see Pine Valley or the National Golf Links of America. However, a discussion of excellent course design would not be productive unless certain layouts were discussed.

Besides, most golfers are shrewd. If they want to see a course and they stay around golf long enough, they eventually meet a friend of a friend who can get them on a famous layout. If you never do get to play these courses, take heart in Elbert Hubbard's words. With just a little bit of effort you will be able to appreciate the finer qualities of these classics, qualities that some of the members who play these courses hundreds of times may not consciously appreciate. Consider how strange it is for someone to make (or inherit) millions of dollars, and join one of these elite designs, yet not have a clue why they paid so much to be there. Thankfully the private courses discussed in this chapter are in good hands. Their members appreciate what they have.

The modern method of judging or interpreting design merits tends to focus on the "experience." Elements such as the mystique of the entrance drive, the square footage of the clubhouse, the density of the men's grill milkshakes and the lavishness of the grass conditioning, all receive emphasis over design integrity.

There is no doubt that these experience-related elements are a part of the fun and no course should be discouraged from creating ambiance. But when talking about course design, the "experience" plays a minor role compared to what the architect accomplished with eighteen holes. You could take all of the elaborate "accoutrements" away from these famous places and still be left with a world-class design. In fact, all of the courses here do not have lavish clubhouses with flower beds lining the entrance drive. These are simple places, even a bit quirky when it comes to their experience. The old-style simplicity and occasional quirks only add to their character.

A motion picture can be shown in a squeaky clean theater with the freshest popcorn, the biggest screen and the sharpest digital sound. The ticket takers could be the friendliest folks on the planet. The movie itself could have dynamic special effects, big-name stars and a dazzling soundtrack. Yet, the story still establishes whether the film left you feeling satisfied. How the plot comes together determines whether the film will hold up over time, and the joy of getting to know the characters determines whether the film will be worth watching again or whether future audiences will want to see it.

In golf course architecture, our characters are the eighteen individual hole designs. The manner in which the architect pieces them together, his routing, drives the story. The architect's ability to put forth a variety of shots while leaving your visual senses satisfied reveals the success of the design.

Four courses have been selected that fall into the greatness category, and like a group of Oscar nominees for Best Picture, each is distinct in style and appearance. Each combines great characters and an original plot. Yet each tells its story with a different twist on the art of golf design.

Pebble Beach and Pine Valley are timeless blockbusters in the vein of *Star Wars* and *Raiders of the Lost Ark*. The National Golf Links is in the vein of an older "independent" film that came along just when the design world needed a fresh storytelling perspective. And Bethpage State Park's demanding Black Course compares to the popular films that feature a serious, hard-driving theme meant to put your game through an emotionally wrenching ordeal.

Each course is evaluated by four noteworthy design elements: how the sequencing of holes lends to the variety and memorability of the course, better known as the routing; the character and design of the greens; the hazards and strategy of the course; and how the design is enhanced by the beauty, experience and atmosphere of the course in question.

Pine Valley Golf Club

Clementon, New Jersey
Opened for play in 1918
Architect: George Crump (with suggestions from many prominent golfers)

> *I remember that when I visited that truly magnificent and truly terrifying course, Pine Valley, I remarked to one of my hosts that if the club had any members who were rather old or fat or unskillful, they must find it very hard work. He scouted the notion and declared that such members were proud as a peacock and as happy as sand boys if they went around in 115 in place of their normal 120. That seems to show that in Philadelphia, at any rate, the poorer golfers are not poor in the manly virtues.*
> —Bernard Darwin

If you pitched Hollywood *The George Crump Story*, they'd laugh and say it sounded like a rip-off of Henry David Thoreau's *Walden*. That is, unless of course you could get Tom Cruise to play Crump, then you'd have a deal.

Over eighty years after Crump died before all eighteen holes at Pine Valley were open for play, his devotion to this remarkable design remains one of golf's most complex and moving stories. The Pine Valley saga started when Crump's beloved wife of only one year died in 1907. The distraught widower set off to the British Isles where he visited family. Crump absorbed the true potential for American golf course design while playing some of England's new inland courses.

When he returned to Philadelphia, Crump found himself lonely and searching for meaning in his life after suffering such an unexpected loss. He had his beloved dogs, his affinity for golf and his passion for hunting. Crump also had devoted friends in the Philadelphia area who, like Crump, were fine golfers. His friends gave him the "brotherly" support to seek out a property suited for a new golf course, especially one that could be played during the winter months when most others were closed.

I think I have landed on something pretty fine . . . a sandy soil, with rolling ground, among the pines. —George Crump

Either on train trips to Atlantic City or during hunting expeditions, Crump located a unique property barely across the Pennsylvania state line in western New Jersey. The financing for a club was put together over the course of a year. Many noted Philadelphians stepped up, including future architect George Thomas and Philadelphia Athletics owner/manager Connie Mack. After a peculiar idea was scrapped that would have given one hole design to each of the first eighteen investors, Crump took on the task of laying out the entire course. He invited all of his fine golfing friends for advice, including A.W. Tillinghast, Thomas, Walter Travis and eventually, the world's most prominent professional architect at the time, H.S. Colt. Crump sunk almost all of his remaining fortune into the course and eventually moved to the site so that he could supervise construction more closely. He built a lakeside cabin where he lived in the Walden-like solitude of the sandy New Jersey pines, feeding hundreds of ducks each evening before settling in for the night to contemplate how best to improve the holes at Pine Valley. Hunting, once Crump's favorite pastime, was banned from the property as his bond with nature grew.

During the lonely nights Crump fretted over the design of each hole, putting countless hours of thought into conceptual drawings and notes. He also grew lonelier and, by some accounts, did not take good care of personal health issues, which led to his deteriorating health, and eventually his death in January 1918. After four years building Pine Valley Golf Club and investing $250,000, Crump died of a brain aneurysm. Four holes had not been completed, but they were laid out by Crump. Hugh Wilson, who designed the famed Merion and was a close friend of Crump, supervised the completion of those holes with the help of his brother, Alan Wilson. The course opened later that year, four years after it had started, and Pine Valley was immediately deemed by many to be the best design in America.

Crump died lonely, and yet, surely felt incredible fulfillment knowing that he had created the greatest course in America. Some have said how sad it is that he never played the completed course, but Crump's mission was to build the best course he could. He pulled it off at a time when people thought he was foolish to build on a sandy and heavily brushed site, a piece of property golf course developers would love to have today.

Crump's is a story worthy of a film, and his masterful golf course is worthy of more study than just about any other in the world.

Routing and Variety of Holes. Pine Valley has a simple and classic mix of yardages, yet the direction of the holes is varied enough to help each hole play differently. The par-4s range in style, while the course only has two par-5s. The ninth does not return to the clubhouse, but it's close enough that golfers can walk in if need be.

The sequence and variety of holes, though nearly a perfect mix,

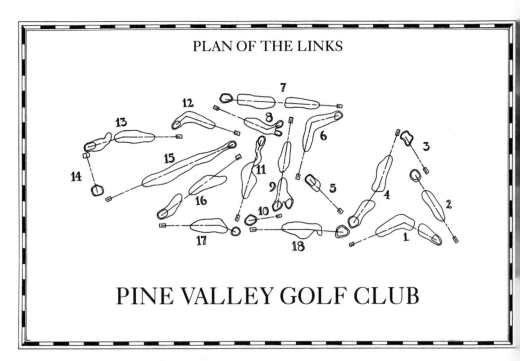

The routing of Pine Valley Golf Club. (GIL HANSE)

does not feel forced to achieve this absolute balance. Pine Valley appears as if Crump found the best features and incorporated them into his design. As difficult as Pine Valley is to play, the course flows beautifully. Each hole is distinct while still sharing a consistent look with the rest of the layout. Some of the walks between greens and tees are very short, others are long and let you clear your mind and enjoy the simplicity of a walk along sandy, pine needle–covered paths.

After you've played one, the next hole is completely different than the previous. And in most cases, more dramatic than the last. This diverse character took several years of work by Crump and many "in-the-field" adjustments to achieve, four years to be exact.

Hazards and Strategy. Many feel that Pine Valley's sandy waste areas are the most attractive hazards in golf, and who could argue? They are filled with multicolored shrubbery and the sand is a rich shade of beige. For the golfer hoping to recover, these sandy areas are full of unthinkable possibilities because the sand is not raked often. Many hazards are placed at just the proper spot, calling on heroic shots to carry them. Each hole at Pine Valley also has a different strategic purpose, but often that is forgotten because each is so punitive of mishits.

Though not an "ideal" design to emulate because it is so difficult for the average player, Pine Valley never was intended to be a leisurely country club course with a swimming pool, junior tournaments, debutante balls and Fourth of July barbeques.

It was designed to be a one-of-a-kind experience, the ultimate test in shotmaking and dramatic golf.

Greens. Evidently Pine Valley was not hard enough from tee to fringe, because George Crump crafted a treacherous set of putting surfaces. They are mixed in size, some are enormous, a few are tiny, but most are mid-sized. Each contains plenty of slope and man-made contour. The greens are also beautifully varied so that no two are alike and each is memorable. Their unforgettable quality is important because Pine Valley becomes more than just a beautiful, penal "test" of shots. Strategic decisions come into play because the fairways are generous and the beautifully contoured greens force you to weigh options.

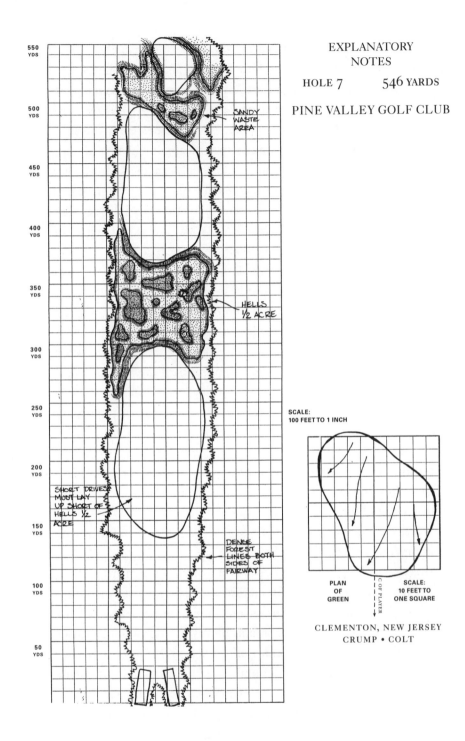

550 YDS

500 YDS

SANDY WASTE AREA

450 YDS

400 YDS

350 YDS

HELLS ½ ACRE

300 YDS

250 YDS

SCALE:
100 FEET TO 1 INCH

200 YDS

SHORT DRIVES MUST LAY UP SHORT OF HELLS ½ ACRE

150 YDS

DENSE FOREST LINES BOTH SIDES OF FAIRWAY

PLAN OF GREEN   C OF PLAYER   SCALE: 10 FEET TO ONE SQUARE

100 YDS

CLEMENTON, NEW JERSEY
CRUMP • COLT

50 YDS

Rendering of the par-5 seventh at Pine Valley Golf Club. (GIL HANSE)

Pine Valley's par-3 tenth hole, just 140 yards. (GEOFF SHACKELFORD)

Modern green speeds make Pine Valley's surfaces a bit too treacherous at times, though some might counter that the fast surfaces uphold the tradition of the course: difficulty. Others would say that well-struck shots reaching the green in regulation should be rewarded with a reasonable chance of two-putting.

Pine Valley's par-3 fifth hole, 225 yards of carry to a severely sloped green. (GEOFF SHACK-ELFORD)

Beauty, Experience, Ambiance. Part of the architect's job is to skill-fully incorporate aesthetics, just like it's a filmmaker's job to tell his story in a visually interesting way. The golf architect must take into account how certain design elements will affect the golfer's experience and help create a unique environment for the player. Pine Valley is nearly perfect on all counts. The course is secluded, making you feel as if you've entered another world when you finally arrive. (And it is other-worldly in another sense: Pine Valley has its own post office and its own mayor.) The clubhouse, food and general golfing atmosphere are unlike anything else in the game, yet if you took all of that away, the golfer's affection for the course would not change. It is, above all else, a masterful design.

Pebble Beach Golf Links

Pebble Beach, California
Opened for play in 1918
Architects: Jack Neville, Douglas Grant, Alister MacKenzie, Chandler Egan and Jack
    Nicklaus

This is the finest strategic course in the world. —Jack Nicklaus

Unlike Pine Valley, where the design genius was apparent from the beginning, Pebble Beach Golf Links *evolved* into a great course.

Pebble Beach has been a work in progress for seventy years now, and some might argue that it is at its finest form as we find it today. Historians might contend that the course peaked in 1929, the year it reopened after Chandler Egan redesigned the original layout. From 1918 to 1928, the layout was a Jack Neville–Douglas Grant design that featured primitive hazards and minimal strategy. Coffin-shaped bunkers and geometrically shaped greens defined the look of the course. However, the two outstanding amateur-golfers-turned-architects created a wonderful routing. This allowed another amateur golfing great, H. Chandler Egan, to eventually heighten the strategic elements, create new greens and improve the bunkering.

During the 1927–28 redesign, Egan created imitation sand dunes that looked like authentic sandbanks. Over the next few years the dunes became too difficult to maintain when the Great Depression limited maintenance resources. The revolutionary dunes were gradually converted to traditional bunkers.

Over the next forty years, Pebble Beach declined. Like an old film slowly deteriorating in a dank basement, the course was neglected, though never to the point that major changes were made. Sometimes financial neglect isn't so bad because it means a design does not have architects making unnecessary changes or planting trees to prevent long hitters from using their skill.

The pattern of neglect reversed when the 1972 U.S. Open was awarded to Pebble Beach. Since then the course has seen a renaissance and new appreciation for its design features. During the late 1990s, millions were spent to upgrade conditions. A program was implemented to reinforce the cliffs, ensuring that the famed eighteenth hole remained attached to California. The bunkers were also given a rugged appearance that helped find a middle ground between the natural look Chandler Egan created and the modern style of a more "defined" bunker.

Still, like that great old black and white film in the basement, Pebble Beach thrives on its interesting mix of characters and the way its sweeping plot ties this variety together. The course is more than just a stunning place to play golf. The holes are compelling to play and the routing pieces them together in such a way that the golfer is taken on a wild journey of ups and downs with an unforgettable concluding twist. Pebble Beach has endured because it combines beauty, strategy and a golfing encounter everyone must try at least once.

Routing and Variety of Holes. As primitive as the bunkering and geometrically shaped greens were in the early 1920s, the Neville and Grant routing was ideal. Many question why these two amateur architects didn't run the first nine holes out on the inland terrain, followed by one long, dramatic return hugging the cliff tops. It's a fair question, because we receive great thrills from a film that starts gently and builds to a climactic finale. But like a complex symphony, the routing of Pebble Beach provides peaks and valleys that make its design a complete test while allowing the golfer to play next to the ocean during portions of both nines.

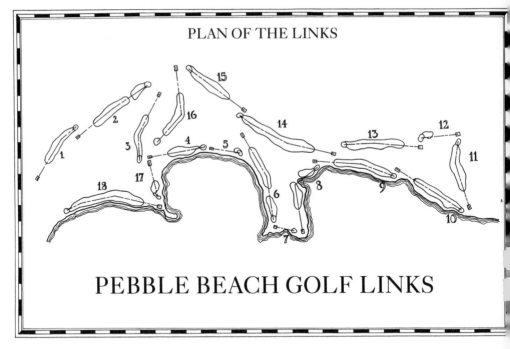

PLAN OF THE LINKS

PEBBLE BEACH GOLF LINKS

The routing of Pebble Beach Golf Links. (GIL HANSE)

The first three holes are often criticized, and unfairly so. They serve many purposes, the most obvious being that they allow you to get your bearings straight. They also give the keen and well-prepared player a chance to get ahead with a birdie or two, because trouble awaits. The third is one of the most interesting par-4s on the course. It is the player's first chance to try a risky tee shot by cutting off the corner of a dogleg, flirting with a ravine. The reward is a better angle to approach the scary little green.

The next set of holes introduces you to the Pacific Ocean. The short par-4 fourth features a landing area guarded by the water, giving the player a whiff of the salty Pacific and the sounds of barking sea lions. Jack Nicklaus's par-3 fifth hole, created in 1999 to fulfill Samuel Morse's dream of another ocean hole, brings the Pacific into play for most of us. The par-5 sixth and the short one-shot seventh then play out to a rocky point, exposing the golfer to the awe-inspiring elements.

The difficult and beautifully designed par-4s at eight, nine and ten separate the real golfers from the awestruck visitors.

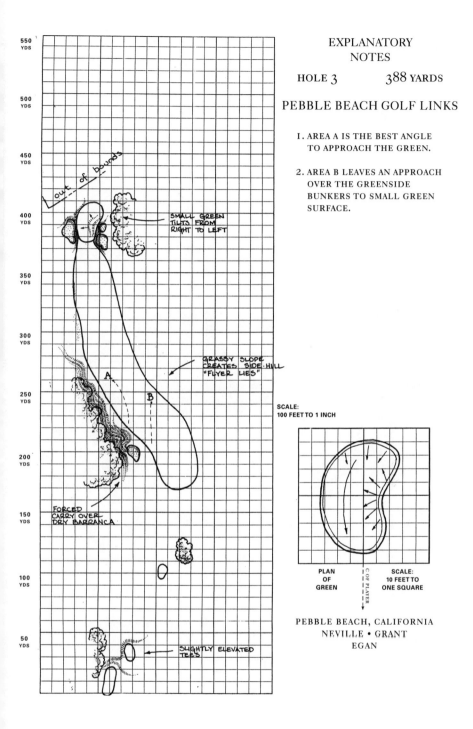

EXPLANATORY
NOTES

HOLE 3   388 YARDS

PEBBLE BEACH GOLF LINKS

1. AREA A IS THE BEST ANGLE
   TO APPROACH THE GREEN.

2. AREA B LEAVES AN APPROACH
   OVER THE GREENSIDE
   BUNKERS TO SMALL GREEN
   SURFACE.

SMALL GREEN
TILTS FROM
RIGHT TO LEFT

GRASSY SLOPE
CREATES SIDE-HILL
"FLYER LIES"

SCALE:
100 FEET TO 1 INCH

A

B

FORCED
CARRY OVER
DRY BARRANCA

PLAN
OF
GREEN

℄ OF PLAYER

SCALE:
10 FEET TO
ONE SQUARE

SLIGHTLY ELEVATED
TEES

PEBBLE BEACH, CALIFORNIA
NEVILLE • GRANT
EGAN

550 YDS
500 YDS
450 YDS
400 YDS
350 YDS
300 YDS
250 YDS
200 YDS
150 YDS
100 YDS
50 YDS

Out of bounds

Rendering of the par-4 third at Pebble Beach Golf Links. (GIL HANSE)

123

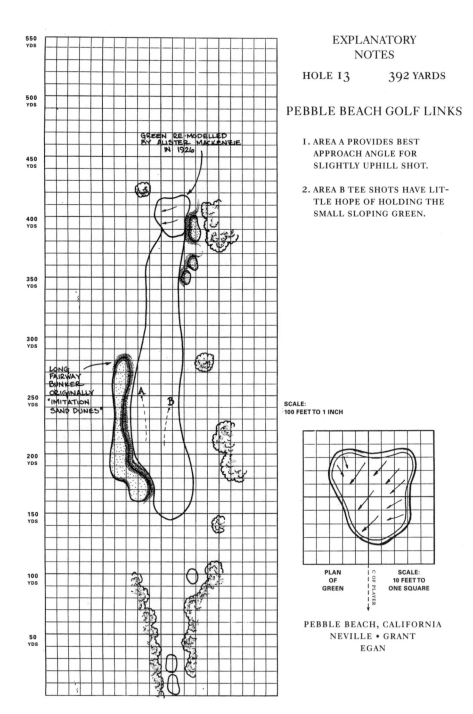

550 YDS

500 YDS

GREEN RE-MODELLED BY ALISTER MACKENZIE IN 1926

450 YDS

400 YDS

350 YDS

300 YDS

LONG FAIRWAY BUNKER ORIGINALLY "IMITATION SAND DUNES"

250 YDS

A

B

200 YDS

150 YDS

100 YDS

50 YDS

EXPLANATORY NOTES

HOLE 13   392 YARDS

PEBBLE BEACH GOLF LINKS

1. AREA A PROVIDES BEST APPROACH ANGLE FOR SLIGHTLY UPHILL SHOT.

2. AREA B TEE SHOTS HAVE LIT-TLE HOPE OF HOLDING THE SMALL SLOPING GREEN.

SCALE:
100 FEET TO 1 INCH

PLAN OF GREEN   C OF PLAYER   SCALE: 10 FEET TO ONE SQUARE

PEBBLE BEACH, CALIFORNIA
NEVILLE • GRANT
EGAN

Rendering of the par-4 thirteenth at Pebble Beach Golf Links. (GIL HANSE)

But no matter who you are, the following six inland holes from eleven through sixteen make it a good time for a break from all of this dramatic seaside golf. Plus, you are seemingly miles from the clubhouse and the course does have to head back, doesn't it? But don't be fooled: Holes eleven through sixteen offer a stretch of inland golf filled with decisions that require as much intelligence as the dramatic seaside holes.

Finally, the course winds its way back toward the ocean on the long par-3 seventeenth, and in the final act of this dramatic tale, you face the ocean-fortified eighteenth. The sequencing provides emotional ups and downs, but each hole asks the golfer to think. Pebble Beach is unique in that it offers its easiest holes at the start, but is a stern test from the fifth hole on. The pressure of knowing you have to start solidly to score well makes the routing unique.

*Hazards and Strategy.*Pebble Beach has seen a constant transformation in its style of bunkering, from coffins to imitation dunes to worn out "sand traps," to today's beautifully rugged pits. Over the years their placement has remained largely the same, and thus, the strategy of the course is intact.

The early years saw those square, crude-looking bunkers with little natural character. Chandler Egan changed that in 1928, introducing imitation sand dunes along with several naturally flowing bunkers similar to Alister MacKenzie's style imitating passing storm clouds. (In 1926 MacKenzie created the basic shape and design of Pebble Beach's eighth and thirteenth greens, but it was Egan who received the commission to redesign the course in 1928.)

Regardless of the look of the bunkers, it is Pebble Beach's ability to pose questions on each shot that makes it so exciting to play for all golfers. It helps that the main hazard you must overcome is the dramatic Pacific Ocean, but the inland holes offer as many decision-making dilemmas as the cliffside holes.

The strategy is often subtle. Perhaps it's a matter of whether to place your drive down the left side of the thirteenth fairway for a better angle of approach to the wicked green. But such simple mind games make Pebble Beach the ultimate meeting of natural and man-made design.

Pebble Beach's par-3 seventh, circa 1929, when the course was dominated by "imitation sand dunes." The dunes were created by architect H. Chandler Egan and superintendent Joe Mayo. (BANCROFT LIBRARY)

Pebble Beach's par-3 seventh today, with man-made bunkers taking the place of imitation dunes. (GEOFF SHACKELFORD)

Pebble Beach's par-4 sixteenth. This is the approach after a well-struck tee shot. (GEOFF SHACKELFORD)

Greens. We often hear about the tiny greens at Pebble Beach lending much of the character to the course, providing its "defense" against great players. They average 3,500 square feet, which is about half of what most courses average. However, the greens have shrunk to the point that a few are too small, negatively impacting the design character (the hourglass-shaped seventeenth green comes to mind as holding much less interest today because there are so few hole locations). The green complexes at Pebble Beach have never been huge, but they do lack some of the thought-provoking hole locations they once provided.

Still, the subtle slopes from back to front or side-to-side allow the strategy to function. And on greens such as the eighth, thirteenth and sixteenth, the slopes are not subtle. They are downright treacherous if you misplace a tee shot or your approach.

Beauty, Experience, Ambiance. The beauty of Pebble Beach is not up for debate. The ocean holes here are not only stunning, each is distinct in character. There is one view in modern design that each golf hole must be a "thing unto itself," so some find it tacky that tourists are hovering around Pebble Beach's first tee area or eighteenth green. Or that a husband and wife are walking their dog down the left side of the sixth hole during the late afternoon. Others don't like the interference of certain roads through the course.

But others find these interferences to be an intriguing part of a round at Pebble Beach, similar to the character that the "distractions" lend to a round on the Old Course at St. Andrews. Some golfers don't mind seeing other people, while other golfers believe a round of golf should be a completely solitary experience. It is a matter of taste. But if you experience Pebble Beach with an open mind, you just might think it's the most enjoyable, exciting and unique golf course in the world. Seeing other people adds to the sense of community and heavenly ambiance that brings people to Pebble Beach and the 17-Mile Drive.

The National Golf Links of America

Southampton, New York
Opened for play in 1911
Architect: C. B. Macdonald

> *There are many features about the National Links which will make the course famous . . . a course has been produced where every hole is a good one and presents a new problem. That is something which has never yet been accomplished, even in Scotland, and in accomplishing it here, Mr. Macdonald has inaugurated a new era in golf.*
> *—H. J. Whigham (Macdonald's son-in-law!)*

While Pine Valley is *The Godfather*, C. B. Macdonald's National Golf Links of America may be golf's *Citizen Kane*. Sure, The National was heralded from the beginning while Orson Welles's masterful film was lucky to even make it into theaters, yet each has proven to be a timeless work of art that is the initial point of study for students hoping to master these respective fields.

The National was built with the intent of igniting a design revolution. Macdonald was (thankfully) not a humble man nor was he shy in stating his goal. At a time when the only new courses being built were downright awful, Macdonald was determined to demonstrate to Americans how golf was played overseas. He had spent a year at St. Andrews and learned about the Old Course from Old Tom Morris. Upon his return to the United States, Macdonald realized the en vogue version of golf architecture in America would not advance the game he loved.

With the National, Macdonald set out to take concepts proven in the British Isles and reproduce them here. Macdonald was not building mere replica holes or a "theme" course. Instead he was borrowing design ideas and placing them where the National's Southampton property allowed for those classic design ideas to be recreated. And like a filmmaker who scrounges touches from their mentors, Macdonald used the proven ideas effectively while adding his own distinct twists. In some cases, his "tribute" holes may have improved on the originals.

Macdonald also created original holes that had nothing to do with famous ones imported from Scotland. All of this was done with the intent of making a statement about the way golf was played in Scotland, the way it should be in America, and how course architecture needed to look to the future. Yes, the National was built with little modesty, but Macdonald loved the game and knew the American version would die without enduring architecture to sustain it. He stubbornly preached his beliefs to ensure that golfers would give the National a chance, otherwise the course might have been a failure.

Like Orson Welles did with *Citizen Kane*, Macdonald never lost sight of the ultimate goal, which was to tell a captivating story, to entertain the golfer. The National proves to have both a fine set of holes for the budding architect to study, while also proving to be as exciting to play as any course in the world. And no course in the world has as many comedic design touches while serving as a complete test of skill as the National Golf Links.

Routing and Variety of Holes. Nothing about the National Golf Links is ordinary, including the clubhouse site and location. Situated *between* the first and eighteenth fairways, the ethereal structure looks out over Peconic Bay with excellent views of the golfers coming and going. The National's set of holes flow amidst what looks to be a basic "out and

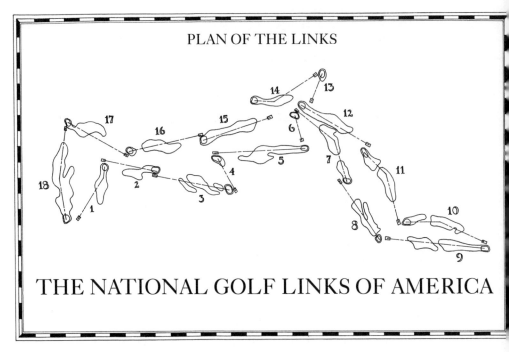

PLAN OF THE LINKS

14   13
17   15   12
16   6
5   7   11
4
18   2   10
3   8
1   9

THE NATIONAL GOLF LINKS OF AMERICA

The routing of the National Golf Links of America. (GIL HANSE)

back" routing similar to St. Andrews. This means the ninth green is at the farthest point from the clubhouse.

However, the bends and shifts in the direction of the holes make it clear that this is no rudimentary routing. From the standpoint of variety, the National offers a little of everything: drama, provocative challenge and plenty of humor. The holes bend in all directions. They are of all different lengths and sizes. Most are wide and large in scale, but each fits the land, forcing a variety of shotmaking possibilities.

Again, the variety is not forced, which is why the course is a true original. Macdonald did not write down a list of holes required to make the perfect course, then check each unit off until he had what would seem "balanced." Instead, he fit the holes to the property and tweaked them to create a genuine variety of shots and looks.

Hazards and Strategy. Macdonald's bunker style combines the deep, almost vertical-faced pits found on many Scottish links with a few irregular curves, bends and different sizes that lend enough of a

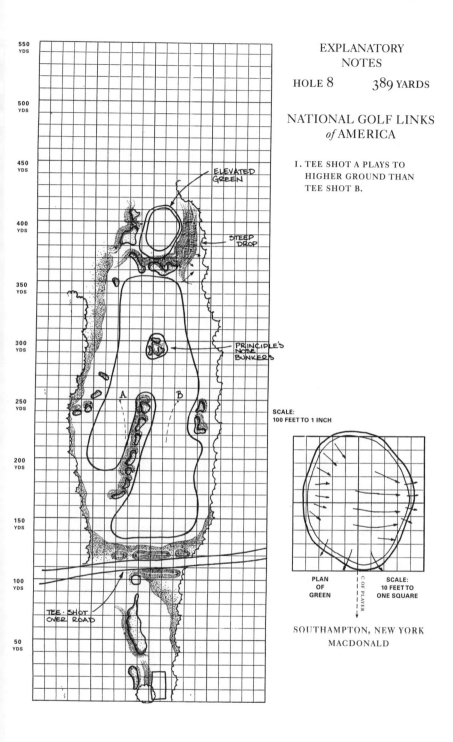

550
YDS

500
YDS

450
YDS

ELEVATED
GREEN

400
YDS

STEEP
DROP

350
YDS

300
YDS

PRINCIPLE'S
NOSE
BUNKERS

250
YDS

A   B

200
YDS

150
YDS

100
YDS

TEE·SHOT
OVER ROAD

50
YDS

EXPLANATORY
NOTES

HOLE 8   389 YARDS

NATIONAL GOLF LINKS
of AMERICA

I. TEE SHOT A PLAYS TO
HIGHER GROUND THAN
TEE SHOT B.

SCALE:
100 FEET TO 1 INCH

PLAN
OF
GREEN

C OF PLAYER

SCALE:
10 FEET TO
ONE SQUARE

SOUTHAMPTON, NEW YORK
MACDONALD

Rendering of the par-4 eighth at the National Golf Links of America. (GIL HANSE)

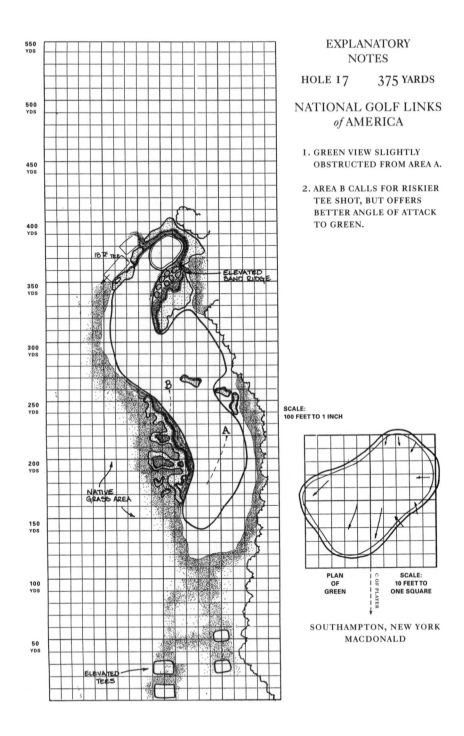

EXPLANATORY
NOTES

HOLE 17   375 YARDS

NATIONAL GOLF LINKS
of AMERICA

1. GREEN VIEW SLIGHTLY
OBSTRUCTED FROM AREA A.

2. AREA B CALLS FOR RISKIER
TEE SHOT, BUT OFFERS
BETTER ANGLE OF ATTACK
TO GREEN.

SCALE:
100 FEET TO 1 INCH

PLAN OF GREEN   SCALE: 10 FEET TO ONE SQUARE

C OF PLAYER

SOUTHAMPTON, NEW YORK
MACDONALD

550 YDS
500 YDS
450 YDS
400 YDS
350 YDS
300 YDS
250 YDS
200 YDS
150 YDS
100 YDS
50 YDS

18 TH TEE

ELEVATED
SAND RIDGE

B

A

NATIVE
GRASS AREA

ELEVATED
TEES

Rendering of par-4 seventeenth at the National Golf Links of America. (GIL HANSE) natural flair. At the time Macdonald built the National, early American golfers had only been exposed to geometric courses with "coffin" shaped bunkers, chocolate-drop mounds and greens sunken into hard-edged bowls to retain water. Natural-looking or -playing golf courses were not a priority to the golf pros laying out those early American courses. So Macdonald brought an overall sense of flair and natural feel to the National that no American architect had ever dared to try before.

Ultimately, the placement of hazards at the National makes the course entertaining to play and study. Macdonald spent seven years conceiving the course, another four building it and the last twenty of his life fine-tuning it. Much of his time was spent adding or removing bunkers, shifting tees and altering bunker sizes to achieve the best strategic possibilities. Some might say Macdonald got carried away because at one time the National was believed to have as many as three hundred bunkers. However, if managed intelligently, there is no reason why the average player should have much trouble getting around the course without losing all hope for mankind. Fairways have been widened again after years of restoration work by course superintendent Karl Olson. Forced carries on the course have always been reasonable while the greens are enormous in order to handle the severe contours. The National is demanding, but most golfers can manage their way around without too much embarrassment.

The "concept" holes patterned after Macdonald's favorites from Europe stand out because, in most instances, Macdonald may have improved on the original. The Redan, originally found at North Berwick in Scotland, was recreated with several twists. Macdonald eliminated the semiblind tee shot aspect that the original has, and shortened the hole by twenty yards. He also created a larger expanse for the golfer to safely aim for, but sloped this area so the player could use the area to work their ball toward the hole. The original Redan at North Berwick is more severe for the cautious player and does not provide the tempting chance to play a run-up shot that Macdonald's version entices the player with.

Greens. They are massive, they are undulating and they are the most fascinating man-made greens in the world. The National's greens are so multifaceted that it is difficult to describe them in a few sen-

The first green at the National Golf Links of America. Seen in the fall when the leaves add even more character, this short par-4 is one of golf's most interesting starting holes. (GEOFF SHACKELFORD)

The par-3 sixth green at the National Golf Links of America. This short downhill par-3 plays to a large, undulating green. (GEOFF SHACKELFORD)

tences. Their ultimate goal was to lend variety to shotmaking and everyday golf. The greens achieved their goal because they call upon so many unique shots and, in most cases, leave room for the careless golfer to hit a green and believe he has found safety, when in fact he'd rather have a bunker shot than a sixty-foot putt.

Beauty, Experience, Ambiance. The course overlooks Peconic Bay in Southampton, enough said? And if there is one course where you are overcome with the "experience" of the day, hopefully it is this one. The intimidating clubhouse is actually warm and inviting inside. It's difficult to see into the windows as you are playing the first and last holes, but inside, the light, airy rooms make it easy to look out across the bay or to watch the golfers play up the eighteenth. Inside is a shrine to Macdonald along with the club's founding members. The early members knew the National was special and that it fostered a movement toward sound architecture, so they honored themselves and the game.

A water tower/windmill sits on the highest hill overlooking the first and sixteenth greens, and provides the greatest man-made landmark on any golf course in America. One element lending subtle beauty to the National is color. The layout is more colorful than just about any in the world thanks to grasses of different colors. You see bright green grass contrasting with the beige bunkers and the sandy native areas. The trees are a subtle mix, again lending variety and slightly different hues, while the occasional splash of water adds yet another dimension.

The entire feeling of the National Golf Links says, "this is the home of American golf, this is how the game is meant to be played and you will grow to like it. If not, then we respectfully ask that you leave us alone and allow us to celebrate the spirit of the game as it was meant to be played." (My quote, not theirs.)

Never have I been so intimidated by a golf course and clubhouse. Yet it was ultimately an affirmative fear, one that puts you in your place if you have lost sight of what golf, course design and tradition are all about. Like filmmakers regularly watching *Citizen Kane*, every golf architect needs to go back to the National every once in a while to be reminded of the daring spirit of C. B. Macdonald, a man who defied conformity and soulless expressions of art. A man who fought for originality in course design so that future generations could find as much joy in golf as he did.

The windmill and water tower at the National Golf Links sits between the second and sixteenth holes, and is visible from miles away. (GEOFF SHACKELFORD)

Bethpage State Park, Black Course

Bethpage, New York
Opened for play in 1936
Architects: A. W. Tillinghast and Joe Burbeck

> *A round of golf should provide eighteen inspirations—not necessarily thrills, for spectacular holes may be sadly overdone. Every hole must be constructed to provide charm without being obtrusive with it.*
>
> *—A. W. Tillinghast*

While we are on the subject of outstanding Long Island golf, discussion must turn to a classic Tillinghast design close to New York City. Just as *The Godfather* is a different type of film than *Citizen Kane*, Bethpage Park's Black Course is a completely dissimilar design when compared to the National Golf Links. Yet each is admirable in its own way.

Bethpage Black is similar to Pine Valley in that some of its features should rarely be emulated the way the National should be, yet Beth-

A warning sign to all golfers prior to teeing off on the Black Course at Bethpage State Park. (GEOFF SHACKELFORD)

page Black is a classic American course that serves some very distinct purposes. Bethpage Black is golf's version of long, serious films such as *Reds* or *Saving Private Ryan*; films that open your eyes to how trying life can be. The Black Course puts you in your place as a golfer, and helps you see the light with regard to those shorter, quirkier and "easier" courses you may take for granted. Best of all, anyone can play Bethpage Black and be put in their place rather inexpensively.

Routing and Variety of Holes. One could argue that the Black Course's routing is an "out and back" setup similar to the National. However, in neither case do you feel like the architect created the sequencing on his drafting board in a matter of minutes. Each course has a distinctive flow like no other in the world, and the routing of the Black may be as unique as any.

The player senses with each hole that you are engrossed or even lost in a sea of trees and hills, but never suffocated by the surroundings. The first hole tees off to a wide-open area where the four closing holes are also in view. After finishing the long par-4 first, the player

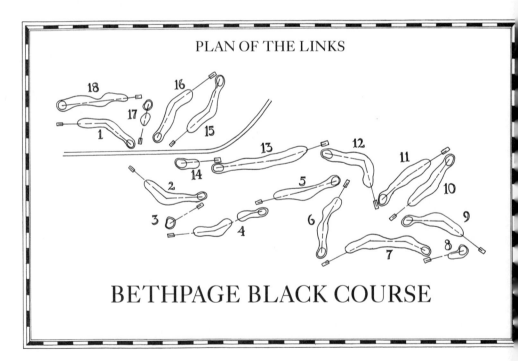

PLAN OF THE LINKS

BETHPAGE BLACK COURSE

The routing of Bethpage State Park's Black Course. (GIL HANSE)

crosses a road and from there the course weaves in, out, up and down a gorgeous tree-lined property. You encounter plenty of sand, native grasses and interesting contours, with the more severe elevation changes tactfully handled by Tillinghast through intelligent planning. After changing direction constantly and presenting consistently difficult holes, the course finally emerges from the wooded area. At the fifteenth tee, you have crossed the road for the finishing stretch. But again, the fifteenth through eighteenth holes each play in a different direction, lending individual character to each hole.

Variety of hole design is where Bethpage Black falls a bit short. However, the lack of par-4 variety was part of this course's intended character from the beginning. It was designed to be a stern, hole-by-hole test with no letup in the two-shotters. The par-3s are well varied in their look and strategy, but three of them play to nearly the same yardage. The two par-5s are wonderful, you just wish there were more of them (the tenth was a par-5). Again though, it was not the intention of the course to provide many birdie holes. This was to be a public version of Pine Valley.

Hazards and Strategy. Strategically, Bethpage features several interesting decisions from the tee and plenty of thought is required on potential lay-up shots. Again, this is as much a course of shaping shots and knowing when to take your licks as it is a course of tempting options. Your troubles can mount quickly if you are not strong enough to know when to fold your hand and take your bogey.

This relentless design characteristic is also why Bethpage Black's design should not be emulated on a regular basis unless you are trying to attract a United States Open. Consistently relentless designs would not be good for the game. An argument can be made that golfers are free to stay away from such a course. They are even warned to at Bethpage with a sign near the first tee. But the modern trend has been for each new course to attempt to emulate the Bethpage Black type of design, and it's not a positive trend. We need variety in the types of courses built, just as much as we do in our individual sets of holes. Bethpage works because there are four other courses to choose from at the very same facility. Each has its own design purpose and audience.

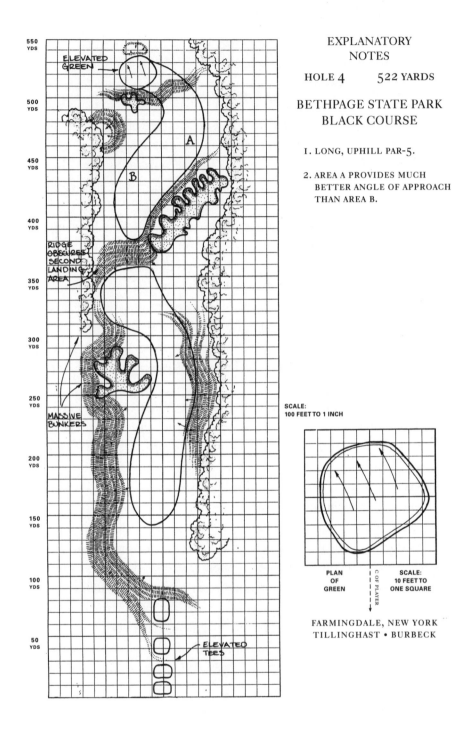

550
YDS

ELEVATED
GREEN

500
YDS

A

450
YDS

B

400
YDS

RIDGE
OBSCURES
SECOND
LANDING
AREA

350
YDS

300
YDS

250
YDS

MASSIVE
BUNKERS

200
YDS

150
YDS

100
YDS

50
YDS

ELEVATED
TEES

EXPLANATORY
NOTES

HOLE 4   522 YARDS

BETHPAGE STATE PARK
BLACK COURSE

1. LONG, UPHILL PAR-5.

2. AREA A PROVIDES MUCH
   BETTER ANGLE OF APPROACH
   THAN AREA B.

SCALE:
100 FEET TO 1 INCH

PLAN
OF
GREEN

C OF PLAYER

SCALE:
10 FEET TO
ONE SQUARE

FARMINGDALE, NEW YORK
TILLINGHAST • BURBECK

Rendering of the par-5 fourth at Bethpage Black. (GIL HANSE)

17th at Sand Hills (GEOFF SHACKELFORD)

18th at Sand Hills (GEOFF SHACKELFORD)

14th at Shinnecock Hills (GEOFF SHACKELFORD)

4th at The National Golf Links (GEOFF SHACKELFORD)

2nd at Somerset Hills (GEOFF SHACKELFORD)

4th at Riviera Country Club (GEOFF SHACKELFORD)

16th at Merion, East Course (GEOFF SHACKELFORD)

15th at World Woods, Pine Barrens (GEOFF SHACKELFORD)

2nd at Cypress Point Club (GEOFF SHACKELFORD)

4th at Baltimore Country Club, East Course (GEOFF SHACKELFORD)

16th at Inniscrone Golf Club (GEOFF SHACKELFORD)

7th at Crystal Downs (GEOFF SHACKELFORD)

12th at Pasatiempo (GEOFF SHACKELFORD)

18th at Pine Valley (GEOFF SHACKELFORD)

13th at Rustic Canyon (GEOFF SHACKELFORD)

14th at Rustic Canyon (GEOFF SHACKELFORD)

17th at Rustic Canyon (GEOFF SHACKELFORD)

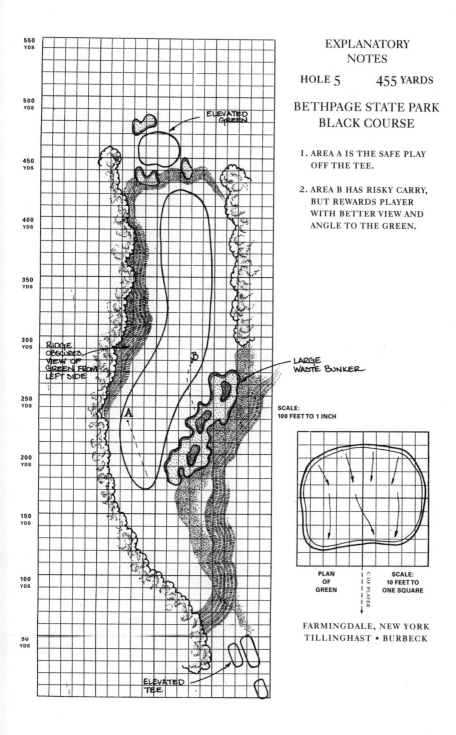

EXPLANATORY
NOTES

HOLE 5   455 YARDS

BETHPAGE STATE PARK
BLACK COURSE

1. AREA A IS THE SAFE PLAY
   OFF THE TEE.

2. AREA B HAS RISKY CARRY,
   BUT REWARDS PLAYER
   WITH BETTER VIEW AND
   ANGLE TO THE GREEN.

SCALE:
100 FEET TO 1 INCH

PLAN OF GREEN

SCALE: 10 FEET TO ONE SQUARE

C OF PLAYER

FARMINGDALE, NEW YORK
TILLINGHAST • BURBECK

ELEVATED GREEN

RIDGE OBSCURES VIEW OF GREEN FROM LEFT SIDE

LARGE WASTE BUNKER

A

B

ELEVATED TEE

550 YDS
500 YDS
450 YDS
400 YDS
350 YDS
300 YDS
250 YDS
200 YDS
150 YDS
100 YDS
50 YDS

Rendering of the par-4-fifth at Bethpage Black. (GIL HANSE)

141

The tee shot on Bethpage Black's par-5 fourth. (GEOFF SHACKELFORD)

The fifth at Bethpage Black tees off over a bunker filled with native grass "islands." (GEOFF SHACKELFORD)

The hazards at Bethpage Black generate great debate among architecture aficionados. Some say they are way too large in scale. Others feel they are not Tillinghast's most artful and certainly weren't helped by the hard-edged look they took on after Rees Jones injected an awkward style during the 1998 Black Course renovation. Others preferred the ragged, rundown look that they had attained from years of play, believing that style fit closer to the Pine Valley–like style of the property. Like a classic film that has been colorized, everyone has their own preference.

There is also the belief that the Black Courses's bunkering needs to be massive in size to match the scale and style of the layout. Either way, the course is always going to be popular, and the heavy play expected in the years following the 2002 U.S. Open will return the softer, more rustic look that the bunkers once had.

Greens. Some traditionalists argue that Bethpage is not among the world's elite designs because the green complexes lack imagination and character. However, this may have been the shrewdest aspect of Tillinghast's design. After all, if the holes are relentless and difficult from tee to fringe, why continue the punishment on the greens? Why not reward the player who has managed to hit them in regulation, as is the case here?

Beauty, Experience and Ambiance. No course in the world, not even Pine Valley, has the mysterious character that the Black's routing provides. Remember, some of the old architects envisioned golf becoming the best alternative to a popular sport such as hunting. They saw golf providing the same man-versus-nature experience without the more gruesome aspects you find in hunting. The notion that they hoped to create, and which Bethpage Black provides better than just about any course in the world, is the feeling of setting out into the woods on a mission to explore the terrain and not knowing exactly what you will find. Every course has this element of mystery to some extent, but Bethpage Black takes on this experience in similar fashion to the first-time filmgoer's experience of *The Godfather II*. The typical three-act filmmaking structure was thrown out the window by Francis Ford Coppola, yet you still experience all of the classic elements and drama.

The par-3 seventeenth on the Black Course at Bethpage State Park. (GEOFF SHACKELFORD)

The story is presented in a completely different and fascinating manner, with its own unique pacing and character.

At Bethpage, Tillinghast ignored the traditional belief that you have "breather" holes and that the ninth green must return to the clubhouse. The result is an unrelenting test that takes the golfer on a long, winding adventure—something all classic courses manage to do.

THE NINTH HOLE

The Architect

*Different Designers and Four Masters: MacKenzie, Ross,
Tillinghast and Dye*

*Building a golf course and then calling in a golf architect afterwards to
remedy the defects is like 'building' your own suit of clothes and then
calling in a tailor to give them style and reinforce the seams so that they
won't rip in vital spots. The way some golf courses rip after being built is
appalling.*   *—Charles Banks, golf architect*

During a modern-day sporting event we hear television announcers
constantly glorify coaches as if they are M.I.T.-educated engineers of
their offenses and defenses, pulling strings as the game goes. Meanwhile the players apparently are mere lackeys, executing what these
geniuses have envisioned. The outcome supposedly rests solely on
which coach outsmarts the other.

It has become a modern American pastime to tout the role of those
in leadership and to underrate or even ignore the efforts of those doing
the dirty work. Whether the leader in question is a coach, CEO, politi-
cian, baseball manager or even a golf architect, the "name" attached to
a venture is considered responsible for all success or failure.

Golf course design has seen the same mythological name status
awarded its architects, to the point that even if an architect's name reg-
isters a laugh because his work is so awful, he is still, after all, a name!
(This reassurance derived from name brands might explain why golf

teachers well-known from regular appearances on instructional shows are now golf architects.)

We hear of "signature designs" by certain contemporary figures, leading us to believe these big names actually designed the course in question. But how many PGA Tour players really spend months, weeks, days or even hours working on the nuances of the design that their name is attached to? Very few. One architect told me he could count the number of *minutes* that the "player" architect was present to collaborate on their Tournament Players Club design. Another friend recounted the excitement of playing an inaugural round with the player-architect of the very course whose opening they were celebrating. After finishing out on the third hole, he asked the famous tour player where the next tee was located. The "player-architect" had no idea.

Talented design staffs and shapers are behind most of the greatest courses ever built, though you'd hardly ever know it. Even if the architect desperately tries to get his associates recognized, most golfers assume it was strictly the architect's vision that brought the project together. But no interesting golf course was built by one person or created because of one person's vision.

Some courses cannot safely put in a public appearance except on the darkest nights. Therefore, I believe it is safer, right at the beginning, to call in the specialist—the golf architect—and place on him the major responsibility for the designing and building of the course.
—Charles Banks, golf architect

The successful architect can envision a finished course, but in order to do so he must assemble a sympathetic team and know when to allow them the freedom to take his ideas to another level. The talented architect is also the one who can filter out the many strange suggestions thrown his way, while keeping an open mind when the least likely of sources comes up with something that improves the design.

Little has changed over the years, though some modern architects would like you to believe they are dealing with much more difficult clients today. They frequently will tell you that the old architects were not restricted with land limitations or nightmarish developers who fancied themselves armchair architects. However, a little research reveals that the developers and committees of early golf courses were just as "helpful" to the old architects, but characters like MacKenzie, Colt, Ross, Flynn, Thomas and Tillinghast figured out ways to prevent this input from having a disastrous effect.

George Thomas had so much trouble with one non-golfer client showing up and sharing ideas that he and associate Billy Bell pledged to talk nonstop between themselves whenever this non-golfer visited to make design suggestions. This proved to be quite a challenge for Thomas and Bell, both soft-spoken, kind individuals who surely respected the man signing the checks.

Since the turn of the twentieth century, when course design became a profession for many, there have been four types of golf course architect. Each "type" has been successful in some form and each method requires a great deal of patience, vision and communication aptitude.

Land Planner

A golf course, like a building, must have character and individuality because no one would be content with a mere reproduction. It is the same problem which confronts the architect of a house when he lays out the accessories and is continually adding new features as they suggest themselves. The plan very rarely is completed to accord exactly with the original intention.   —*Tom Simpson, golf architect*

The land-planning approach to design relies almost solely on topographic maps, in-office planning work, and the presentation of detailed grading plans. The architect makes a visit to the site, and does most of, if not all planning on paper. He creates beautiful computer-aided drawings that look glamorous. Dense rolls of detailed plans are then sent to a contractor to interpret, with help interpreting along the way.

The land-planner method began in rudimentary form with Tom Bendelow during the early 1900s, and evolved to the point that a more complex form of land planning now thrives as the most popular approach to design. For a nominal fee, Bendelow would stake a site in a day or two, leaving behind instructions for whoever built the course. Only in a small percentage of cases did he return to see how the course was constructed.

As the century ended and most golf architects studied landscape architecture in college, intricate grading plans and lavish color renderings replaced Bendelow's stakes and allowed the architect to never leave his office. County and city governments require intricate drawings and detailed descriptions to approve a modern-day design; the landscape-architecture approach has therefore become a necessity to deal with some municipalities.

Unfortunately, when courses are built straight from plans like a house, the results are often quite ordinary and sometimes downright lousy. The designs built off paper look as if they were designed with little genuine care for natural features, or you see too many whirling lines, as if the designer tried to make it look like the course was not built on a computer. More important, many of these designs fail to function as well as they could because there was limited supervision during construction, meaning no one was present to analyze whether these newly shaped landscapes worked as golf holes or could be maintained by a superintendent.

World- or Regional-Traveler Architect

Why should an architect have to saddle himself with one or two projects, when six or seven could be had? This has led to the franchise mentality which plagues so much of golf course architecture, producing a sameness to many layouts built during the last twenty years . . . as a result, there is a tendency to rely on what has worked in the past and to shy away from the unconventional or the innovative.   —Gil Hanse, golf architect

The "World-Traveler" designation classifies most of the major "brand-name" architects we know from 1950 on. In modern times the world-traveler designation has come to include many lesser-known designers who take on four to six projects per year and fancy themselves as the next great worldwide architect. Wannabe or legitimate, the world traveler creates courses with a staff that churns out extensive plans. Once construction begins the architect can visit to appear in those embarrassing photographs, replete with an entourage clad in expensive sunglasses and designer shirts, standing around looking at blueprints.

Developers pay lavishly to hire world-traveling architects and even pay for their private jet fuel, just to have those few hours of bonding time and photographs taken with the big name. Meanwhile, the course is constructed by a contractor that specializes in golf course construction and perhaps even the architect's recognizable style. The contractor tends to repeat what the architect did on the previous project unless he's directed otherwise. Though this approach appears repetitive and leads to manufactured-looking courses, some clients feel comforted knowing their course will look very similar to the architect's last acclaimed design. Unfortunately for golfers, such similarities may prove comforting enough to get them to play once, but repeat visits become uninteresting.

My favorite golf course construction stories come from those who work on-site for world-traveler architects. The shapers who have worked for these architects can tell you about the day the big-name architect made his third and final contractually obligated visit prior to the course being seeded. Stories of architects getting lost on their way to the site, having to be briefed on details of their design en route and even their disregard for the people who work hard for them, tend to paint a rather bleak picture.

It is not unusual for the world-traveler architect to modify one bunker or green design during these cameo site appearances, even if it will come at great expense since the project is almost complete and built to the plan specifications. You can imagine the world traveler making his grand appearance with a photographer in tow and an entourage of financiers concentrating on his every move.

The world traveler then announces that a green about to be seeded must be torn up, and lowered by eight inches for better "visual deception." Or maybe the architect decides that an entire bunker needs to be shifted a measly four feet forward to catch a long hitter's drive. As soon as the world-traveler architect hops on his private jet to attend his next staged site visit, the ordered changes are rarely made because the construction crew realizes that the architect will never notice whether the changes were made when he returns for opening day.

Here's the best part. Several times when changes were ordered but not implemented because of time or financial constraints, the architect has been known to return and look at the finished product that was supposed to have been altered. These architects have been known to pat themselves on the back for remembering that they made that last-minute design change, and congratulate themselves with a "look how much better it is now" comment.

This is not to say that the concept of traveling extensively and charging for your name is a bad thing, since people are often willing to pay handsomely for this kind of design and derive satisfaction in playing such courses. Name architects sell real estate. But it takes someone with a special talent to travel the world and create lasting architecture with individual character.

The Player-Architect

If you see a player out in public having dinner, chances are he's with his boring money manager or some boring rich guy he hopes to design a golf course for. —Dan Jenkins, writer

With the exception of certain designers like Bobby Jones, Ben Crenshaw, Tom Weiskopf and a handful of others, this phenomenon has to be the strangest of all in contemporary golf. A project hires a solid architect who will probably give his best, but ultimately they decide the project needs more name-drawing power, so a Tour professional is paid anywhere from $75,000 to $500,000 to lend his name, visit the site two or three times, and perhaps play eighteen holes on opening day.

You can understand this phenomenon when names like Palmer and Nicklaus sell millions of dollars in real estate, or their name helps bring people to a place that otherwise would not get much attention. It is the lesser-known Tour player-architect phenomenon that makes many scratch their head. Tour players who have won a single tour event are announcing their intention to start a design firm or join an established architect. All at added expense to projects, with little or no expertise added to the final design.

Even if the players were genuinely designing, it does not ensure they are going to create good holes. As Bobby Jones said, "No man learns to design a golf course simply by playing golf, no matter how well."

Assuming there is actual design input, good players tend to think of their own game. They have a difficult time envisioning how others play. Sure, they might say how they notice their "pro-am partners tend to slice" or some other myth that drives design. But it takes a great deal of time looking at each individual hole design, in person preferably, to consider the games of different golfers—time that good players usually spend playing, practicing or posing for pictures.

The Hands-On Designer

Designing and constructing a golf course is an evolutionary process. It is a process of starting with an idea, a concept, and then adapting to the changes that occur to that concept in the field. —Bill Coore, golf architect

This category includes most of the old architects recognized today as "masters," including the four featured in this chapter. Some will argue that Donald Ross and Alister MacKenzie were not hands-on architects, but instead, the first world travelers. True, they were not as hands-on, but even as much time as they spent traveling and working out ideas from an office, a train or, in MacKenzie's case, trans-Atlantic ships, both Ross and MacKenzie were excellent communicators who spent time on-site during construction of their most noted project, for significant periods of time.

Donald Ross never did see several of his courses in completed form, but his intricate plans were well conceived. More importantly, the plans were carried out by a group of construction experts who could have been master architects on their own, and who had Ross's approval to deviate where necessary to create better holes or to deal with unex-pected situations. Still, Ross's best work was at Pinehurst or in the

Northeast where he spent summers and could visit during construction.

Today, a number of architects are returning to the field. They are creating small offices to handle the most basic paperwork issues while devoting much of their time to their projects in the field, not sitting at a drawing board. Instead of amassing a large staff of technicians creating grading plans and computer-aided designs, they are hiring a team of trustworthy shapers who move from project to project, similar to the setup Ross and MacKenzie employed.

With the on-site attention of an architect, outside contractors are now only part of the equation instead of being the on-site design representative and supervisor of the project. Much of the designing takes place as construction commences, allowing for more flexibility as the project moves forward and as ideas evolve.

So why is this on-site time so vital during the routing of the holes and later on, during construction?

Besides the obvious reasons that any kind of personal supervision and time devoted to an art is likely to yield better results, it must be remembered that a golf course site is as large a canvas as an architect will find (except for Frederick Law Olmsted's commission to design Central Park in New York!). A golf course has a minimum of one hundred and fifty acres, up to as many as a thousand acres to work with. A canvas that large is not going to reveal itself in a short time, no matter how many topographic maps the architect has at his disposal.

Besides serving as a canvas for architects to create artistically beautiful landscapes, the golf course must also function well to be enjoyed, maintained and to be profitable. Without time spent considering and adjusting the functional and scientific side, the finished product is bound to have problems that will require expensive patchwork efforts once the course is open. So on-site design can help prevent future problems, because the construction process is much more art than science.

Many of the architects who devote their time to on-site supervision are genuine characters. Thus, their on-site presence surely lifted the spirits of those around them carrying out the less attractive but still important tasks. With everyone in the dirt doing work, the entire team is more liable to create a better course.

Most of all, the time spent on-site ultimately helps familiarize architects with the terrain, shapes their ideas, and allows them the time necessary to figure how best to take advantage of natural features. Give any talented architect time to tinker with a design and they are going to get more out of the land than an architect who spends his time drawing plans, going to cocktail parties and attending ribbon-cutting ceremonies.

An architect's earnest hope is, without doubt, that his courses will have the necessary vitality to resist possible adverse criticism, and will endure as a lasting record of his craft and of his love for his work.

—H. S. Colt, golf architect

Understanding the difference between the various approaches to design will help you see why the following designers were selected as "great architects" worthy of further discussion. They were creative visionaries who balanced the art, science and communication skills required to create a sound design and, in essence, to "sell" their ideas. Much of their passion to promote their designs comes from a love for golf and the hope that the people who played their courses would experience fun and adventure.

Alister MacKenzie, Donald Ross, A.W. Tillinghast and Pete Dye have been praised, even worshiped by some and branded "master" architects. Each has been lovingly disparaged by frustrated golfers, a condemnation that some architects relish. After all, what good is the architect if he fails to create holes that occasionally provoke passionate discussion and emotional reactions?

The primary purpose of this chapter is to explore the elements that elevated these men to the status of master architect. It would be simple to repeat a few of their philosophical remarks on design because their philosophies were vivid and interesting, but if you have the opportunity to play one of their courses, such anecdotes may not help you appreciate their accomplishments nor help you sort through their design ploys. Instead, here is an overview of each designer's approach to architecture and what attributes make them worthy of master status.

ALISTER MACKENZIE

Born: August 30, 1870, in Yorkshire, England
Died: January 6, 1934, in Santa Cruz, California

Career Summary:

(BOB DAVIS)

- Raised in Scottish Highlands, received Bachelor of Medicine degree
- Served as Alwoodley Golf Club Green Chairman in early 1900s, worked with architect H.S. Colt in redesigning the Alwoodley course
- Won first prize in 1914 *Country Life* magazine design contest
- Served as physician during Boer War and World War I, credited himself with saving thousands of lives during wars thanks to implementation of his camouflage theories
- Created own design practice during the 1920s and traveled the world
- Designed Cypress Point, Pasatiempo, Crystal Downs and Augusta National in a four-year span
- Died broke in 1934 before publication of his second book, *The Spirit of St. Andrews*. Was owed several thousand dollars by Augusta National for his design, but was never paid

Notable Designs:

Alwoodley Golf Club (1907 redesign, with H. S. Colt)
Royal Adelaide Golf Club (1926 redesign)
Royal Melbourne Golf Club—West Course (1931, with Alex Russell)
Kingston Heath Golf Club (1928 redesign, with Alex Russell)
Cypress Point Golf Club (1928, with Robert Hunter)
The Valley Club of Montecito (1928, with Robert Hunter)
Pasatiempo Golf Club (1929, with Marion Hollins)
Augusta National Golf Club (1932, with Bobby Jones)
Crystal Downs Country Club (1933, with Perry Maxwell)

Alister MacKenzie preached a consistent belief when laying out a golf course: Design a course that is pleasurable and interesting for players of all levels. MacKenzie crafted adventurous designs without resorting to gimmicks or lavish features that modern architects fall back on too easily.

Bobby Jones, who selected MacKenzie to design Augusta National Golf Club, wrote, "Dr. MacKenzie has long contended that a golf course, in order to hold interest for any amount of continuous play, must offer adventure. His conception is that nothing is as tiresome as certainty, and he blames the plethora of prescriptive courses, where every shot is known and ordered in advance, for the prevailing tendency to regard the score, rather than the playing of strokes. . . . Dr. MacKenzie has proved that it is entirely possible to construct a course that will provide interesting yet not unreasonable problems for every golfer according to his skill."

MacKenzie injected options into his holes. He wanted you to have to work to figure how best to use a small mound next to the green, or why you had better not miss the green long. These subtle features constituted the "little things" that made his courses such a treat for golfers of all levels to test the first time around, as well as the one hundredth round played.

His construction firm also introduced the most remarkable and original bunkers the game has ever seen. The distinctive style of large pits with sand flashed up the irregularly shaped faces became a renowned MacKenzie trait, thanks to his incorporation of irregularly shaped capes and bays. But unlike modern designers who you'd swear use the same machine-molded bunker cutter from course to course, each MacKenzie bunker has its own character. The capes and bays have individual personalities like each cloud in the sky will have its own distinct features. MacKenzie's primary bunker builder actually gained most of his inspiration from passing storm clouds.

MacKenzie was not the hands-on architect some would like to think. The doctor was willing to travel and sell his services all over the world because he found trusted associates throughout to supervise the construction of his designs. MacKenzie and his second wife Hilda were noted ballroom dancers and loved to enter competitions while traveling on various trans-Atlantic voyages. He shipped his beloved DeSoto to England so he'd have proper transportation, and rarely has a photograph of him appeared where he was dressed in anything but plus-fours, white shirt, tie and often a Scottish driving cap.

When MacKenzie traveled to Australia during the mid-1920s, the trip resulted in two designs consistently ranked among the top twenty in the world. He spent just six weeks there but managed to forever leave his mark. How did he do it?

MacKenzie relied on his sharp wit, imagination and, most of all, his persuasive communication skills. More importantly, he discovered a trusted associate in each part of the world where he worked: Robert Hunter in northern California, Perry Maxwell in the Midwest, Alex Russell and Mick Morcum in Australia and Wendell Miller in the eastern United States.

MacKenzie was similar to the masterful film director who may not be as well versed in lighting, sound or cinematography as he could be, but, like those special directors, he possessed an overall vision for design with an ability to communicate what he envisioned. MacKenzie surrounded himself with quality people and trusted them to create the elements he was in search of. And surely they came up with a few brilliant touches of their own. MacKenzie instilled a passion for his work that inspired those around him to devote the energy and detail work necessary to craft masterful designs. The "fun" of playing a MacKenzie course comes from this sense of joy that was injected into the construction process.

The attention to detail is evident in the courses of MacKenzie today, even though very few exist as he left them. Golfers sense a unique feeling to each of his designs but often can't describe what feels special. MacKenzie's secret: routing.

The doctor refused to follow any kind of prescribed sequencing of holes or "balance" in his designs. The ground dictated the type of golf holes he would lay out and construct, which is why no two of his courses look or play the same. Yet you can spot a MacKenzie course right away based on certain features, such as the distinctive bunkering and the gentle use of small hillocks around greens. Even the occasional boomerang, horseshoe or tooth-shaped putting surface was a MacKenzie trademark to promote exciting hole locations.

Most architects struggle to create the special aura that a MacKenzie course offers. Because like great land planners in the vein of Frederick Law Olmsted, MacKenzie could figure out how best to fit holes onto a property and situate a golf course to evoke a comfortable, settled connection to the ground. His course routings are always functional and original, but rarely do they fight the contours of the property. His tees, bunkers and greens have character created through careful construction. Their scale is never too big or too small, always just right.

Most of all, MacKenzie courses are full of subtle surprises, which goes back to what separated him in the eyes of a discerning client like Bobby Jones. His designs give the impression that you and your golfing friends are setting out on an adventure, and you aren't sure what to expect from hole to hole but you have the feeling it will be enjoyable. The surprises MacKenzie has waiting make his courses exciting to look at and fun to tackle, yet never overwhelming to the eye.

Dr. MacKenzie always points to old St. Andrews to illustrate what adventure on a golf course can mean. There, certainly, one does not have one's course from tee to green plotted by the man who designed the layout. A considerable amount of room is always offered off the tee to allow a player to attack his problem in a way that suits his own tastes. But the game is always full of surprises until one has made a real study of the course. It is a lasting thrill to be forever discovering new slopes and rolls and hazards, which do not at first strike the eye, but nevertheless are of immense importance in the correct playing of the hole. This is what the doctor means by adventure. —Bobby Jones

MacKenzie spent a year mapping the Old Course and it served as his career-long inspiration. He named his second book *The Spirit of St. Andrews* because he believed the Old Course was the ultimate layout to emulate both strategically and in the shaping of contours. MacKenzie also admired the Old Course because it could be played by any level of golfer, including the old man who could not hit the ball "as far as the lusty youth could kick one." Yet St. Andrews requires more intelligence and shotmaking skill than any course in golf. That unique combination of playability and mental challenge is what Bobby Jones

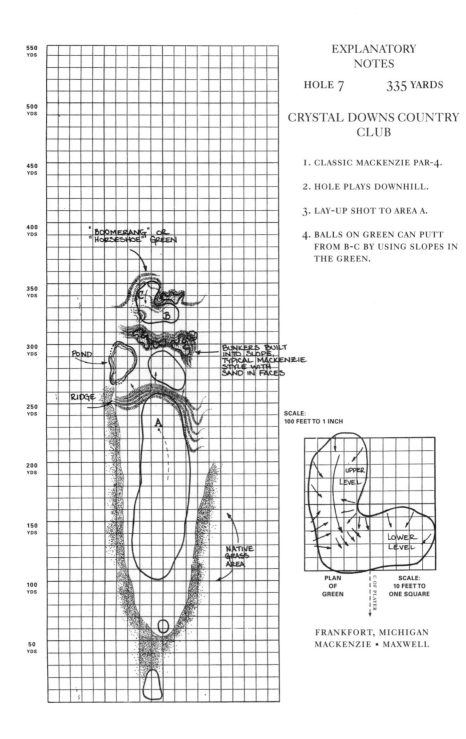

The par-4 seventh at Alister MacKenzie's Crystal Downs Country Club. (GIL HANSE)

hoped to accomplish with his dream course at Augusta National: challenging for the good player, but plenty playable for the average man.

MacKenzie and Jones actually sought to use design ideas found on the seaside, sandy links courses and place them amidst the hilly, Georgia pine–covered terrain at Augusta. It was a bold notion for any architect to consider pulling off, yet they managed to make it work.

From day one, their version of Augusta was playable for Jones's amateur golfing friends and yet compelling for the world's best professionals. Most of all, Augusta National exuded that feeling of adventure. You never knew what to expect each time out. We still do not know what to expect to see there in modern times, even as the course is nearing the complete loss of its original flavor. That's because no one created a more subtle mystique and sense of fun than MacKenzie. It is just a shame so little of MacKenzie's adventurous design is available for golfers to enjoy.

(USGA)

DONALD ROSS
Born: 1872 in Dornoch, Scotland
Died: 1948 in Pinehurst, North Carolina

Career Summary:

• Grew up playing Dornoch course and became fascinated by golf
• Served an apprenticeship at St. Andrews under Old Tom Morris
• Returned to Dornoch and became course greenkeeper, also worked as a clubmaker
• Emigrated to America in 1899, hired to build and maintain Oakley Golf Club in Boston
• In 1901 remodeled and added nine holes to Pinehurst Resort for the Tufts family
• Made many contacts at Pinehurst to design other courses, eventually started his own practice
• Designed or remodeled nearly four hundred courses, including some of America's most famous

Notable Designs:

> Pinehurst Resort #2 (1903–1948)
> Brae Burn Country Club (1912)
> Wannamoisett Golf Club (1914)
> Scioto (1916)
> Oakland Hills (1917)
> Interlachen (1919)
> Inverness Golf Club (1920)
> Oak Hill (1923, 36 holes)
> Salem Country Club (1925)
> Franklin Hills Country Club (1926)
> Seminole (1929)

Designing 399 courses over a forty-year period is not the best prescription for creating timeless masterpieces. And with these 400 or so commissions spread out across America, how could Donald Ross have possibly left a positive mark?

Imagine a filmmaker pumping out three feature-length films a year, a reasonable equivalent to the ten-golf-courses-a-year average Ross produced. The chances are not good that the filmmaker would achieve a high success rate with such an output.

Painters create portfolios as large as Ross's, but they'll freely admit there are many works in their collection that they are afraid to look at or which were experimental.

But a majority of Donald Ross's designs are excellent and some are brilliant. This might be difficult to believe today when looking at many of his designs, since so few resemble their original state. Through analysis of photos, memories of older golfers and by experiencing many interesting holes that still exist, however, it becomes apparent that Ross shared the same qualities MacKenzie preached: Ross could locate the key features on a property and make the most of them, even when some of the properties were not very interesting. And he designed with a subtle, loving touch that reflected his love for nature and golfers.

After figuring out the routing of a course, this often signaled the end to Ross's time on-site if he had ever even visited the site (this was the case a few times where developers or municipalities merely sent him a topographic map and paid for a routing and set of drawings). In most cases where he visited the site, Ross would return to his office and create a set of plans for the golf course. Most of his time was spent on detailed green sketches that would make most modern architects dizzy with awe because of their consistent originality and ingenuity.

Once the drawings were complete, Ross would then have one of his talented supervisors carry out the work, with most of the green designs coming close to what he sketched. Ross was more involved in some projects than others, notably Pinehurst's #2 course and many Northeastern efforts. These also happen to be his best golf courses.

One thing Ross and his team managed to do consistently, whether present on-site or not, was to design ingeniously contoured greens. You may have heard the commonly thrown about "Ross greens" phrase, but rarely has anyone been able to define them. Like trying to simplify the style of Mozart, Monet or Capra, it can't be done. Variety was taken to new heights by Ross. His imagination could work from behind a drafting table and create intricately designed green complexes from his office. Some were more fun to play than others. Others might even make you laugh, such as those when Ross used small "pimples" to add a distinct character to an otherwise round, flat green. Occasionally Ross would "crown" the green, creating a putting area shaped like an upside-down cereal bowl, though this effect was used in limited ways and is a fallacy regarding his style.

Ross's beautiful course renderings and accompanying comments are stored safely at the Tufts Archive in North Carolina and have been used by many historians and architects to help restore Ross designs. Like a director's storyboard, the drawings consistently tell the story of each course.

Ross did devote himself to the Pinehurst #2 course in an almost obsessive-compulsive manner. He worked for years fine-tuning #2, creating a course so complex and fascinating that, like St. Andrews, it tends to be considered overrated or peculiar by some golfers on the first or second trip around. Over time, however, Pinehurst #2 reveals its genius like any masterpiece.

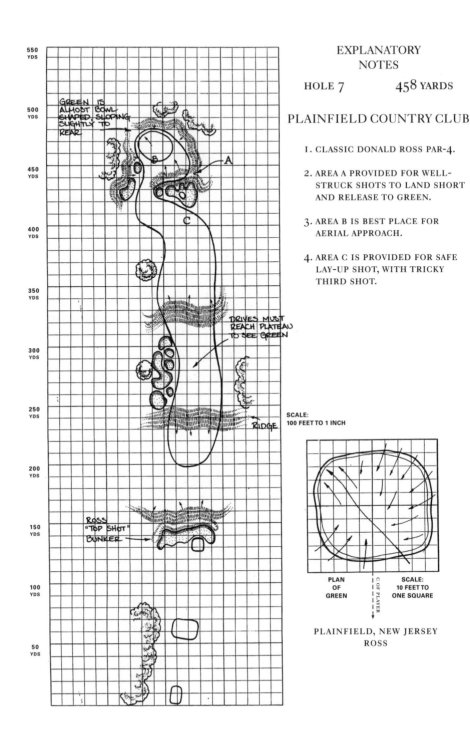

EXPLANATORY NOTES

HOLE 7   458 YARDS

PLAINFIELD COUNTRY CLUB

1. CLASSIC DONALD ROSS PAR-4.

2. AREA A PROVIDED FOR WELL-STRUCK SHOTS TO LAND SHORT AND RELEASE TO GREEN.

3. AREA B IS BEST PLACE FOR AERIAL APPROACH.

4. AREA C IS PROVIDED FOR SAFE LAY-UP SHOT, WITH TRICKY THIRD SHOT.

SCALE:
100 FEET TO 1 INCH

PLAN OF GREEN   C OF PLAYER   SCALE: 10 FEET TO ONE SQUARE

PLAINFIELD, NEW JERSEY
ROSS

Labels on diagram: GREEN IS ALMOST BOWL SHAPED, SLOPING SLIGHTLY TO REAR. / DRIVES MUST REACH PLATEAU TO SEE GREEN / RIDGE / ROSS "TOP SHOT" BUNKER

The par-4 seventh at Donald Ross's Plainfield Country Club. (GIL HANSE)

Thanks to Ross's use of strategy, natural contours and land planning, his design at Pinehurst is one of the ultimate thinking and shot-making tests in golf. It also has more to reveal than most golf courses in the world—that is, if the golfer is patient. The same could be said for all of Ross's courses, actually. He did not create flashy, "look at me, I'm Donald Ross" designs. Instead, they were subtle and dignified designs that respected their natural settings.

Pinehurst notwithstanding, how could Ross still be considered a master with a portfolio of designs so large? Some might argue that he stretched himself too thin and he reportedly admitted this fact late in his career. Some argue that his courses weren't as consistently dramatic or artistically interesting to look at as MacKenzie's or Tillinghast's. But Ross was a soft-spoken man, and not an outgoing salesman like other architects. He was, however, a keen businessman with a sense for sound, restrained golf course character.

Ross consistently created enjoyable courses that utilized the simplest of natural features, such as ridges or rolls in the ground. Like his home course at Royal Dornoch in Scotland, Ross designs feel good when you play them; they are never overwhelming, but never so simple that they seem dull. His work is comfortable to look at because he never overwhelmed the land with massive features. And when you consider the number of holes Ross built and the enjoyable rounds of golf he has influenced, no architect took sound design to larger audiences than Donald Ross.

ALBERT WARREN TILLINGHAST
Born: May 1874 in Philadelphia, Pennsylvania
Died: May 1942 in Toledo, Ohio

Career Summary:

• Born into a wealthy family and once said: "I never finished a school I went to."
• Nicknamed "the Terror" because of tempestuous childhood

- Introduced to golf in 1890s in Scotland; took lessons from Old Tom Morris
- Hired by family friends to design Shawnee Country Club in 1907, soon started design business
- Worked as editor of *Golf Illustrated* for several years while becoming well-known architect, also noted for his photography, artwork and piano playing
- One of the founders of the PGA of America, he later consulted for the PGA by traveling the country to analyze courses for the local PGA pro
- Moved to California in 1937 to open antique shop and briefly partnered with Billy Bell, died in obscurity five years later

Notable Designs:

Baltusrol Golf Club (1922, 36 holes)
Baltimore Country Club (1926, East course and routing for West)
Bethpage State Park (1935, consultant three courses)
Brook Hollow Golf Club (1921)
Fenway Golf Club (1924)
Newport Golf Club (1924 redesign)
Philadelphia Cricket Club (1922, Flourtown Course)
Quaker Ridge Golf Club (1926)
Ridgewood Country Club (1929, 27 holes)
San Francisco Golf Club (1915)
Somerset Hills Golf Club (1917)
Winged Foot Golf Club (1923, 36 holes)

In contrast to Ross's gentle touch, A.W. Tillinghast was and remains golf architecture's ultimate eccentric. His wide-ranging portfolio of classic designs displayed humor and quirkiness. Yet, any Tillinghast course you play is a solid test of skill from the first hole to the last. And even though "Tillie" was quite the comedian, he knew how to build sound holes that provoked a variety of reactions from the golfer. The ability to create with sometimes outlandishly small greens or other oddball features is a tribute to Tillie's ability to balance his eccentricity with proven design principles.

If Tillinghast had been a painter instead of the architect, writer, musician, fine furniture collector and Broadway producer that he was, his career might be compared to that of Vincent van Gogh. Tillinghast constantly varied his design style from project to project, much like van Gogh repeatedly toyed with different brush strokes and colors in a quest to find new and interesting ways to present his ideas.

Unlike Ross and MacKenzie, who left subtle hints behind of their presence, Tillinghast's touch is more difficult to trace. Some of us enjoy finding those little mounds or distinctive bunkers that remind us we are playing a certain architect's course. Finding signs of Tillinghast's touch is more difficult. He was not afraid to play with different bunker styles or a variety of green-complex designs. Yet, somehow in this constant shifting of visual styles, Tillinghast created sound holes because of his consistent use of strategy and reliance on other features.

Consider his two most famous courses, Winged Foot's West Course and Baltusrol's Lower Course. Both United States Open sites were built two years apart and within short distance of one another. Yet few golfers could guess they were designed by the same man. Winged Foot's West Course features propped up greens guarded by beautiful sand-faced bunkers. Each bunker has individual character, created by interesting grass capes and bays. The Winged Foot holes are defined by their greens, while the tee-to-fringe portion of Winged Foot is fairly simple but ultimately as challenging as any course ever built.

Meanwhile Baltusrol has more variety in the look and character of the holes; the bunkers are grass-faced in style as opposed to the sand-flashed look found at Winged Foot; and Baltusrol has a unique routing that includes back-to-back par-5s at the end of the round. Yet all of these unusual quirks function in a stylish manner, so classical that Baltusrol has hosted as many U.S. Opens as any course in the world.

In 1918, a few years before he created Winged Foot and Baltusrol, Tillinghast was even more extreme in contrasting his design style. He created San Francisco Golf Club in California with large, sand-faced bunkers that contained so many capes and bays around their edges they looked like old, sand-colored baseball mitts strewn about the property. The same year, Tillinghast designed Somerset Hills in New

Jersey, a shorter, funkier course that may be as interesting as any design ever created in America. Little about the design features could be called natural. Somerset includes odd, almost cone-shaped mounds, named the "Dolomites" after the rocky Italian mountain range. The greens are downright offbeat, with wild contours and dramatic corner hole locations. The sequencing of the holes follows no set pattern except that the nines return to the clubhouse. Yet the course presents a solid challenge like no other and is near the top of many architects' list of favorites.

Tillinghast did have one identifying trait that he left behind on nearly all of his designs. He called it the "Sahara Hole." At Pine Valley they called it "Hell's Half Acre." Either way, Tillinghast loved creating a large forced carry area at the halfway point of a long par-5, the idea being that it placed pressure on the tee shot to hit a solid drive. Otherwise a decision on the second shot would be necessary: play over the sandy area or lay up and require at least four shots to reach the hole. Such a design is considered "penal" by many golfers and understandably so because it puts such a premium on length and accuracy. But to Tillinghast, putting the Sahara desert midway through a three-shot hole solved the problem of par-5s that lack an interesting tee shot or any kind of strategic decision after the drive.

Like van Gogh, Tillinghast died penniless in 1942 with little fanfare. His accomplishments were not realized at the time, nor was he really known until 1974 when United States Golf Association director Frank Hannigan wrote an essay detailing Tillie's life and times. Only then did it become apparent that Tillinghast, after his "misspent" youth, devoted his life to making golf fun for millions of players. His influence through his extensive writings and a portfolio of courses was vital to the acceptance of many of the more eccentric, but ultimately amusing, design ideas the art has ever seen.

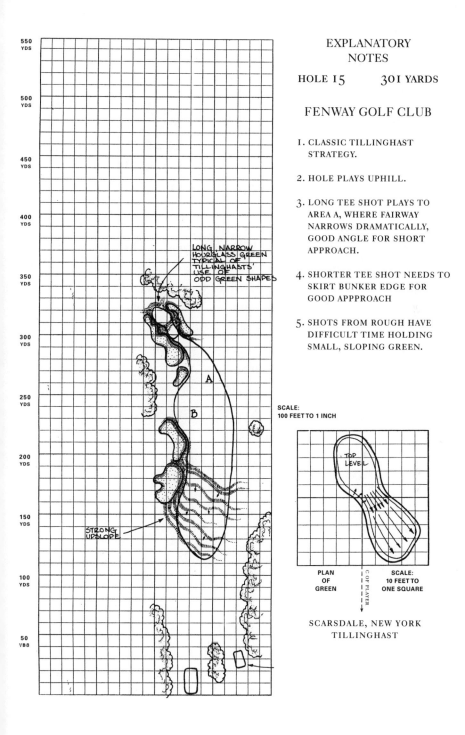

EXPLANATORY NOTES

HOLE 15   301 YARDS

FENWAY GOLF CLUB

1. CLASSIC TILLINGHAST STRATEGY.

2. HOLE PLAYS UPHILL.

3. LONG TEE SHOT PLAYS TO AREA A, WHERE FAIRWAY NARROWS DRAMATICALLY, GOOD ANGLE FOR SHORT APPROACH.

4. SHORTER TEE SHOT NEEDS TO SKIRT BUNKER EDGE FOR GOOD APPPROACH

5. SHOTS FROM ROUGH HAVE DIFFICULT TIME HOLDING SMALL, SLOPING GREEN.

SCALE:
100 FEET TO 1 INCH

LONG NARROW HOURGLASS GREEN TYPICAL OF TILLINGHASTS' USE OF ODD GREEN SHAPES

STRONG UPSLOPE

TOP LEVEL

PLAN OF GREEN

℄ OF PLAYER

SCALE:
10 FEET TO ONE SQUARE

SCARSDALE, NEW YORK
TILLINGHAST

The par-4 fifteenth at A. W. Tillinghast's Fenway Golf Club. (GIL HANSE)

PETE DYE

Born: 1925 in Urbana, Ohio

Career Summary:

- Excellent amateur golfer, met wife Alice in college
- Worked as life insurance salesman in Indianapolis

(**GEOFF SHACKELFORD**) • Served as green chairman at Country Club of Indianapolis, supervised course redesign

- By 1963, had designed several courses, and toured Scotland with Alice
- Influenced by Seth Raynor and William Langford's Midwest designs
- By mid-sixties was incorporating Scottish look while returning strategy and other features not seen in American design at that time
- 1969 opening of Harbour Town with Jack Nicklaus made him famous
- Over the next twenty years built numerous world-class courses while teaching younger architects like Bill Coore and Tom Doak
- Dye does some of his own shaping work, Alice has changed most architects' approach to where "forward" tees are placed

Notable Designs:

Crooked Stick GC (1964)

The Golf Club (1967)

Harbour Town Golf Links (1969)

TPC at Sawgrass (1981)

Long Cove Club (1982)

PGA West—Stadium (1986)

The Ocean Course at Kiawah Island (1991)

Whistling Straits (1998)

No person has arrived on the architecture scene and made more of an impact than Pete Dye did in the late 1960s. Even though we all have our own reaction to his island greens and railroad ties, the impact of Dye's style is often lost in the constant debate over whether his courses are "fair" or not. That may be Dye's greatest contribution. He made people talk about architecture again. His courses created a sense of excitement that golf needed.

Dye, and his talented partner co-designer wife Alice, played much of their golf on the Midwest designs of William Langford and Seth Raynor. Both of those early-twentieth-century architects created steep grass-faced bunkers with large undulating greens, and even the occasional island green surrounded by *sand*. Langford and Raynor were different than the other "Golden Age" architects because their style was a cleaner, Americanized, almost engineered version of the great links of Scotland.

After they married, the Dyes took their now infamous trip to Scotland which, in talking to Dye, is a bit overrated in its influence on his style. He is more inclined to tell you that he loves the work of "Mr. Raynor," and that the links of Scotland merely confirmed his belief that he needed to get out of the insurance business and into the design world.

When Dye realized he was in the wrong line of work, architecture was dominated by an assembly-line mentality with cookie-cutter bunkers appearing identical from course to course. The general look of American courses had shifted to tree-lined layouts that reached 7,000 yards and generally made the game difficult in a less than exciting way. More than the difficulty, architecture dominating American golf from 1950 to the early '70s was devoid of character, warmth and humor. Dye was determined to provide an alternative approach.

Say what you want about the "naturalness" or lack thereof in his courses, but Dye's funky-looking mounds and pot bunkers have character. There is a look of irregularity to his style that makes his courses appear appealing to the eye. Dye's work does not contain the flat, regular look of so many designs from his era. His smaller greens and rolling fairway contours shocked golfers at first sight. Now those features are considered common on the palettes of many modern designers, all because of Dye.

Pete Dye's most important contribution was to the strategic side of modern golf. He believed that the average American course was becoming a test of who hit their ball the straightest, not which player could combine physical talent with a strong mind. Dye knew that the one way to trip good players and give the crafty average player some help was to reintroduce decision-making to golf courses. Bunkers in

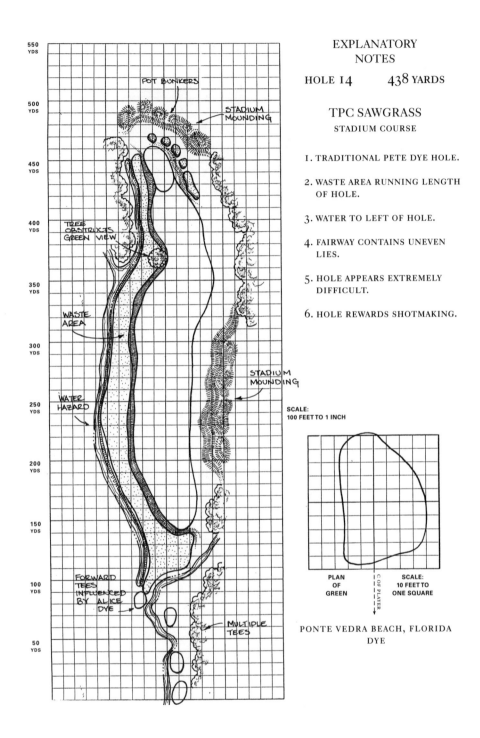

HOLE 14   438 YARDS

TPC SAWGRASS
STADIUM COURSE

1. TRADITIONAL PETE DYE HOLE.

2. WASTE AREA RUNNING LENGTH OF HOLE.

3. WATER TO LEFT OF HOLE.

4. FAIRWAY CONTAINS UNEVEN LIES.

5. HOLE APPEARS EXTREMELY DIFFICULT.

6. HOLE REWARDS SHOTMAKING.

SCALE:
100 FEET TO 1 INCH

PLAN OF GREEN   SCALE: 10 FEET TO ONE SQUARE

PONTE VEDRA BEACH, FLORIDA
DYE

550 YDS
500 YDS
450 YDS
400 YDS
350 YDS
300 YDS
250 YDS
200 YDS
150 YDS
100 YDS
50 YDS

POT BUNKERS
STADIUM MOUNDING
TREE OBSTRUCTS GREEN VIEW
WASTE AREA
STADIUM MOUNDING
WATER HAZARD
FORWARD TEES INFLUENCED BY ALICE DYE
MULTIPLE TEES

The par-4 fourteenth at Pete Dye's TPC at Sawgrass. (GIL HANSE)

170

the middle of fairways, blind approaches for poorly placed tee shots, and deceiving forced carries that tempted you to bite off more than you could chew. All were elements Dye brought back to golf design.

Like Tillinghast, Dye has always created courses with a sense of humor. His drollness keeps golfers coming back, even if they believe a Dye course means play will often seem unfair or too penal. The air of humor in Dye's work keeps things buoyant while you struggle to find balls and make a bagful of double bogeys. You also know what you are getting into when you sign up for a tee time at a Dye course. This advance notice may ease some of the pain compared to courses where you didn't know who the architect was, or why you walked off feeling so beaten down.

Alice Dye has been a key contributor to her husband's work and to all designs of the modern era because she insists on improved forward tee areas. She continues to study every possible way to get golfers to play the proper set of tees for their games and, most of all, to make the game more interesting for shorter-hitting golfers. Many think that designing forward tees is simply a matter of placing a tee as far forward as possible, but Alice Dye has insisted on these tees not only being forward, but in places that give the shorter hitter the same strategic decisions to deal with as the good players who are teeing off from the back tees. It sounds like a simple concept that you would expect every architect to have followed for years, but not until Alice Dye came along were the forward tees given much thought. Nor were tees placed for seniors or beginners.

More than any architect in the game, Pete Dye may be remembered less for his courses and more for his impact on the profession. He took proven, classical design looks and interpreted them in his own distinct artistic style, creating golf courses that look like nothing anyone else could have imagined. Maybe he used a few too many railroad ties or island greens for some golfers' liking. Bob Hope said he's the only architect capable of building a course that could burn down.

But few will deny that the prospect of experiencing a Pete Dye course for the first time is always going to be an adventure. How many modern architects consistently create the kind of interest and sense of excitement that golfers relish in a Pete Dye design?

The Tenth Hole

Mind Games

Outsmarting the Architect and Managing Your Thoughts

The object of design, as has been mentioned, is to create difficulties (and, in a modified sense, illusions), not to explain them; to outwit the expert or at least to set his brains to work to find the best solutions. In a word, the object is to make him conceive the big idea and attempt the utmost that skill and nerve may suggest to execute it. —H. N. Wethered and Tom Simpson

Course management has long been the least understood aspect of the game. No matter how many hours they may watch *Golf Academy Live*, golfers still succumb to the most basic of architectural ploys. The recent wave of golf psychology books and magazine instruction articles has brought attention to the "mental side" of golf. Still, it is remarkable to see how little awareness there is for the strongest component of Tiger Woods's game: management of the design in front of him along with his ability to deal with changing conditions and adapting to scenarios that arise on the course.

The increasing number of golfers who go through lengthy preshot routines and other assorted mental checklists does slow the game down more than we'd like. However, such preshot preparations have helped many talented players raise the level of their game while allowing plenty of average players to elevate their golf to new heights.

Still, many players fail to understand that improvement does not come from hitting more "perfect" shots than they used to. Advancement comes with more manageable misses. Better scoring starts by hitting fewer disastrous shots. Sports psychologists constantly preach to golfers that they must accept their faults and aim to improve their misses. To do this, we must acknowledge the often ego-deflating notion that most of our shots will be less than perfect.

Ben Hogan consistently talked about a typical round including only seven or so shots that he hit the way he wanted, which to some degree is true for most golfers. During an eighteen-hole round, the player who misses their shots the best will likely shoot the lowest score, win a match, or simply enjoy their round the most.

Thus, managing shots so that you know where to "bail out" or how to go about properly calculating your options poses the trickiest of all course-management issues. Many golfers are trained to ignore the obstacles placed before them and instead focus on where they want to hit their shot. Others do it naturally. Either way, golfers are often instructed to visualize a shot reaching a goal, and trained to erase images of everything else. You must only focus on a positive outcome, or so some sports psychologists suggest.

This seems logical, right? All of us have experienced those rare moments when we dial into the target and ignore distractions with ease. But those "zone" moments are atypical.

To be successful on a consistent basis, the player needs to develop a system that allows them to get into the architect's mind without overanalyzing the situation at hand. Part of this system includes the golfer accepting his limitations when analyzing how to handle a strategic situation. This difficult sort of self-awareness poses the most delicate of all course management theories, yet is essential to outwitting the architect.

Golf is a game of balance. The man who knows the value of each of his clubs, and who can work out when it is proper to play one and when to play another, succeeds at the game. The ability of a golfer to know his power and accuracy, and to play for what he can accomplish, is a thing which makes his game as perfect as can be while a thinker who gauges the true value of his shots, and is able to play them well, nearly always defeats an opponent who neglects to consider and properly discount his shortcomings.

—*George Thomas*

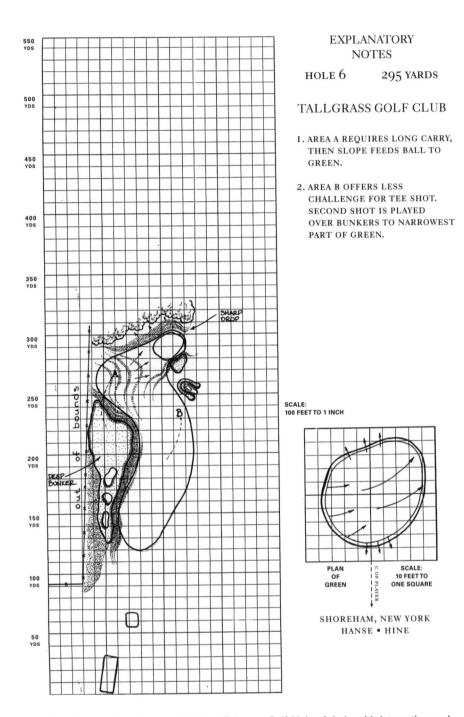

550 YDS

500 YDS

450 YDS

400 YDS

350 YDS

300 YDS

250 YDS

200 YDS

150 YDS

100 YDS

50 YDS

out of bounds

DEEP BUNKER

SHARP DROP

B

EXPLANATORY NOTES

HOLE 6   295 YARDS

TALLGRASS GOLF CLUB

1. AREA A REQUIRES LONG CARRY, THEN SLOPE FEEDS BALL TO GREEN.

2. AREA B OFFERS LESS CHALLENGE FOR TEE SHOT. SECOND SHOT IS PLAYED OVER BUNKERS TO NARROWEST PART OF GREEN.

SCALE:
100 FEET TO 1 INCH

PLAN OF GREEN   ℂ OF PLAYER   SCALE: 10 FEET TO ONE SQUARE

SHOREHAM, NEW YORK
HANSE • HINE

Rendering of the short par-4 sixth at Tallgrass Golf Links. A hole with interesting and difficult-looking options, but local knowledge reveals that the hole is quite simple if the player can acknowledge their own limitations. (GIL HANSE)

The wise player calculates the options at hand, then visualizes the option he would like to attempt, but he also must consider the areas where a slight miss can land safely. (Assuming that the architect has provided a place for a safe play.) This is the player who can "properly discount his shortcomings," which is George Thomas's succinct way of saying, "if you remain aware of your limitations but not encumbered by them, you stand a chance of visualizing the shot that best takes advantage of the architecture before you."

This basic analytical approach to golf architecture is essential to scoring. Yet we see only a few golfers who *enjoy* the challenge of assimilating the information presented by architects. Most, including some outstanding players on the PGA and LPGA Tour, tend to blame the architect when their on-course choices result in poor outcomes. But certain players come along every generation who savor options. They love having to sort out possibilities and come up with the appropriate club selection and shot.

> *The clever golf architect understands the psychology of the game, and*
> *exploits it in his design in a variety of ways.*   —*Tom Doak*

To take your game to the proverbial next level, it is important to acknowledge which school of design is driving the architect's philosophy. Some architects, like those in the framing school covered in the Third Hole, are not trying to play with your mind. Such design is meant to ease any burdens you might have and present soothing landscapes. If there is pressure to play a particular shot, it's strictly a physical limitation that must be overcome, usually requiring a shot hit high and straight. There is little in the way of subtlety or trickery in "framing" architecture, because everything is before you. Awareness of these design traits can help eliminate much of your preshot planning and self-examination regarding possible design ploys, because there aren't any!

The framing designs are very popular for beginners or on a tournament course where the golfers expect that every hole will be a fair one requiring little or no thought. Unfortunately, golf without decisions becomes banal and tedious on repeat visits. The courses separating themselves over time create both a great mental and physical

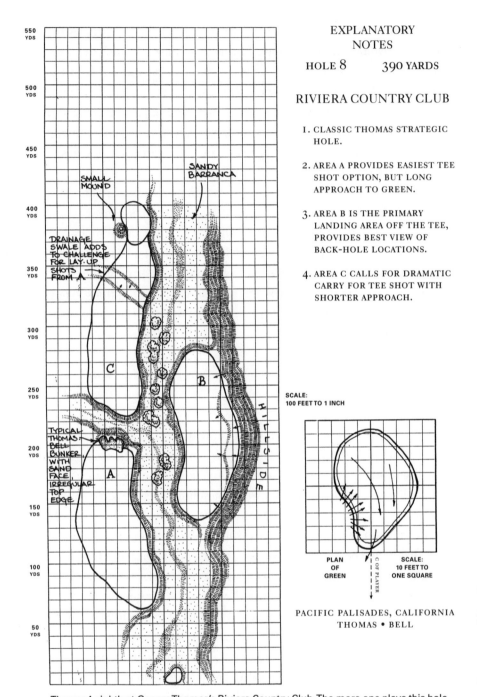

RIVIERA COUNTRY CLUB

1. CLASSIC THOMAS STRATEGIC
   HOLE.

2. AREA A PROVIDES EASIEST TEE
   SHOT OPTION, BUT LONG
   APPROACH TO GREEN.

3. AREA B IS THE PRIMARY
   LANDING AREA OFF THE TEE,
   PROVIDES BEST VIEW OF
   BACK-HOLE LOCATIONS.

4. AREA C CALLS FOR DRAMATIC
   CARRY FOR TEE SHOT WITH
   SHORTER APPROACH.

SCALE:
100 FEET TO 1 INCH

PLAN
OF
GREEN

C OF PLAYER

SCALE:
10 FEET TO
ONE SQUARE

PACIFIC PALISADES, CALIFORNIA
THOMAS • BELL

The par-4 eighth at George Thomas's Riviera Country Club. The more one plays this hole, the more thought impedes one's ability to decipher his options. It is the architect's hope that the player will outthink himself by drifting from his game plan, or succumbing to temptation to try an option that is just out of reach. (GIL HANSE) challenge, while also continually impressing us with their sheer beauty. They reward local knowledge, yet find a way to make us invent new shots every time around.

When you get those dudes thinking, they're in trouble.

—*Pete Dye, on touring pros*

Pete Dye presents design ploys in direct contrast to the framing approach, yet his courses are just as popular and dramatic the first time around. On repeat visits, you find that the strategies Dye employs are interesting but fairly simple *if* you are able to look past the many dramatic obstacles he lays out before you (railroad ties, nasty mounding, elevated greens, deep bunkers, etc.). But how many of us have the strength of mind to simplify all of the information a Pete Dye course presents? It's not an easy task, as we see during the Players Championship at Dye's TPC Sawgrass design, where the best players in the world are mentally teased and tortured.

When you play a Pete Dye course you need to immediately recognize that he throws more at you than you really need to know. His goal as an architect is to distract you from the obvious, to complicate your pre-shot plans. Dye busies the landscape to encourage the imagination to conjure up flashes of all of those nasty-looking hazards, so that you ignore the generous areas he leaves to play safely.

When you can acknowledge this visual-torture style that Dye and other architects such as Robert Trent Jones present, you have won the battle. When you turn down the volume on hazards, tall grasses, lakes or out-of-bounds, you can outwit the architect. Focusing on the basics (fairways and greens), your mind can pinpoint the proper strategy and help you recognize what shots can and cannot be played. With the possibilities more clearly defined, you stand a better chance of pulling off a confident stroke.

A man has got to know his limitations. —*"Dirty" Harry Calahan*

Golf architects recognize that most players have trouble accepting which shots are not in their repertoire. The clever course designer expects that you will not "properly discount your shortcomings."

However, if you have an awareness of your limitations, you will be able to tackle the strategies of a course with better judgment. When you are presented with tempting design or enticing hole locations, accepting your limitations will allow you to manage your game confidently and not fall for an architect's tricks. This does not mean you have to shut down your imagination and deprive yourself of the thrill of going for a par-5 in two or aiming at the hole location behind a bunker. Awareness of your limitations is merely a means of understanding how to lower your score, manage a match-play situation or eliminate common mistakes.

> *The player may experiment about his swing, his grip, his stance. It is only*
> *when he begins asking his caddie's advice that he is getting on dangerous*
> *ground.* —*Sir Walter Simpson,* The Art of Golf, *1897*

Most architects expect golfers to obsess over numbers and absorb way too much information. They know most players will worry about yardage, the par of the hole, or that players will simply overload on useless facts. In this day of white jumpsuit–clad forecaddies, sprinkler head yardages, GPS systems, detailed course guides and input on how to play a design from just about anyone with a pulse, course management often comes down to who weeds out unnecessary information best.

One great modern golf myth is that you use yardages "to the hole." This is a product of our shift to "target" golf, our interest in statistics and the overall aerial-attack style of modern golf. However, most well-designed holes still reward shots that are played short of the flagstick or to the sides of a hole location and sometimes beyond the hole location. Shotmaking is an art form, not a science.

Architects often count on you to play a full shot straight to the "pin high" yardage. They place hazards to catch these shots, or contour greens in such a way that every play except the shot straight to the hole will prove to be the wisest option.

Architects also rely on the player to lock into an almost robotic mode whereby the player knows how far they hit a certain club, and when that yardage comes up, the player automatically reaches for the appropriate iron. Is it ego that prevents us from taking one more club to play to the uphill green site, or two more clubs to hit a longer, lower shot that compensates for a stiff breeze? Either way, the best architects know they only have to create subtle features because golfers create many hazards for themselves.

> *Don't worry about par. The practice of printing par figures is literally a*
> *mental hazard.*   *—Bobby Jones*

Par. It could be the most overrated, misunderstood, mind-boggling word in golf. In the context of course management, it is every architect's greatest weapon against the golfer hoping to match or break par. No matter how little thought an architect puts into his design, par nearly always presents a quandary for the proud golfer.

If a player is not focused on the bunkers, lakes, creeks, rough or nasty contours, they have been known to focus on the par. Perhaps because the handicap system is based on our score in relation to par on each hole, or maybe because par is held up by tournament golf committees as some holier-than-thou standard. Either way, golfers are suckers for par.

Many times, a hole earns the label of playing as an "easy par." Therefore, taking anything higher than a par is frustrating for many players. Or perhaps another hole is a "tough par," one of those par 4.5s like the Road hole at St. Andrews. So after positioning themselves with a good tee shot, golfers are tempted to pull off a bold stroke in order to have a chance at making a hard-fought par, when a lay-up would have set up the chance for an up-and-down and, at worst, an easy bogey.

Par's effect on your game is also vastly underrated once you've recorded one. Or not recorded one.

For instance, if you take bogey on a short par-5 where you normally expect to make par or maybe even birdie, such a misstep invariably adds pressure to your management of the next hole. Or if you par a hole you normally make bogey or worse on, the tendency is to approach the next hole a bit more aggressively. After all, you just made par and you've got some strokes to spare, so why not be aggressive on the next tee?

The easiest way to eliminate this common misstep is to rely on the classic "one hole at a time" approach. But even the strongest of minds can't resist attacking a new hole with memories of the previous hole.

The object of a bunker or trap is not only to punish a physical mistake, to punish lack of control, but also to punish pride and egotism.
—Charles Blair Macdonald

Pride. This complicates the art of course management. Whether the architect is very subtle or completely over-the-top in his design presentation, the trick for the player is to ignore pride-related factors such as par. Forget what you are "supposed" to do or not do in various situations. Golf provides an excruciating amount of time and experience to help you consider options between shots. You have to set your ego aside and use that time to decide on the simplest, most logical play at hand.

Pride explains why sports psychologists preach the concept of a quiet mind and minimal processing of information. The longer you contemplate a stroke, the better the chance your ego will consider too many possibilities. When you understand that much of golf architecture is designed to distract, disorient and unsettle your thought process, you will be a long way toward learning how to shut out those distractions. You might even move closer to the state of mind that all great players share: relishing the challenge.

Certain golfers become excited by options or dilemmas. They are inspired by the chance to use their creativity to overcome the best the architect offers. If these great minds fail to pull off a shot, they simply accept that they did not carry out the stroke they envisioned. Their pride is not damaged nor do they blame the course, they even take pride in having tried the bold stroke. Their ego is satisfied that it accepted the challenge and things simply didn't work out.

The great courses entice the player to outwit himself. —Tom Doak

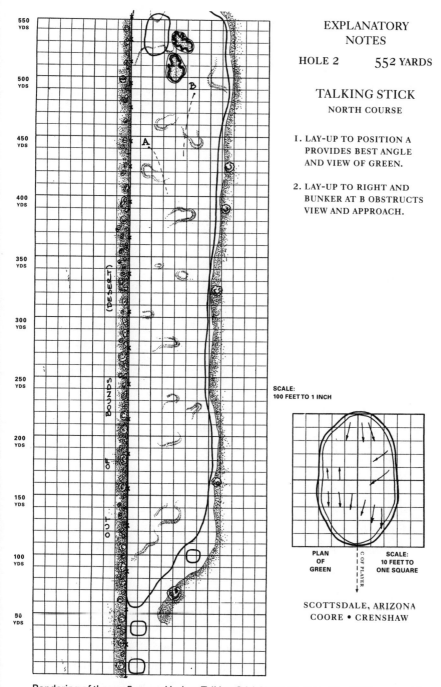

550 YDS

500 YDS

450 YDS

400 YDS

350 YDS

300 YDS

250 YDS

200 YDS

150 YDS

100 YDS

50 YDS

(DESERT)

OUT OF BOUNDS

B

A

EXPLANATORY NOTES

HOLE 2   552 YARDS

TALKING STICK
NORTH COURSE

1. LAY-UP TO POSITION A
   PROVIDES BEST ANGLE
   AND VIEW OF GREEN.

2. LAY-UP TO RIGHT AND
   BUNKER AT B OBSTRUCTS
   VIEW AND APPROACH.

SCALE:
100 FEET TO 1 INCH

PLAN
OF
GREEN

C OF PLAYER

SCALE:
10 FEET TO
ONE SQUARE

SCOTTSDALE, ARIZONA
COORE • CRENSHAW

Rendering of the par-5 second hole at Talking Stick North. Designed by Bill Coore and Ben Crenshaw, this par-5 plays straight away with out of bounds down the left. Ample fairway is provided, but the out of bounds still draws most players near or over it. A subtle, fascinating hole that ultimately rewards local knowledge over time. (GIL HANSE)

Some of our favorite holes reveal themselves to be very simple when you weed out all of the noise and break them down. If you take the four greats featured in the Seventh Hole, you find that after sorting out all of the distractions and options, the options are pretty simple. The great holes leave decisions and options up to the player, instead of forcing themselves onto the golfer. They consistently reward shrewd judgment and shotmaking. But as architect Tom Doak points out, the great ones "entice the player to outwit himself."

Whether it is due to how the hazards are placed, or the angle in which a green sits, or a particular hole's location in the course of eighteen holes, the best designs tempt players to overanalyze. They lure you into considering wild scenarios, some of which are brilliant, others of which are unwise. Some holes are so simple that they make the player suspicious, fueling phobias over unseen possibilities that do not exist.

The great holes also are designed so that a preround game plan is either essential to stick to, or completely useless! Consider the previously discussed par-3 twelfth hole at Augusta National. The long, narrow green is guarded by Rae's Creek. On Sunday of the Masters, we all know that the hole will be placed on the far right side of the green. Players know they should not play straight toward that hole location because the goofy wind shifts conspire with the angle of the green. Yet, no matter what their game plan was heading into the final round of the Masters, players always seem to fight the obvious choice and do something foolish. This is one hole where their preround plan of attack toward the center of the green is *always* correct.

Other great holes demand on-the-spot creativity, making preround game plans problematic. Most do-or-die holes are better approached without a plan because formulaic approaches to them only complicate golfers' ability to wade through the options at hand. Instead, the players' instincts the moment they step on the tee will serve them better. Certain holes reward those who process the conditions before them or the state of their round, and will most likely yield better results.

In the case of our four "great" holes, the Road hole at St. Andrews, the thirteenth at Augusta, the tenth at Riviera and sixteenth at Cypress Point, each can be planned out in advance. Yet something about these holes and the rest of the course around them tempts players to alter their game plan when they step on the tee. Many times, deviating from the plan is a sound move, sometimes not. Usually the elements require on-the-spot calls, which is always a sound reason for altering a plan. Or perhaps your game just doesn't feel right to try the preplanned shot, also a legitimate reason to deviate from the plan.

However, if you attack certain holes more desperately than planned, be careful. Game-plan changes made out of desperation lead to high-risk plays, particularly on a hole with dangerous options.

The golfer has more enemies than any other athlete. He has fourteen clubs in his bag, all of them different, eighteen holes to play, all of them different, every week; and all around him are sand, trees, grass, water, wind . . . in addition, the game is fifty percent mental, so his biggest enemy is himself.
—Dan Jenkins

With these general ideas in mind, remember the following seven course management principles that are related to golf architecture.

1. **View hazards as a challenge, not your enemy.** Consider the approach Tiger Woods, Bobby Jones, Jack Nicklaus and Ben Hogan brought to a course: they loved to be presented with a chance to outsmart the design. They were excited by thought-provoking holes. Even if you don't have an ounce of their shot-making talent, their mental approach was driven by the love of relishing all challenges. They worship strategic courses because they enjoy the opportunity of sorting out all of the options, and choosing the best plan of attack, knowing that winning the mental battle will put them ahead of most other golfers. Also, this approach gets your mind working proactively, in a "how can I conquer this hole" mode instead of a more fearful, defensive state.

2. **Be aware of your limitations when analyzing the design.** Acknowledge but don't dwell on the limits of your swing or short game. Focus on the shots you feel you have the best chance of hitting so that you can plan an approach based on your playing style.

3. **Be weary of an inflexible preround game plan.** It is one thing to have a plan of attack in mind for each hole. It's another to think you must stick to your plan or else you are somehow falling apart at the seams. The best golf architecture forces a few spontaneous decisions, so don't question your courage when you find yourself deviating from a plan, especially because of unexpected weather conditions or when you just don't feel you can play the shot at hand. Too many golfers are made to feel guilty by modern sports psychology for altering their game plan, but interesting golf architecture mixed with changes in conditions nearly always force unplanned, on-the-spot decision making.

4. **First instincts are best.** Your initial thoughts when stepping on the tee or in tackling a recovery shot are often the wisest. The longer you think about a shot, the more likely you are to be lured into a reckless play.

5. **Acknowledge and take advantage of design features.** Architects often create features to give the wise golfer something to "work" a shot off of or an area for a shrewd lay-up shot. Contours, mounds, rolls and safe lay-up areas are almost always present, but rarely obvious, because you are distracted by the more terrifying-looking hazards. Also, some architects design holes where you can catch a glimpse of flagstick locations from other holes. Many times golfers complain that a blind shot or large green seemed "unfair" in trying to determine where the hole was located. However, in many of those cases the architect saw this problem coming, and gave you the chance to preview that green from a prior hole. Or, if you just walk twenty paces to your left or right, you'd be amazed what things you might see!

6. **Learn the architect's school of design and tendencies before playing.** Knowing the architect and what kind of design philosophy drives his work will help you better prepare for and understand design features of a course. For instance, many architects reward the placement of shots with nothing more than a better view of a green or the ability to see a hazard that is not visible from another place on the hole. If you know ahead of time what the architect's basic tendencies are toward this kind of subtle

strategy, you will be in a better position to analyze the course before you.

7. **Avoid dwelling on numbers.** Par is the single biggest distraction of most golfers. Each stroke in golf should be played based on what is before you, what your chances are of pulling off the shot, and if wiser options exist. Par should never enter into this equation. Also, be careful with yardages and how you use them, particularly on courses in extreme conditions, particularly those playing dry and "fast." Yardages to the hole are useless in fast conditions.

Do not give the architects the power that they hope you will give them. Treat the architecture as an enjoyable challenge to overcome. Locate features that help you visualize the shaping of shots, and take advantage of design elements that might even give you a favorable bounce. In time you will find that architecture is manageable. In most cases, the architect has provided plenty of chances to overcome the design.

The Eleventh Hole

Training and Daydreaming

Training Your Design Eye and Daydreaming on the Links

One who would know the soul of golf must begin as would one who will know the soul of music. There is no more chance for one to gather up the soul of golf in a hurry than there is for that same one to understand Wagner in a week. —*P.A. Vaille,* The Soul of Golf, *1912*

Like any challenging risk-reward par-5, the result of training your design eye and learning to daydream on the links will reap enormous benefits for your game while adding to your enjoyment of golf courses. There is joy to be found in analyzing an architect's design and then, as Jack Nicklaus does to distract himself from the languid pace of play, to daydream, pondering how you would have designed the hole you are playing. Or how you would fix a hole should you find yourself anointed the next U.S. Open "doctor."

But if you over-train your design eye, you risk becoming a certified architecture junkie, incapable of playing golf without noticing most design features. Hazards may enter your thought pattern the night before your next round. Or as you drive to the course, features you've noticed may quietly enter your mind. You could even become so aware of your surroundings that you morph into the poor golfer Walter Simpson wrote about in 1887, the one who cannot enjoy anything that gets in his way, including laughing children in the backyard just off the fourth fairway.

> *For the golfer, Nature loses her significance. Larks, the casts of worms, the buzzing of bees, and even children are hateful . . . rain comes to be regarded solely in its relation to the putting greens; the daisy is detested, botanical specimens are but "hazards," twigs "break clubs." Winds cease to be east, south, west or north. They are ahead, behind sideways. And the sky is dark, according to the state of the game.*
>
> —*Sir Walter Simpson, 1887*

On the other hand, if your trained eye recalls features such as a helpful mound that you can play a shot off of, then your training becomes useful. Or perhaps you remember a greenside bunker is placed deceptively short of the putting surface, reminding you to trust the yardage even though the shot may seem shorter than it appears. You can employ your trained eye and use a selective memory of design features to your advantage.

> *There is one thing in the game of golf which is entirely dreary and depressing, and that is looking for balls. Moreover it is depressing not only for those who look, but for those behind who have to wait while they are looking.*
>
> —*Bernard Darwin, writer*

If you find yourself waiting for the group ahead to locate a ball, daydreams of redesigning your home course can become an excellent distraction when your mind normally might obsess over the next shot. Daydreaming has also been cited by many champions as a way to ease pressure during a competitive round. However, if your daydreaming inspires you to join the local green committee, you risk becoming the most hated golfer at your course. After all, golf course committee members have a well-known propensity for sharing redesign ideas during nineteenth-hole conversations. When that occurs, we know you've taken the art of daydreaming too far.

So with this precautionary discourse complete, let's tread the fine line between refining your eye and learning how to analyze design features without letting it become a fatal addiction.

Training Your Design Eye

> . . . *the possession of a vivid imagination, which is an absolute essential in obtaining success, may prevent him [the architect] from attaining a position among the higher ranks of players. Everyone knows how fatal the imagination is in playing the game.* —*Alister MacKenzie*

Noted crime novelist Michael Connelly says he rarely reads mysteries by other writers in his genre and region, even though he was inspired to write because of his love for such novels. Connelly simply cannot read the books without analyzing what the author is trying to do or without noticing which tricks the writer is employing. It is unfortunate he no longer can enjoy reading what seems like a good mystery to most of us, but then again, would Connelly be as good at his job if he did not have such a discerning eye?

In golf architecture, our objective is to help you identify the basics of design while still permitting you to maintain your golfing peace of mind. Just like the wine enthusiast who evaluates a merlot and still enjoys the company of friends sharing the bottle, you should be able to identify designs with character and interesting features, while still enjoying your regular game. We all have a hobby or business that we know the inner workings of, often to the point that it becomes difficult to appreciate the most basic pleasures it may bring. Golf architecture is no different for some, once they open the curtain and see how Oz is really pulling the strings.

PGA Tour professionals have a trained eye for design, or at least, that is the rationale behind hiring so many of them to be "player architects." However, their design taste tends to center around how a course fits their game. They know a great design when they see it because it is comfortable to their eye (i.e., their game). They are also quick to label a course unfair if they find themselves uncomfortable on that particular design, or they simply cannot figure out how to overcome the architectural ploys. And we all are guilty of judging courses by our scores or how the course fits our game. But there is more to training your design eye than analyzing how it affects scoring or how you believe shots were fairly or unfairly received.

Most of us have a song we don't really want to hear because it reminds us of a time in our lives we'd like to leave behind. Even though the song is wonderfully composed, is it the song's fault that it happened to have come on the radio at an inopportune moment?

So is it reasonable to judge the architect's work because our game is off? Of course not.

Course maintenance should also not determine whether a design receives high or low marks. Evaluating design by the quality of maintenance is a bit like finding fault with the architecture of a baseball stadium because the floor was sticky beneath your seat. Or disregarding the merits of a painting because you felt the museum air temperature seemed too cold for your taste.

Some things are not under the golf architect's control, particularly the difficult task of maintaining a golf course. If the maintenance is consistently lacking on repeat visits to a course, that becomes a different matter. The merits of a design should not rely on how pristinely manicured the turf and bunkers are. However there is no denying that an interesting design needs quality maintenance to expose the best playing features. If a course consistently fails to maintain the prescribed look to its hazards or never offers a reasonable playing quality with its greens, you are not going to encounter the architecture as the architect had hoped.

In attempting to grasp the integrity of a design, there are three general areas to focus on that should help you train your eye without getting so deeply involved that you can't take the club back. Those areas include the character and scale of the design features, how the strategy of the hole functioned (if strategy was present at all), and, after you've played the course, how memorable the features were.

Ground Features and Scale

The scale on which one makes rolls and mounds depends on the scale of the existing contours, otherwise your creations will not balance with the landscape.

—George Thomas

Three factors tend to determine our level of attraction to a hole, whether it is the first time we see it or during multiple visits. The laws of *naturalness, irregularity* and *randomness* characterize the most consistently interesting, popular and beautiful holes in golf.

Overdone ground shaping or hazards placed only to penalize nearly always annoy golfers the first time playing a hole. In time, we tend to become even more conscious of those features that appear out of place. Furthermore, extremely natural and rugged-looking courses also become more attractive as you appreciate how they fit the landscape.

You will often see modern designers use a lake to guard a green. But as you walk the fairway leading up to the green, you may notice the ground immediately before the lake actually sits at a lower level than the lake itself. Now, in nature, have you ever seen a lake at a higher level than the ground immediately around it? A crowned lake? Of course not. Yet in golf this has become a modern construction trend and your first sign that the architect and construction team did not appreciate the fundamentals of nature.

Mounds are trickier to gauge, but in general, the softer the look of a contour and the more gently it ties in to the surrounds, the more likely you are to find it attractive. A row of steep, conehead-shaped mounds rarely takes on attractive character, particularly when they are arranged like a single-file line of obedient soldiers.

Scale is also an important attribute of golf course construction and your eye's reception of design features. If a setting for golf is wide and grand in scale, larger features will fit better. If a hole is narrow, its green small and the bunkers undersized, then the scale of all features should be restrained.

However, there can be exceptions as long as they are carried out gracefully by the architect. Many believe that the size of a green must be dictated by the length of a hole: small greens on short holes, large greens on long ones. Yet some of the most interesting holes are those where the architect defied this mantra, and built an enormous green on a short par-4, or a small, unprotected green on a long par-5.

When it comes to the shapes of bunkers and greens, analyzing the concepts of *irregularity* and *randomness* requires your attention. In time, you will begin to notice the difference between green contours, mounds, drainage swales and bunker shapes crafted with care versus those that look artificial. We all have seen cloverleaf-shaped bunkers that register the thought, "haven't I seen this someplace before?" We've also seen the hole design the architect beamed up from one of his favorite award-winning efforts and loves to repeat because it has proven to be a dependable formula.

We've even seen rows of mounds or bunkers that look more like a nursery of hazards instead of randomly found features in nature. Take that same nursery of bunkers and disperse them in *irregular* fashion, and they take on a far less offensive appearance.

The looser, more impressionistic style of bunkering tends to fit the irregular lines of nature and makes for more interesting golf if the architect incorporates his bunkers well. The cleaner, harder and sharper the edges, the less natural they appear.

The most popular holes usually have hazards that appear "randomly" placed and constructed, even if their placement was carefully conceived by the architect. The more random certain design elements appear, the more immune to criticism most features tend to be. The more man-made they appear, the more irritating they are likely to be, particularly if they are only placed to inflict penalty.

When analyzing design turns to features on the ground, the planting of trees or the maintenance of hazard edges, ask yourself whether the features display the fundamental laws of naturalness, irregularity and randomness.

Is There Any Strategy?

The tilt of the green or its molding, the undulations here and there, the position of the bunkers, the openings for certain shots—these are the

*methods an architect uses to present the problems. Simply to make holes
difficult to play is not at all the point. That would be an easy matter, and
unfortunately it is too frequently done by the inexperienced. To make them
thrilling to play, to make them force you to play certain shots, and even to
reach certain positions in order to have a chance to play such shots—these
superlatively fine qualities residing in first-rate holes are the result either
of exceptionally desirable terrain or the product of an exceptionally
talented architect.*   —Robert Hunter, golf architect

There should be some challenge in understanding the strategy of a
hole the first time around, otherwise what fun would it be to play the
hole again and again? Many architects are told to make a hole understandable to speed up play, but ultimately, such holes become boring
on repeat visits because there is little to discover. Worse, there is no
reward for having gained some local knowledge during your initial
playing.

Rarely do straightforward holes contain different options for play
based on weather conditions or differing hole locations. The sense of
discovery and adventure endears us to holes we admire, which is why
judging a design based on one round is always a risky matter.

Avoid analyzing the strategic merits of a hole from the tee. Perhaps
after you've played it or while you are waiting for a friend to putt out,
take a look back and consider how the hazards were placed, how the
green sat in relation to the fairway, and whether a well–thought out
plan would have been rewarded over a less intelligent attack.

It is easy to overrate your most recent experiences on a hole or to
criticize the design because it did not reward your approach shot. But
maybe your ball hit a hard spot on the green and you were unlucky. Is
that an architectural flaw or just bad luck?

After you've played a hole, reconsider its merits no matter what
your score. Ask yourself, if I had placed my tee shot or approach differently, would the hole have rewarded my shot? Is a riskier play
rewarded over a safer play? How would the design work under different conditions, with different hole locations?

Holes with dramatic risk and reward options prove easier to evaluate than more subtle designs. The question of analyzing a risk-reward hole reverts back to temptation. If the tee shot tempted you to undertake a bold shot while dangling an equally tempting safe play before you, then its risk-reward strategy worked. If either shot—the risky play or the safe play—was clearly the wise alternative for all players all of the time, then the strategy is absent.

Remember, the architect's goal is to make you fret, to make each option enticing, to ask you to make tough decisions, to reward you for making the best choice and, finally, to ask you to follow up that decision up with solid shotmaking. If you are rewarded in these situations, the architect has created an interesting, fun hole.

One more area should be considered in judging the strategy of a hole. If you felt a hazard was out of place or unfair, ask yourself, did the architect place that bunker to make the hole more interesting, or was it there merely to penalize?

Was the shot to the green obscured because you placed the tee shot in the wrong position, assuming another option was available? That would be a clever design touch. But if the architect did not provide a place to hit the ball in order to open up a view of the green, then the design was not as well conceived.

Every hole is different, but when it comes to analyzing strategy, remember concepts such as temptation and the notion of comedy in design. Remember that some architects are trying to present original ideas. Often, design features that seem ridiculous on first glance, in hindsight actually give you a chuckle and, in time, become fun to play.

Memorability

When you play a course and remember each hole, it has individuality and change. If your mind cannot recall the exact sequence of the holes, that course lacks the great assets of originality and diversity.
                                                            —*George C. Thomas Jr.*

One trick in analyzing golf course design is figuring out when and how to think about a course. Some designs are so bland that only a handful of holes are memorable within hours after you've stepped off the last green. However, the less you analyze the design while on the course, the better off you'll be. Let time sort out the nuances and annoyances of the course. The more you remember of a course after you've played, the better the design.

Some holes are memorable because they are awful. They are garish, goofy or just plain impossible to play. But when you are sitting around after playing or perhaps on the way home from a trip, that is the opportune time to think back to a course. The interesting holes that immediately come to mind usually stick with you for a reason: They had character and they functioned well. They were interesting.

Like a great film or music injected with some complexity, the best golf courses tend to get better long after you've played them. Initial reactions, even postround thoughts, are dangerous. In time, your emotions forget what the hole did to your game or elements that initially struck you as odd, because time allows you to sift through the information and tells you which designs were distinctive.

When you are faced with a deep bunker or a risk-reward scenario, it's difficult to separate personal results from your view of the architect's work. The more time you have to get away from a hole and the more often you are reminded of its features, the more likely something about the hole worked. That is the time to dig in and analyze the elements that make the hole memorable. By doing this, you'll improve your eye when you encounter interesting features in the future. Maybe it was one tiny little bump in the green that made the entire strategy of a hole work. Or maybe it was the character of a bunker or the tilt of the green that made the hole stand out.

Many experienced armchair architects recognize the need to postpone judgment after they go to a lavish course with wonderful service, perfect maintenance, and a fun game with friends. In time, they still cherish those elements, but they also take a more constructively critical look at the design. Time has a funny way of helping us refine our view of any art form, moment in history or business deal. Golf architecture is no different.

Dead or Alive?

*Vitality is another quality that is essential. Instinctively we feel that one
course is alive, another dead and insipid, lacking energy of expression. We
look for the unexpected note and a pleasantness of line. Every curve
should have a spring in it, and no straight line should ever be quite
straight. Generally the detection of these slight differences is purely a matter
of feeling which once experienced is not likely to be forgotten.*

—*Tom Simpson*

If all else fails but you still want to look at design features and figure out why it looks good to you compared to others, the difference
may come down to the concept that Tom Simpson pointed out: Does
the hole look dead, or does it look alive?

Does a bunker have a lively, fresh appearance or is it sterile and
flat? Does a hole fit the land in a way that looks dull or vibrant? Sometimes there is no technical, analytic explanation as to why our heart
gravitates toward certain holes. Often, a painting simply appears warm,
fresh and inviting to us. There is no other explanation. It just has life.

Daydreaming on the Links

*Like so many golfers, I became an "armchair architect" at an early age,
constantly visualizing ways to improve my home course, Scioto, in
Columbus, along with, as my wings spread, many of the others I
played . . . more and more, I began to ask myself whether it was possible to
create something more interesting and inviting.*   —*Jack Nicklaus*

Developing on-course armchair-architect sensibilities can be fraught
with dangerous possibilities. What is the reward for dreaming about how
you would redesign a hole while you are playing? Is the temptation
worth the risk?

After all, if design daydreaming helped Jack Nicklaus pass time on
the course, why can't it help other golfers get through a slow day or
pass time on a dull layout?

Just like training your design eye, daydreaming opens your mind to possibilities that never existed before. You'll notice things you probably never detected, meaning the next time you play a hole your selective memory may not be so selective. Assuming you come up with a brilliant design revelation, maybe even an eye-opener that you think MacKenzie in his prime could never have imagined, you may feel compelled to share your idea.

> *Criticizing a golf course is like going into a man's family. The fond mother trots up her children for admiration. Only a boor would express anything else than a high opinion. So it is a thankless task to criticize a friend's home golf course. "Where ignorance is bliss 'tis folly to be wise." It is natural one should love his home course. He knows it, and with golf holes familiarity does not breed contempt, but quite the reverse.*
> —*C. B. Macdonald*

Even if you daydream something so brilliant that no one can deny your foresight is anything but wonderful, such suggestions will be taken as disparaging criticism. And if your playing partners are dues-paying members or just regulars at the local daily-fee, you will probably offend them. So when you daydream on the links, rule number one is simple: Keep ideas to yourself. Rule number two is a bit more complex: Remember why you are daydreaming.

If play is slow and you are waiting for a green to clear, go ahead and imagine some design alterations. Daydreaming can be a wonderful tool to relax the mind and erase less than attractive thoughts about your swing or shot outcomes. If the hole you are redesigning is sadly overbuilt and offensive to the entire golfing populace, fine, daydream away. And if the hole is so dull it would drive even the most tolerant golfer to skip it, fine again.

However, if you fantasize about redesigning a hole because you have trouble playing it, then it's time to put the brakes on. When you are telling yourself that a design is too difficult, stop. Or if you think the architect is unfairly punishing your game and therefore you begin to daydream, this can only lead to negative thoughts when it's your turn to play. Furthermore, such daydreaming will magnify the difficulties of the hole during future rounds.

I think it's true that we create our own pressure. If you think about water
to the right and a trap to the left and all the things that can go wrong, then
you're creating your own pressure.   *—Tom Weiskopf*

With an understanding of the pitfalls of playing on-course armchair
architect, lets get to the fun part, redesigning. There are two types of
holes that should cause you to daydream: the banal, boring design or
the sadly overbuilt hole. Each requires a unique approach.

The Banal, Boring Hole

It has often been suggested that an uninteresting hole might be improved by
lengthening it, but it would be a safe axiom to adopt, "It will only be made
worse and take longer to play. Shorten it and get it over."
                                                      —Alister MacKenzie

We've all played a hole where even the quietest mind will specu-
late whether the architect could have tried any harder to make the hole
less interesting.

Usually these boring holes rely on nothing more than trees lining
the fairway for their interest, and we all know how tedious and penalizing playing through too many trees can be. Maybe the hole escapes
criticism because the surrounding environment is beautiful or the
course is well maintained. Still, these banal holes are often bunkerless
and lack any appealing contours.

Your focus in redesigning boring holes should be on strategy, not
the easier notion of rearranging the landscape with multiple hazards.
The overcooked, throw-out-every-idea-in-the-book method of redesign
is often the easy solution, but it is not a very effective way to spice up a
golf hole. Instead, your challenge is to find a feature, whether it be the
tiniest ridge near the green or the gentle angle in which the green sits.
Then take advantage of whatever feature your eye catches and use it in a
strategic fashion.

Search for a way to make players of all levels consider their options.
Perhaps you would simply place a tiny bunker in the center of the fairway, 235 yards off the tee. This would force all golfers to think their

way around the bunker. The shortest hitters would have to ask themselves, will I be able to get by the bunker in two shots? Most average golfers would ask, will my best drive reach that little bunker? Will longer and more aggressive players be tempted to drive over the bunker?

Either way, with a minor addition you've added numerous possibilities to a once dull hole.

Perhaps a hole has a nice bend to it and an aggressive drive could be rewarded for cutting the corner. But as the hole sits now, drives turning around the bend find that the green doesn't reward their aggressive play, or maybe even penalizes the bold but successful tee shot. Your goal as armchair architect is to make the green more interesting. You have to come up with a redesign that rewards the aggressive and accurate player, while gently inconveniencing the less assertive player. The key here is not to get carried away, but instead, to find a subtle means of adding intrigue to the hole.

The Sadly Overbuilt Hole

I may be wrong, but I believe that the golfers of today want originality.
Even those who are not particularly analytical sense the difference between
a purely natural hole and one which suggests the artificial.

—A. W. Tillinghast

The sadly overbuilt hole is your chance to be more creative. If the original architect rearranged the land and threw in seemingly every idea from his bag of gimmicks, then you have the freedom to do what you want. Fire up the bulldozers, free up the budget and have at it!

To keep this daydreaming process constructive, the first objective should be to figure out how to turn an overdone hole into one that can be made more fun for *all* golfers. The holes where the architect got carried away usually are built with only the scratch player in mind. Your task could mean filling in bunkers and lakes, or bringing out the chain saw to remove garish palm trees that aren't native to your state.

But maybe the hole is not salvageable. Maybe it is so bad that you need to borrow Carl Spackler's dynamite recipe. Do a service to golfers everywhere and blow it up. Roll out the bulldozers and visualize how you would redo the hole so that it takes on some character, while making it functional from a strategic and aesthetic point of view. This could take on any number of redesign options, but again, show restraint. Try to keep the island green in your back pocket, and visualize a minimum number of bunkers that will cause the most trouble for the good player, while not over-penalizing the rest of us.

> *When discussing the question of altering a hole, the chief consideration that should exercise the mind is "Are we going to add appreciably to the interest and excitement of the hole?" Unless we are convinced of this we should leave it alone.* —*Alister MacKenzie*

Remember, do not daydream because you have trouble playing a certain hole or a hole seems unfair to you. Taking this stance will lead you down a dangerous path, one that blames the architecture for your bad breaks or poor course management. Sure, it is okay to blame the course now and then instead of being too hard on yourself, but do not make it a habit.

Instead, daydream when you sense the architect either did not do enough, or worse, over-designed. Find an attractive balance in your mind that would make play more interesting for all golfers, but still reasonably fun.

And again, resist the greatest temptation of all: sharing these redesign ideas with your playing partners.

The Twelfth Hole

Design Talk

Understanding the Language of Architecture

*Terms such as birdie, bogey, driver and five iron are familiar to us today,
but would have been unrecognizable by golfers a century ago. If you asked
your caddie for a baffing spoon, what club (in today's terminology) would
you receive? A wedge!*

*—Raymond Floyd (the baffing spoon was the nineteenth-century
version of a 9-wood)*

The rhetoric of golf is often viewed as insider's jargon, only understood
by ardent students or stuffy old rules officials clad in their faded bucket
hats and gray polyester slacks. But you do not have to be a golf snob to
understand the basics of design talk.

Understanding correct terminology is in your best interest because
it is one less thing to feel anxious about in a game that causes so much
anxiety. Learning some key terms will not take long and it will put you
at ease when talking about course design. Furthermore, many golf
snobs misuse the terms discussed in this chapter, so if nothing else,
knowing the correct usage will make it fun to correct one of those golf
blowhards.

The language of design can sound a bit overwhelming and obnoxious to outsiders. There are those times when certain golf television
announcers say such ridiculous things that it makes us long for the days

when Henry Longhurst or Ben Wright would demonstrate how to use golf's formal terminology. Most golfers can spot a novice or a non-student of the game right away based solely on how that person refers to various elements of golf. It is not a disgrace to be ignorant of certain golfing terms, because few golfers are ever properly introduced to the language and etiquette of the game the way old-time golfers were during their youth: through caddying.

However, we all want to feel comfortable playing this most awkward and humbling of games. Knowing how to "talk golf" is a confidence booster no matter how bad your game is. Especially when the golf turns from a leisure-time activity to a serious business affair, as it so often does these days. And knowing the difference between various design terms will lead to more enjoyable and comfortable postround banter. Here are a few definitions of key terms, offered in a helpful, somewhat nonpurist spirit.

Bunkers on the King's Course, Gleneagles, Scotland. Though they appear to be traps, call them bunkers to avoid reprimand from a golf purist. (LYNN SHACKELFORD)

Bunker versus Sand Trap

Throughout this and all my other writings on the game, I have used the word 'bunker' in what I have understood to be the traditional golfing sense, meaning a pit in which the soil has been exposed and the area covered with sand. I regard the term 'sand trap' as an unacceptable Americanization. Its use annoys me almost as much as hearing a golf club called a "stick."
                                                                    —*Bobby Jones*

Even as a full-fledged architecture junkie, I'm not offended by those who say "trap" or "sand trap." Some traditionalists lose their minds, however, when golfers refer to bunkers as traps, or worse, sand traps. The USGA's executive director annually makes a point during U.S. Open telecasts to remind people they are bunkers, not sand traps. Don't ask me exactly why there is such a vital delineation between the two. After all, "trap" takes on an intimidating aura that the modern-day bunker seldom presents. In fact, many bunkers are no longer traps, but instead, better places to miss your ball than the rough surrounding the bunker.

Either way, call them bunkers and you'll avoid a lecture from a golfer who probably called them sand traps at one time too.

Links

Nature was their architect, and beast and man her contractors. In the formation and overall stabilization of our island coastlines, the sea at intervals of time and distance gradually receded from the higher ground of cliff, bluff and escarpment—to and from which the tides once flowed and ebbed. And as during the ages, by stages, the sea withdrew, it left a series of sandy wastes in bold ridge and significant furrow, broken and divided by numerous channels up and down which the tides advanced and retired, and down certain of which the burns, streams and rivers found their way to the sea.
                                                                —*Sir Guy Campbell*

There are very few genuine "links" courses in the world. By strict definition, around one hundred and sixty. Nearly all are in Scotland,

England, Ireland or Northern Ireland, with a few others scattered about Europe.

Links describes a specific type of sandy soil that is created by the meeting of river and sea terrain. It is land the ocean once covered; but thanks to the sea salt left behind, links became areas unsuitable for farming.

In America, we've come to call any course a "links-style" design when the layout is treeless and somewhat flat. Or a course is labeled a links when it's within a few miles of a natural body of water, and thus, may be exposed to the occasional whiff of sea breeze more than the normal layout.

Pebble Beach is not a links course. Perhaps to some it is a links-style course because it can get windy and the course plays along the sea, but it is not a links. And in the true definition of links style, it also fails because the soil is more clay than sand, meaning there is an absence of drainage that allows for firm turf, and thus, few bump-and-run shots to be played.

There are properties in America that come close to capturing the linksland *elements* which lead to genuine links-style golf (porous soil,

Bandon Dunes Golf Club in Oregon, a world-famous course. However, it is not a links in the true definition. (LYNN SHACKELFORD)

The seventeenth at Ballybunion's Old Course, Ireland. This famous course sits on linksland. (LYNN SHACKELFORD)

fescue grass turf, native grasses in the roughs and the characteristic undulations that appear to have been formed by water movement): Sand Hills in Nebraska, Shinnecock Hills and the National Golf Links on Long Island, and the Bandon Dunes complex in Oregon. These examples stretch the definition of links, which certainly does not diminish the quality of their designs. They just are not true links.

Signature Hole

> *. . . a dreadful cliché that probably has done as much harm as any phrase I can recall.* —Tom Fazio, *on the term* signature hole, *2000*

> *We want all the shots at Berkeley Hall to be signature shots.*
> —Tom Fazio, *2001*

To be blunt, avoid using "signature hole" under any and all circumstances. The phrase has been popularized by shrewd marketing folks for advertising purposes, and by television announcers who don't know any better. I've heard many players arrive at a course they've never seen and ask the local assistant pro, "Which is your signature hole?"

There is no special signature-hole committee that visits and anoints one particular hole as worthy of signature status, nor is there a national registry of signature holes.

Why does the use of signature hole rankle traditionalists and architecture fanatics? For most, it is a sad day for architecture when golfers have been led to believe that there can only be one exceptional, memorable hole per eighteen, instead of several outstanding holes surrounded by many more memorable ones. Of course, when we grouse about this trend toward one outstanding hole and seventeen ordinary ones, one of the marketing folks is bound to interject, "We don't like to think of our course as having one signature hole. We like to think we have eighteen signature holes."

Signature Design

Give your course a signature.

—1960 ad for architect Robert Trent Jones Sr.

Robert Trent Jones was the most popular architect during the 1960s, cranking out ten to fifteen courses per year worldwide. When he developed a set style, Jones began referring to certain courses as signature designs. It was a nice way of saying that he was not there much, but that his staff would incorporate the typical Trent Jones look.

Today, we could only wish that architects would give projects the attention Trent Jones paid to his work. When you hear "signature design," it's your cue that the architect was almost never involved with a project, probably visiting for a photo session or two and opening day. If you asked the signature designer to describe his design today, he would have trouble taking you through all eighteen, uh, signature holes.

Flag or Flagstick versus Pin

. . . while a flagstick almost invariably has a flag attached to it, usually with a numeral on it indicating the correct number of a hole, it does not

have to. Merion . . . has wicker baskets attached to its flagsticks rather
than actual bunting.   —*Charles Price*

Certain golfers hate it when an announcer says that a player is going for the *pin* or is *pin high* or can't reach today's *pin placement*. Evidently they should say the player is going for the hole. The ball is "hole high" or the player is unable to get to today's "hole location."

Pin does sound a bit too much like a bowling term, but personally I find flagstick and hole location just as awkward. When possible, I say "hole location" but usually end up uttering *pin placement*. Meanwhile, flagstick seems pretty harmless too.

So if anyone gives you trouble, remind them that flagstick has appeared in rule books since 1875. Pin did not make an in-print appearance until 1893, and that was in a book of poems, which may explain why the edge goes to flagstick. However, hole location is the preferred choice even though it has no discernable origin!

Then again who cares? We all know what is being talked about, whether it's a pin, a flagstick or a hole location.

Green fee or Green Committee, not Green*s* Fee or Green*s* Committee

Three years efter Allan deed I cam to keep the Green here.
                                              —*Old Tom Morris on St. Andrews*

Another misuse that does not get noticed by most golfers, but just to be safe you have been warned: The proper usage is green fee or green committee or greenkeeper, not greens.

Golf Club versus Country Club

In the British Isles and most of continental Europe, as everybody knows
by now, golf clubs have been traditionally just that: golf clubs, places
where you play only golf, with a house attached in which you hang up your
hat, change your shoes, and later have a quick drink with your
companions while you add up the scores. British clubs have no bridge

games, fashion shows, or cocktail parties; no car dealers, insurance
brokers, or stock-and-bond dealers moonlighting on the first available tee;
no real estate salesman trying to sell you a condominium in which you can
hear your next door neighbor reading a newspaper.   —Charles Price

Master writer, historian and observer Charles Price would never
have guessed that the misuse of "golf club" would be so different in
today's game than the confusion he lamented back in the early 1980s.
With the turn of the century onslaught of "upscale daily-fee" courses,
better known as public-courses-that-charge-a-lot-to-play, many of
these pricey facilities have sought to give their course a little extra
edge. So instead of naming their layout the Experience at Burro Bridge
Golf Course, they change "Course" to "Club." These are not clubs,
but instead, public golf courses.

Still, what Price bemoaned in his day was the confusion between a
country club, where golf was just part of the equation amidst swimming pools and tennis courts, versus a true golf club where our beloved
sport was the focus:

How, then, do you tell a golf club from a country club, since no one can
tell anymore where the suburbs leave off and the country begins? Well,
to start with, no self-respecting golf club has a clubhouse with Muzak in
it. Neither does it hold wedding receptions, singing lunches for groups
like the Rotarians, nor birthday parties for anybody less than ninety. It
will not tolerate bingo parties or casino nights to raise money for the new
zoo. It does not hire car valets who have never shifted gears, lifeguards
who might not know how to swim, or golf pros who wear pink shoes. It
will not countenance fat ladies in Bermuda shorts, portable radios on golf
carts tuned to the Super Bowl, or Sunday-morning comedians whose
idea of humor is telling you you're standing too close to the ball after you
hit it.

What's In a Name?

Come to Quarry Ranch Country Club and Residential Community.
Garden homes on the rim, one ninety and up. Live the dream life at St.

Quarry Muirfield Golf and Racquet Club. Town houses, patio homes,
condos. Quarry Oaks, Quarry Palms, Quarry Village. All I want's in
on it.   —*Tommy Earl, in Dan Jenkins's* Rude Behavior

The late 1990s boom in golf construction meant that several thousand new courses arrived within just a few years of each other. Many tried to elevate themselves by piecing together what seemed like elegant, tradition-rich names.

I will concede that the golf world does not need another course named Hillcrest or Riverside. But how long-winded and strange can some golf course names get? Imagine the honest folks who work at some of these places. People who want to take pride in their work, only to have to mumble to friends and family their otherwise attractive course's kitschy name?

The name of a facility can tell you a lot about its character, its purpose as a (gulp) "product," and just how seriously it takes its architecture. The simpler the name, the more likely the course has a classic design that respects its environment. The more schmaltzy the title, the more likely the architecture takes on characteristics of the name.

My plan is to call the whole community Tumbleweed Pointe. Put an e *on*
the end of it . . . because that e *ups the price of a spec home by twenty*
thousand dollars. That's all the e *does.*
                    —*Tommy Earl, in* Rude Behavior

Attempts to Make a Name Looke Elegante. Someone takes a simple word like Point or Old and tacks on an *e* in a desperate attempt to convince people that the course has ties to old money or Mayflower voyagers. Or in Tommy Earl's case, adding twenty thousand to the price of a spec home.

Dial 911. Fire marshals must cringe when hearing all of the variations on "Burning." Trees, Oaks, Ridges, Bushes and even Sands are ablaze these days.

The LINKS Connection. Isn't it fascinating when tree-lined American inland golf courses with heavy soil become links? Names like the

Rain Forest National Preserve Golf Links or the Links at Sycamore Jungle abound. If there is an award for "Best Performance by an Oxymoron in a Golf Course Title," it would inevitably go to one of the many links with trees.

Animals Doing Strange Things. There are golf courses named for running blackwolves, rabbits that dance, roosters running, puppies in creeks, eagles that are doubled and raccoons doing things that don't even make sense. Animals *can* be incorporated effectively in a golf course name, as long as they are not *doing* something.

Strange Pines. Again, there are plenty of ways to use pines in a pleasant, timeless manner. Pine Tree, Pine Valley, Pinehurst, et cetera. But why the desire to have pines doing something? They are not contortionists. Yet there are golf courses with pines that are bent, circled, coosa'd, dodgered, moody-quiet and knotted. Talk about tough material for the logo designers to work with.

THE [Fill in Links, Experience, Challenge or Tradition] AT THE [Fill in Course Locale or Theme Here]. Fifteen years from now, these are the names that may eventually (if not already) earn the "What were they thinking" award? Golfers will look at this plethora of longwinded designations like we look at bell-bottoms and eight-track tapes today.

The fill-in-the-blank names seem to try for a mystical, otherworldly resonance. Things like, the Soulful Challenge at Chicken Soup Bay or the Don't Sweat the Small Stuff at Blissful Creek Ranch and Riding Club. How can any golf course with such a long-winded, over-the-top title become the topic of conversation when half the talk involves sorting out names?

Now, you might be thinking, there is the National Golf Links of America. But C.B. Macdonald backed up this audacious name with architecture like no one had (or has) ever seen.

Augusta National Syndrome. The formula is simple. Take your course location or even the club founder's last name, then slap on "National." This is your indication of a club hoping to host a national event while remaining ultra-exclusive the other fifty-one weeks of the year. Even if it sounds wretched to take their town or state name, these courses assume that if they add National to their title, they suddenly have the Augusta National of their region. The funny thing is, few of these places actually have a national membership or a design anyone would talk about nationally. Just an attitude.

> *"Does the club have a name?"*
> *"St. Andrews at Spark Plug Mall! We broke concrete this week."*
> —*Dan Jenkins,* Designers and Developers

Now that I've offended half of the golf courses built since 1980, let's move on to a subject that is beneficial to everyone's game and understanding the courses you play: maintenance.

But remember, what's in a golf course name?

Everything.

The Thirteenth Hole

Understanding Maintenance

A Simplified Look at Greenkeeping and How to Better Understand Conditions

I'm going to be the head greenkeeper, hopefully within six years, that's my schedule. I'm studying a lot of this stuff so I know it, you know. Chinch bugs. Manganese. Nitrogen . . . you know.

—*Carl Spackler, in* Caddyshack

Golf course maintenance is often viewed as a mysterious, even complex topic unworthy of a golfer's attention. Yet most players feel free to offer their opinion about what the local superintendent is doing wrong or how he could do his job better.

To speak with some knowledge base, the novice golfer does not need to know the difference in growing habits between A-4 Bent versus L-93, or understand the harmful effects of nematodes. But all players should be aware of certain basic principles to improve their game and to better appreciate the effort that goes into maintaining a golf course.

During the 1990s, turfgrass science and respect for golf course maintenance personnel made enormous strides. More advanced grasses were developed and new methods were created to maintain turf, all of which allow superintendents to provide better playing conditions. This has led to better widespread greenkeeping than at any time in the history of golf. The job of course superintendent has always been the most important for the success of any course, but only recently have courses begun to value their superintendents and maintenance staffs by paying handsomely to retain top quality superintendents, mechanics and reliable staff members.

Do you know what I just saw? A gopher!
Do you know what gophers can do to a gawlf course?   —Judge Smails

Of course, there is the Carl Spackler issue. Because of Bill Murray's quirky assistant-superintendent character from the 1980 film *Caddyshack*, some superintendents may find the use of various Spacklerisms in this chapter a bit disconcerting. There may be some truth that Murray's character created a negative perception of golf course superintendents, but based on the respect most golfers have for their "keeper of the green," concern over Murray's depiction of a marijuana-smoking, gopher-chasing nut who fantasizes about members' wives is nothing more than silly paranoia.

However, many superintendents still have not matched the popularity of the local pro because they do not develop the suave communication skills that golf professionals have from years of teaching golfers and handling tricky political situations. Superintendents are busy solving problems and rarely want to listen to local golfers tell their horror stories. So most golfers have not engaged in conversations with the superintendent, nor are they aware of how much maintenance affects their game or the inability to improve their scoring.

Cool-Season Grasses

I invented my own kind of grass too. You know that? This is registered.
Carl Spackler Bent. This is a hybrid. This is a cross of Bluegrass,
Kentucky Bluegrass, Featherbed Bent, and Northern California
Sensimilla.   —Carl Spackler

With the advent of new grasses, the differences between warm- and cool-season grasses may become nonexistent within the next ten years. Why does that matter? Because it means even better playing conditions await, particularly for those in warm climates where finer, better playing grasses are not currently an option.

For now, it is still useful to know the difference between warm- or cool-season grasses. Differentiating between the two provides a logical starting point for any discussion of maintenance.

The best-known cool-season grasses are the various bents, ryes, fescues and poa annuas. Cool-season grasses are a more delicate species that prefer weather from 55–85 degrees. Cool-season grasses tend to exhibit a lush, rich shade of green. Their finer grass blades create better and faster surfaces, particularly as closely cut putting surfaces. Since they are finer bladed grasses, they also prefer less golf course "traffic." The drawback with a cool-season grass is obvious: When the weather gets warmer, it is tougher to maintain cool-season grasses at low mowing heights with lots of play. They suffer stress more rapidly and are prone to die unless kept wet. And under certain circumstances, when kept too moist, they become prone to disease.

Rye grass is commonly used for fall overseeding of fairways and tees where golf is played year-round, lending a fresh splash of green in places like Scottsdale and Palm Springs. However, rye is a surprisingly hardy grass that has been known to stunt the growth of warm-season grasses like Bermuda, zoysia and kikuyu grass, which is why some courses avoid costly rye grass overseedings that might slow down the reemergence of the primary summertime turf. Modern rye grasses are hardier than ever, making them a popular choice for year-round use in warmer climates.

Poa annua grass is classified as a weed, but commonly takes over courses in cooler regions and can provide an excellent playing surface. It is the primary grass on what are considered some of the best putting surfaces in the world. But "poa" requires the attention of a talented superintendent, because it is prone to disease, struggles in hot weather and requires delicate maintenance practices.

Warm-Season Grasses

It's a little harsh. —Carl Spackler, on his "registered" bent

Found in balmy, tropical regions of the world, warm-season varieties consist of Bermuda, zoysia and kikuyu grasses that thrive during warm days and nights. They are found on tees, fairways and "fringes" but less often in greens because they do not have thin blades like most cool-season grasses.

However, the next major advance in golf will be the widespread use of fine-blade Bermuda grass for putting surfaces. Many of these new Bermuda grasses have blades so thin that they look and play like bent grass to anyone except turfgrass professionals. But unlike the cool-season grasses, they are hardier and thus should improve putting conditions on courses with heavy traffic. They will also allow layouts in warmer climates to maintain firm, fast greens year round. Most warm-season grasses should cost less to maintain and require less water, a savings that hopefully will be passed along to golfers when such grasses are established.

As a fairway surface, most of the warm-season varieties are best because they provide a dense "turf" feeling underneath your ball and they handle the various forms of golf course traffic well. When used for the rough, many of these grasses can become unwieldy if not kept at a low height (1–2 inches). Their tough, wiry blades tend to suck balls to the bottom when left at 4–5 inch heights, which is why the USGA prefers to avoid Bermuda grass rough for the U.S. Open.

Short Grass

In golf architecture, tightly mowed grass is the nearest thing we have to a land mine. The average golfer sees acres of manicured grass and is encouraged to swing without fear. But the clever architect can utilize short grass in several ways to increase the difficulty of the course, and it will have the greatest effect on better players who recognize and fear the problems it will present. —Tom Doak

Architects inspired by links-style golf believe that the most interesting hazard of all is short grass. Most links courses we see during the British Open are lined by tall "native" grasses that swallow up balls. Unfortunately, most links courses are made interesting and challeng-

Ballybunion, Old Course, Ireland. Note how the short grass surrounding the green accentuates the impact that the lefthand slope has. (GEOFF SHACKELFORD)

ing by the expansive areas of tightly mown turf, with the tall but sparse native-grass areas off to the sides that appear much more difficult than they really are.

Not only does short grass make the game more fun for those who like to play bump-and-run shots, tightly mown grass brings features into play when the fairway comes close to the edges of, say, deep bunkers. Short grass also feeds the slightest mishit shots off a green and into what Americans generally call "chipping" or collection areas. The inclusion of such areas has proven to be one of the most interesting features in modern-day American architecture.

Bobby Jones and Alister MacKenzie relied on short grass to create challenge in their 1933 Augusta National design. Pinehurst #2 is extremely difficult because its crowned greens feed uncontrolled shots to short-grass areas around its greens. In both cases the courses are not made easier with short grass. They are more difficult and interesting because the short grass creates decision-making options, while also sending errant balls away from the prime areas of play without punishing golfers with lost balls.

Short grass is deceiving because it creates multiple playing options that tall grass won't allow. How many times have we seen a player in deep rough simply chip back out to the fairway? Meanwhile the player with a good chance to get their club on the ball has a decision to make: does he take the risky play or play safe? We often see good players make bad decisions in these instances, and end up registering a higher score than the players who did not have decisions to make.

Architects will continue to use short grass as a hazard around greens now that the grasses are developed to tolerate lower mowing heights. Many golfers tend to be less afraid of using a putter from off a short-grass collection area because they find it less intimidating than a lofted wedge shot.

However, when faced with short grass around a green, scratch golfers tend to think too much about their options: Do I play the old links-style "bump-and-run" shot? Or should I putt the ball through the fringe-height grass even though it may get an unpredictable bound? Or, maybe use the lob shot even though there is less margin for error when playing a lofted club off of a "tight" lie?

Scratch players are less likely to pull off a great shot if they have options to mull over and the slightest bit of doubt, which is why architects are using short grass in place of greenside bunkers. As maintenance practices improve and costs can be controlled better than in the past, superintendents are becoming comfortable with maintaining more fairway area than rough. Not only does this make the game more forgiving for most golfers, but it also adds strategic possibilities that make golf more interesting for all.

Long Grass

Narrow fairways bordered by long grass make bad golfers. They do so by destroying the harmony and continuity of the game and in causing a stilted and a cramped style, destroying all freedom of play. —Alister MacKenzie

As short grass comes back in style, long grass is being seen for what it is: boring, stifling and irritating. No golfer enjoys looking for balls or chipping sideways out of five-inch rough.

Players searching for lost balls, the primary reason long grass is such a nuisance. (LYNN SHACKELFORD)

The par-4 ninth at Maidstone Club, Easthampton, New York. Though it looks severe from a distance, this long grass is actually sparse and thus makes it easy to find your ball. (GEOFF SHACKELFORD)

Sheep at Lahinch mow the long grass quite effectively. (LYNN SHACKELFORD)

The USGA has used rough as the primary method to place a premium on straight driving off the tee, and as the Masters has proven with its modern addition of a "second cut," narrow fairways guarded by straight rough lines leads to less interesting golf than a course of primarily short turf. Long grass stifles creativity and shotmaking off of the tee and around greens, and ultimately does not necessarily "identify" the best golfer. In fact, it often slows wayward shots from reaching trouble.

On paper, fairways bordered by thick rough sound like a proven formula for producing great golf. This formula would expose "accuracy," but what it actually rewards is straight play involving little shotmaking creativity. Rough also tends to have a stifling effect on everyone's swing. So be wary of playing the course that thinks it is hosting a U.S. Open on a daily basis. Such a layout can severely damage your ability to swing fluidly and without restraint. Such courses have been known to lead golfers down bizarre swing paths, fostering patchwork fixes or faulty swing compensation requiring months of repair.

Flyer Lies

Judging the flyer has sadly become a dying art. —David Feherty

If your ball lies in grass at 3/4 of an inch to 2 inches, with enough grass blades nestling themselves between the ball and clubface at impact, you *might* have a "flyer lie." *Sometimes* at impact, the grass blades will conspire with your clubface to put overspin on the ball, sending it distances you never imagined. That's a "flyer." However, there is no way of actually knowing for sure when the flyer will occur, but it usually happens when you can make solid contact with the ball and grass blades are in between.

There will be times when your ball sits up higher in rough grass than normal, with little interference from the grass between club and ball. Next thing you know, your 8-iron shot has traveled 165 yards into someone's backyard.

Fairway Contours

Fairways should be irregular in shape and not like bowling alleys extending through the woods.   —A. W. Tillinghast

Much of a course's character can be detected by looking at the contour lines of its fairways. The narrow, straight-lined look is not particularly appealing, nor does it cause the player to think about much other than trying to hit their drive as straight as possible. (And doesn't that get tiresome?)

The bowling-alley style came about during the 1940s and '50s when fairway irrigation systems were installed and courses became more selective as to where they would maintain fairway height grass and where they would place less priority on maintaining grass. The advent of irrigation systems created the distinction between fairway and rough; prior to that architects were not concerned with the delineation between the two. They merely wanted fairways to be generous, surrounded by less consistently maintained turf.

Opposite of the narrow bowling-alley look is the layout that tries to use fairway contours to look natural. They mow a series of wavy, whirly lines that move in and out but fail to appear natural. Those constantly shifting lines look nice on paper, but when actually cut, the wavy look never quite works. Also, if a green is designed to be attacked from a certain side of a fairway, the wavy lined contour makes it hard to pinpoint an area that you want to play to in order to have the best angle to the hole, reducing strategic interest and increasing our annoyance with whoever created all of those wavy lines. The best cure for all of this fairway contour nonsense: Fit any and all curves with existing features or bends in the hole.

Grain

> . . . at some point we are going to have to figure out what we really want from our golf courses. Do we want interesting tests of skill with lots of character and perhaps a little grain on the greens? Or do we want level but slick putting surfaces that only make the game less interesting?   —Pete Dye

There is a famous golf announcer who talks about the concept of grain and how it will affect a putt, even as a tournament is played on greens that could never have grain because of their grass variety. Or he'll talk about grain even though he knows the putting surfaces are mown at $1/8$ inch, about as low as a mower can go before it starts hitting roots and soil. This particular announcer receives letters from superintendents around the country who beg him to get his facts straight so golfers will not complain about grain on their home course greens. But to no avail. He keeps on talking about the grain.

Grain is the effect of grass growing toward the sunny western side of your course, assuming you have grainy greens. Grain is still found on certain older varieties of Bermuda and bent-grass greens or on courses that mow greens at higher cutting heights. If the grass appears shiny in one direction and dark in the others, balls will be heading down grain when rolling over the shiny sections.

Grain affects how much break a player should read into a putt, and if you are putting directly down or into the grain, the speed of your putt will also be impacted. But with today's lower mowing heights, high-tech grasses and devices that "verti-cut" the tops of longer grass blades, the concept of grain is disappearing in modern-day golf. Sure, Augusta National mows its fairways toward the tees in hopes that the grass grain pointed at the players will slow down the roll of long drives. But again, when grass is cut at such low height, the impact is minimal.

If you look at a green and have trouble deciphering whether grass blades are clearly growing in a certain direction, then you are not likely to have grain affecting your putts. If you can step away, look at the grass color and not see radically different shades when looking at the turf from different angles, then it is unlikely you will encounter putts that require consideration of grain.

The Stimpmeter

The aspect of the game you lose with green speeds averaging somewhere between 11–13 on the Stimpmeter is the ability to build contour into your putting surfaces . . . when you take contour out of the greens and speed them up, you only make the game easier for the average-putting Tour pro, and harder for the club player. —Pete Dye

As grass strains improve, superintendents have been able to cut greens at low heights and not worry about the health problems associated with grass scalping. The average green speed has risen and we hear television announcers and golfers talk about their speed reading on the "Stimpmeter."

The implement in question is a simple three-foot-long piece of metal, the width of a golf ball. You lay one end on the ground, and hold the other end high enough so that a ball gently rolls down the metal ramp and onto the green. From there, you measure the distance the ball rolled on a flat part of the green, then repeat the process twice more. Then roll the balls three more times in the opposite direction. Measure the distance the ball rolled each time, with the average distance of all six rolls creating your Stimpmeter reading. That is why you hear people refer to greens rolling nine feet, or ten and a half feet on the Stimpmeter.

Generally, greens roll in the seven-to-nine-foot range today. Sixty years ago greens "Stimped out" in the five-to-seven-foot range, though Pete Dye argues grain was more prevalent back then and thus distances ranged from four to ten feet depending on which direction you were putting. Watching old golf films, you may see Dye's point. Some putts look painfully slow, while others have a quickness to them similar to modern speeds.

When greens start rolling in the ten-foot range and higher, you are talking about very fast surfaces to putt. Thirteen feet on the Stimpmeter puts you in Augusta National Sunday-afternoon-of-the-Masters territory. The problem with our green speed obsession is that it has placed the priority in green construction and maintenance on achieving a certain numerical pacing standard instead of what common sense tells you is the best speed for the health of the grass.

The Stimpmeter has stifled the creativity of many architects before they even start construction of a new layout. If for whatever reason a course wants to attain green speeds above ten on a daily basis, they often select a certain variety of grass that will allow for this. The architect then must design around this selection, and he cannot build many interesting contours or slopes when he knows speeds will be so high.

Imagine an artist using bright colors for a morbid subject matter because he knows ahead of time that the painting will be displayed in a dark room. Shouldn't the subject material and the need for whatever color required take priority, with the room's lighting adapted to the art? Placing the emphasis on speed over character is like building a concert hall and designing the building with sightlines as the focus instead of acoustics. Are you there to look at the orchestra or hear the music? In the Stimpmeter age, some courses need to ask themselves, are golfers there to look at the ball roll fast, or are they there to have fun negotiating challenging but still reasonable putts created by interesting contours? Golf has seen some downright insane green speed "norms" take precedence over design, all to the detriment of interesting greens and, oftentimes, healthy turf.

The "USGA Green"

When I retire I'm going to get a pair of gray slacks, a white shirt, a striped tie, a blue blazer, a case of dandruff, and go stand on the first tee so I can be a USGA official.   *—Lee Trevino*

You may hear people mention that a course has USGA greens. Or perhaps in justifying a costly reconstruction, an old course needs USGA greens to improve conditions. (This is an interesting concept considering the U.S. Open has only been played on a handful of courses with a full set of USGA greens.)

Instead of building a putting surface atop some nice native soil like they did in the old days, the USGA green creates an eighteen-inch-deep subsurface system with carefully placed layers of different materials. A sandy soil mixed with organic material serves as the primary surface that grass grows on. This system allows water to drain while also creating a perched water table underneath the surface that retains enough moisture in the root zone to encourage roots to search deep down for water, making the roots stronger and leading to healthy greens.

The construction of a USGA green requires a surprising amount of precision. Builders have to match each layer of gravel and sand from top to bottom, meaning the bottom of the subsurface system has to match the contours that we putt over for the green to function properly (at least in theory). As you might imagine, trying to match the different layers takes time and money, not to mention that such precision makes it hard for architects to create greens with that old-style character found on non-USGA greens.

Virtually all courses today are built using this method or modified variation called the "California" green. Architects are comfortable with USGA greens because they are reliable for the superintendent who has to maintain them and absolves them of liability should the greens not grow in properly. Creatively they are a nightmare to design and build, and financially they are expensive.

There are many interesting alternative construction methods used these days to counter the cost and creative difficulties of using a USGA green, so if you hear a new course is not using USGA green specifications, do not assume this will lead to problematic greens. There is a good chance the turf consultants have developed an easier green to maintain, while the architect was given the chance to build more interesting green contours that will putt just as beautifully as a USGA green.

Bunkers

Bunkers are not places of pleasure; they are for punishment and
repentance.   *—Old Tom Morris*

Of all the elements that a superintendent must give attention to, the bunker may be the most elusive. Growing grass has become the easy part of golf maintenance. Keeping sand raked regularly and at the consistency golfers want has become a difficult, almost impossible task. Particle sizes are sent to labs, different sands are put in test plots for committees to weigh in on. Synthetic lining is even put in some bunkers to prevent "contamination" of those mysteriously popular blinding white sands.

A typical bunker at Maidstone Club, Easthampton, New York. There is just enough trouble here to cause doubts, but also the opportunity for a recovery shot. (GEOFF SHACKELFORD)

Bunkers with "irregular" and natural-looking edges on the eleventh at Easthampton Golf Club, New York. (GEOFF SHACKELFORD)

The modern-day touring professional and single-digit players have declared that the bunker must be "fair" above all else and superintendents now spend as much as half their time trying to find the perfect sand and maintenance practice to make bunkers "fair." The depths of sand must always be uniform and the texture of the sand consistent throughout the course. Many golfers concur, because who can ever forget that awful lie that cost them a match in the Palmer Flight of the Mayflower Cup?

Golf course superintendents are pressured by committeemen and tournament competitors to convert these hazards into areas as playable as the fairway, or else risk losing their job. Other courses waste thousands of gallons of water hosing down sand to keep it from getting too fluffy, while PGA Tour sites have even been asked to mix expensive tennis court clay into their sand so that PGA Tour players will never have to face a fluffy lie or "fried egg" (better known as a plugged lie).

This does not mean that all superintendents or architects should restore Oakmont's old "furrowing" rakes, because that takes the hazard element too far and discourages recovery shots. After all, the best hazards are those that allow for a dashing recovery from time to time.

Such shots are fun while the awareness that we might have a chance to hit a recovery tempts many of us into aggressive shots with the hope that even if we land in the hazard, we still might have some hope of recovering.

The presentation of the bunker is also one of the architect's favorite "paints." Some designers like to create ragged, eroded-edge hazards that appear old and natural. Others prefer clean, cloverleaf shapes, and still others will use them symbolically (fish, mermaids, Mickey Mouse, etc.). All bunkers require maintenance, no matter what look the architect hopes for. Add the pressure of presenting manicured sand on a daily basis, and you see why superintendents want architects to build fewer bunkers.

Visit Your Superintendent

Is this your place, Carl? It's uh . . . really . . . awful.
—*Ty Webb, visiting Carl Spackler's Bushwood living quarters*

The best way to gain insight into your home course or a tournament layout is to talk to the superintendent. So much can be learned about the playing characteristics of the course from a knowledgeable superintendent. As long as you are not asking for advice from the superintendent during a competitive round, you are not breaking the rules of golf.

Superintendents are not like Carl Spackler, living down in a dumpy maintenance building, spending their evenings making clay model gophers and using leaf blowers to dust their bookshelves. However, some superintendents take pride in setting their course up for an event and will leave it up to the golfers to acquire some local knowledge during pretournament practice rounds.

Assuming you call a superintendent to gain a few tips about the course conditions, here are some questions to try asking. Remember, don't ask the superintendent these questions in an accusatory manner, but simply as a curious golfer looking to understand the course a little better. If you approach a superintendent this way, you are likely to pick up some surprising insights.

A well-dressed "greenkeeper" at Royal County Down. (LYNN SHACKELFORD)

Do You Plan to Change Watering or Mowing Practices for the Tournament? This will tell you what to expect when it comes to the firmness of fairways and greens if you are hoping to gain pre-tournament insight. Understanding how the maintenance may deviate from normal maintenance practices will help you anticipate changes in green speeds and also allow you to consider alternative strategic approaches to certain holes. Firmer fairways might force you to use a different club off a tee, or faster greens might remind you not to miss your shots in certain areas around various hole locations. "Double-cutting" greens will obviously increase speed and firmness.

Remember, the firmer and faster a course, the more design features come into play. Many courses will change dramatically in tournament conditions simply because of less watering by the superintendent or a different mowing regimen.

Have You Added Any Sand to the Bunkers Recently? This allows you to check out certain bunkers or at least become aware of possible differences in sand texture. When new sand is added to bunkers, it is not as compacted as sand that has settled for some time, meaning there is an increased chance of buried lies in hazards with fresh sand. This is an important piece of knowledge to have, particularly when you are confronted with a tempting shot. If you are aware that a bunker has new, fluffy sand, the risky shot becomes more perilous, maybe even too dangerous to try.

Do Some Greens Drain Better Than Others? No matter how scientific green construction gets with a subsurface system, all greens drain differently. Some greens will hold shots better than others, while others will putt faster even if they are maintained the same way. You don't necessarily need a superintendent to tell you this, because in your own play you can sense if a green is firmer or softer than others. As a general rule, greens exposed to wind or sitting at higher elevations will nearly always be just a bit drier, firmer and faster.

Are There Any Optional Tees That Might *Be Put into Play?* Some courses offer a variety of tee shot angles for holes or they simply like to mix up the yardages during tournament play by dramatically shifting tee markers. Or sometimes the tournament tee is closed during practice rounds. The superintendent may not give you the exact setup plan, but he probably has been told which tees to have prepared for an event. If you preface your question with "might" or "possibly," you'll increase the likelihood that the superintendent will tip you off as to possible alternative course setups. This comes in handy prior to a practice round because it allows you to survey yardages in advance and helps provide some idea how the optional tee might change your strategic approach to the hole. Confronting those situations before tournament play will give you an edge over players who are flustered by such surprises.

How Accurate are the Yardages on the Course? Ask the superintendent how precise the sprinkler head yardages are or if the local yardage book is reliable. He will probably say that everything is fine, but you never know. He might mention a few yardages that people think are incorrect, or make suggestions about which yardage system is the best to consult.

> *If the importance of course management is diluted in favor of uniform courses, air golf, power golf, or easier courses that popularize the game, we've made a grave mistake. Golf is a game of uncertainty—in the player, in the design of the course, and in the bounce of the ball.*
>
> —*Robert Brown,* The Way of Golf

Questioning the superintendent is important if you are looking for an edge in your everyday one-dollar Nassau, a local city championship, or if you are just curious about the inner workings of your home course. You'll never be able to understand some of the bounces you get or some of the bad lies that turn up on a golf course. It's a game of chance, and always will be no matter how well maintained a course may be.

However, understanding maintenance can help reduce the element of uncertainty and ease the pain of bad breaks that seemingly were inflicted by the superintendent, but were actually Mother Nature–induced. Knowing the intricacies involved in the maintenance of your home course will make it easier to manage your game more efficiently and confidently.

If you do track down your superintendent, don't forget to thank him for his efforts. He might be so flattered that he will throw one last nugget of local knowledge your way.

The Fourteenth Hole

Rustic Canyon

The Making of a Modern-Day Golf Course

> *Time.* —*Ben Crenshaw's response, whenever asked what leads to
> interesting course design*

I have listened to various tour players and fans approach Ben Crenshaw and ask him what is the single most important element of course
design.

He always replies, "Time."

Not strategy. Not money. Nor a glorious site by the ocean. He doesn't
even say something like, "creating a variety of holes," or "hiring the best
team of shapers you can find." Or my favorite mantra from modern architects who never seem to actually do what they say: "We build courses
challenging for the top players, yet playable for the everyday golfer."

Time.

I never could figure out what he has been talking about and always
assumed the "time" answer had something to do with Ben and his
design partner Bill Coore's careful approach to design.

After having spent nearly two years walking a site, attending bureau-
cratic meetings and finally seeing a course completed, I finally understand exactly what Ben Crenshaw has been talking about. Just as time
allows us to reflect on a film, music or business deal, all the time you can
possibly have is vital if you hope to design a course with character.

If you want to involve the best people and ultimately construct the course as inexpensively as possible with as many interesting subtleties, time is essential. Most of all, if you believe in creating holes that are fun for every level of golfer and still reasonable to play, you need time to sort out the possibilities and weigh alternatives as the construction progresses.

> *There just isn't a whole lot of home cooking anymore, everything is microwaved.*
>   —*Bill Kittleman, longtime Merion golf pro, on modern golf design*

I first met Gil Hanse when he was finishing the construction of Inniscrone Golf Club in Pennsylvania. He was nice enough to arrange visits to several fine courses in the Philadelphia area and to introduce me to his friend and collaborator Bill Kittleman, the longtime pro at Merion and one of golf's genuine characters. After dinner at Merion, Gil suggested that if a project ever came about in my hometown and I was interested in getting my feet wet, that he'd be interested in taking on a lowly golf writer such as myself. I was honored but did not set about looking for a site when I returned home.

Few sites in Southern California come along that have the potential to be anything but ordinary at best. Developers here seem to always pick the worst sites imaginable for building a golf course. They look for land near freeways or atop mountains, or both. There have been very few layouts constructed in recent years where the average golfer can afford to play, walk and have any fun. For the most part golfers in this course-thin market have rejected the many new layouts because of cost and difficulty, problems that are easily attributed to poor site selection.

In Ventura County, seven hundred acres of county-owned land became available for a long-term lease in 1999, with the lessee having the right to develop a "moderately" priced public course. The only developer to bid on the project was a former American Golf Corporation executive starting his own company. To get the course built, he was going to have to approach the project differently than was the standard practice in the region. The property was environmentally sensi-

The view from above the front-nine property for Rustic Canyon prior to construction.
(GEOFF SHACKELFORD)

tive and quite beautiful, maybe too beautiful to develop into a golf course since so few tracts like it still exist in the area. Horse riders, joggers, bird watchers, and legions of hikers have used the land for as long as anyone can recall.

The best terrain ran along the base of beautiful sage and cactus–covered canyon slopes. This arroyo is almost two miles long, running in a north-south direction, and has 243 feet of elevation change from top to bottom, though walking it you would be hard-pressed to guess there is so much slope.

Because the best land for golf runs north to south, the site would be excellent for avoiding holes playing into the morning or setting sun, but less than ideal if you wanted to play directly against or downwind. Most golfers would rather deal with sideways wind gusts than holes playing into the sun, so in that sense, the site was close to ideal. A native habitat area runs down the center of the canyon and would prove to be the biggest environmental obstacle. Thankfully, this area and the lack of dramatic elevation change scared away one developer and his architect from wanting to develop the site. I thank them daily for passing up the opportunity.

The county of Ventura has talked about building a golf facility on this tract several times, but ultimately pulled out each time because of

The view from above the back-nine property for Rustic Canyon just prior to construction.
(GEOFF SHACKELFORD)

environmental concerns or neighbors who understandably opposed development. The county considered creating an archery center to host the 1984 Olympic Games, and in a moment of extreme myopia, a water-amusement park. Thankfully, their insistence on a golf course won out. The site lends itself to a sensitively routed golf course that would add a minimal amount of traffic to the local neighborhood of middle-income homes.

The proposed thirty-six holes were whittled down to eighteen and the design promised to create a low-profile, environmentally sensitive course that would bring affordable golf to Ventura County (and much-needed revenue to a struggling parks department). Through my dad, the developer became aware of my interest and the idea of bringing in someone like Gil Hanse, who builds interesting courses without massive earthmoving. During various meetings with local agencies, I soon learned that the lack of earthwork was key to selling the course to the strong environmental movement working to preserve Ventura County's many beautiful areas.

After meeting with the developer on site, Hanse Design was hired and took on yours truly to help with the planning and preliminary design phase of the course, and then to stay on and help during construction. The initial work entailed attending numerous on-site meetings with biologists, engineers, local representatives of California Fish and Wildlife, the Army Corps of Engineers and the U.S. Fish and Game Departments. Those last two agencies are the key to getting any golf course approved in the United States.

The Approval Process

The current environmental situation is that the general public has exaggerated fears of environmental impacts and "environmentalists" have too little information to satisfy those concerns. . . . The result is a rather lengthy and costly permit process during which the golf course developer must prove his innocence. —*Michael Hurdzan*

Because the site contained a sensitive wildlife "channel" running down the center, there has always been great concern over what would happen if golf was introduced to the arroyo formerly known as Happy Camp Regional Park. (No, there was never consideration given to using the Happy Camp name, especially now that you know my feelings on golf course names.)

Many believed a golf course would cover this beautiful habitat area in turf, even though it is filled with fascinating forms of shrubbery, cactus, poison oak, a deep channel, beautiful sandy areas and a nasty form of broom that looks very similar to gorse. As soon as anyone with knowledge of great golf courses saw the channel, there was no question that it would become a feature unique to the course. There is nothing quite like it that I have seen on any golf course because the plant material combines a desert look with broomlike shrubbery found on old Scottish links. Sure, golfers will lose balls in this rustic habitat area, but it will also lend beauty and individuality to the golf course.

The decision to keep this sensitive area intact surprised the various agencies so much that they did not understand how or why we were leaving it alone (other than cart path crossings). They became suspicious, which led to one of the few misunderstandings between the developer and county during the approval process. Our intention to leave the sensitive area alone was soon clarified and along we went. By preserving this native habitat channel, we were leaving sensitive plant material in place. This meant we were also preserving the primary breeding corridor for the local coyotes, birds, frogs, lizards and snakes.

The other surprising issue that came up in on-site meetings was the concern these agencies had with introducing the modern "look" of golf to a beautiful site. Those who had the power to cause problems for our project expressed concern with modern golf's massive earthmoving and the over-irrigated look of courses. They did not want the incorporation of non-native trees or grasses or blinding white bunker sand.

Can you blame them? Palm trees, huge mounds and large lakes with streaming fountains would needlessly scar a beautiful landscape.

By walking the site with us, they saw how we planned to "place" the course onto the site instead of "erecting" a course there. Many seemed pleased, though still suspicious. Not until we walked all eighteen holes with a member from each agency did they begin to accept what we were actually saying.

There was, however, one biologist in particular who seemed more concerned with getting his way than what was logically best for the safety of golfers, and it resulted in some tense moments. Even with our theme of low profile golf and a "rustic" look to the course that would include use of native grasses and minimal irrigation near the sensitive areas, this one gentleman insisted we place split-rail fences to line the entire sensitive habitat channel that runs from the top end of the design all the way down to the lower end, some 240 feet below. Fencing would have affected half the holes on the course. Furthermore, to have a split-rail fence running along the entire channel would have been expensive, unsightly and unsafe. And how many golfers are going to obey a rickety wooden fence and stay out of the hazard when their brand new four-dollar golf ball is in view?

We argued that the presence of snakes and poisonous plant material is enough for most golfers to stay out of the area. However, the biologist held firm, suggesting that we needed to have fencing immediately in front of one of the par-3's tees. This meant golfers would have to risk teeing off over it with low shots possibly ricocheting off the wood and causing a potential safety nightmare, not to mention silly golf giving new meaning to the term "forced carry."

After years of hearing from architects how awful the approval side of design can be and how us golf writers have no idea how hard it can be, I agree that it is tough when some folks have to get their way, in spite of logic. Almost everyone we encountered was simply doing their job, however, protecting the interests of their organization.

The Design Process

There can be no really first class golf course without good material to work with. The best material is a sandy loam in gentle undulation, breaking into hillocks in a few places. Securing such land is really more than half the battle. Having such material at hand to work upon, the completion of an ideal course becomes a matter of experience, gardening and math-ematics.
—C. B. Macdonald

Amidst all of these meetings, Gil Hanse was open to my thoughts on the routing and individual hole designs. We initially worked on routings separately, Gil doing one on paper from his home office in Pennsylvania while I created one by walking the site. When we eventually met on the site with our two maps, it was surprising how similar we were in places and how different in others. As an amateur router of golf courses, I had come up with a good number of holes that became part of the final course, but there were serious problems.

Even with the number of interesting possibilities, the routing was stuck in certain places and I had trouble finding a way out. I became so caught up in some features that I could not notice other opportunities. So after days of staring, erasing and probably stepping much closer to snakes than I'd like to know, there were several key areas that prevented the plan from becoming a flowing eighteen. There were holes I knew would be exciting because there was no denying how good they already looked just sitting there. A few had such perfect features that I wondered if they were abandoned holes from a golf course that once existed. It is amazing how delusional you can get some days in the hot Southern California sun.

Gil and associate Jim Wagner arrived to complete the routing and quickly spotted solutions to the weak points and insisted on other key changes that took the course to another level. After three days, they had made several adjustments that never occurred to me in the hours staring at various features. Surprisingly little time was spent looking at alternative routings because once we had pieced the puzzle together, it seemed to flow naturally, though only time would tell if we had taken advantage of the best features.

As I walked the land and talked out loud to ward off any unfriendly visitors (until I found out that snakes can't hear), all I could think of was the golf architect who only routed holes from his drawing board. Gil Hanse had penciled a routing on paper just to have a starting point for discussion, but never believed it would amount to much more than that. He knew there would be no way to figure out the best sequence of holes other than to get out and walk the site, throw ideas around with others and debate the merits of different combinations. It is not an easy process, but it is quite satisfying once the pieces all come together.

Once the routing was set, I had the fortune of living only forty-five minutes from the site, so for a year I visited the property once a week and sketched out design ideas, working on one or two holes at a time. These drawings led to strategies we would start with going into construction, though I was well aware that once Gil and Jim were here to build the course, the original ideas would evolve significantly. We all agreed it was vital to go in with some clear thoughts about the goal of each hole and its basic strategy so that we were aware of each hole's purpose in the course of the round.

As soon as the native grasses and shrubbery were cleared from the site, new ideas and several wild ground features revealed new possibilities.

Design Style and Theme

Why can't people build rustic courses anymore? —Alice Dye, golf architect

Throughout our various meetings with the planning agencies, many would ask, "So is this going to be a 'links-style' course?" I never knew how to respond to such a question, because the traditionalist in me wanted to explain that the city of Moorpark was several miles from the ocean and, thus, this was not a true links. But I knew such a caustic reply would not help the process, and understood that "links" was a concise way of describing the look we hoped to achieve: firm turf, open and rolling fairways, and an absence of man-made water and trees. Eventually, the development team settled on the name we liked most, Rustic Canyon, and the theme of a "rustic" course developed.

When I toured Alice Dye around Riviera during the American Society of Golf Course Architects' visit to Los Angeles in 1998, I showed her areas under the groves of eucalyptus where the club's grass-loving ownership was making an extreme effort to grow turf, all to the detriment of eucalyptus trees that were showing signs of disease caused by overwatering. In her usual concise, to-the-point manner, Mrs. Dye asked, "Why can't people build rustic courses anymore?"

She was referring to the look of many older layouts that featured tightly mown fairways and nicely groomed greens and tees. However, everything else about these old courses had an irregular, "links-style" or rugged look: native grasses and patches of clumpy grass in the roughs, brown and red bushes popping up in sandy waste areas to create a natural appearance, jagged-edged bunkers, with eroded edges or weird plant material occasionally popping out of the sides. Rustic.

When I told Gil Hanse of her comment, it stayed with us and ultimately became the theme that would lend itself to our site and help win over the Moorpark community that recently has seen new golf courses built that were anything but rustic. Some may struggle with the rustic concept at first, but we think the style of the course, the setting, the character of the holes and the reasonable cost to play will ultimately win people over. Rustic doesn't mean the course will look run down or play poorly. In fact, the wide fairways should be quite lush, but areas off to the sides of play will hopefully not get much irrigation, and thus, will take on a rough, irregular appearance that will help the course fit with the native surrounds. Many modern layouts are adding native grasses and other "rustic" areas, better known as waste areas. They can look wonderful and should save water, but often irrigation hits these areas. This causes an overgrown look that is too lush, making them difficult for finding and playing balls.

Even though Gil Hanse, Jim Wagner and Gil's other associate Rodney Hine are building such interesting bunkers these days, the number of large, man-made hazards at Rustic Canyon was going to be minimal. We decided that the sandy soil of the site lends itself to "waste" bunkers. The emphasis will be on strategy that uses natural features as a priority, with bunkers added to compliment the unique contours. You will have to see the ground for yourself to understand why we fell in love with it and worked so hard to preserve all of the little bumps and natural drainage swales.

The routing includes three short par-4s, five par-5s (including back-to-back three-shotters on nine and ten), and five par-3s of varying length. The quirky variety was created by routing around the features that existed, and frankly, par-5s and par-3s are more fun to play for most golfers than a course with an overabundance of long par-4s. However, the back nine routing centered around two lengthy par-4s, the fourteenth and sixteenth holes, which were apparent in character before any earth was moved.

The key to the course sustaining itself for everyday play will be the width of the fairways, the variety of holes and the moderately sized greens. Width and larger greens also create different strategic scenarios from day to day, not to mention making the maintenance easier over the long term. The more I looked at the possibilities of this site and saw so many older courses, the more I have become fascinated with large greens. Small greens, basically anything under 4,200 square feet, tend to be overrated in modern golf as the ultimate sign of architectural brilliance. Mind you, this is coming from someone who grew up playing tiny sets of greens and loves the character of a smaller putting surface. Too many small greens on one course, however, ultimately limits playing options and the character of the golf.

The Construction Process

In golf construction, art and utility meet; both are absolutely vital; one is ruined without the other. —*George C. Thomas Jr.*

Much of Rustic Canyon's design was developed during the construction process. Some of the changes to our initial thoughts were made to improve design character, and some were compromises to accommodate the irrigation system, maintenance, carts and other function-related issues.

The normal modern-day project goes something like this: Developer hires architect who creates plans; architect recommends contractor who is hired to carry out the plans; contractor builds course with architect supervising construction. Depending on the architect, shapers who specialize in the architect's work may be employed. The irrigation system, agronomy of the course and the entire infrastructure are created by the contractor with the architect and superintendent consulted from their spots on the sideline.

Rustic Canyon was different because the developer and the architect worked together as the contractor. A small construction company did handle the fine grading of tees and the initial placement of the greens mix. Gil Hanse and Jim Wagner would build the bunkers, greens and tees. I managed to learn the bulldozer enough to handle certain menial clearing and dirt pushing tasks (and was glad to do it). Of course, for the first forty hours or so on the bulldozer, I looked a bit like Woody Allen in *Annie Hall* trying to drive a car. Plenty of stops and starts, near accidents and going backward when I meant to go forward.

The tenth green is where my shaping prowess finally was allowed

Gil Hanse, Jim Wagner and Geoff Shackelford at Rustic Canyon. (TOMMY NACCARATO)

to bequeath permanent features on the property, and even there I was just trying to not do any damage. The contours that resulted in the green were strictly accidental, but after Gil cleaned them up they did appear to look like gently rolling steps on the long green, which was affectionately known as the lap pool since it's forty-seven yards long and only sixteen yards wide. I also spent a good three weeks fidgeting with the third hole, moving mounds and piles of various dumpings from the rest of the course, trying to make sense of a hole with one hundred and fifty yards of width and three hundred yards of length. I can only imagine what some of the passersby were thinking watching the bulldozer twist and spin in strange directions.

Construction of any hole, no matter what the process is, goes in the same order for just about everyone. The hole design is "roughed" out, with the green usually built first. It is "cored" out and something close to the final contours are actually created on the green well floor. The irrigation crew then comes in and installs the irrigation system while the golf course builders work on the next hole. Once the primary irrigation is installed, the shapers return to the hole to do the all-important finish work. This includes work on bunkers, approaches and tees along with blending the sandy greens mix into the surrounds of

The author at work, transplanting a yucca found in the hills surrounding Rustic Canyon.
(TOMMY NACCARATO)

the green, a dreadful task that I spent much of my time on, but which is important to creating an old-style look of a seamless transition from fairway to green. Irrigation is finalized, the ground is seeded and the hole is finished.

Installing the irrigation system so that golfers will not see clumpy, sloppy-looking ground is a difficult and ongoing task to complete. As is creating a finished bunker, or a smooth but interesting green surface. Meeting the needs of drainage is an integral component to the day-to-day maintenance of a course, and thus often gets in the way of some design ideas as you rough-shape the holes.

Also having a hands-on approach allowed us to work closely with irrigation contractor Charlie Amos and his hardworking crew. They were willing to deviate from irrigation plans where necessary to create better holes, fewer irrigation control boxes in view and a more efficient use of the irrigation system. Such "in the field" adaptation only occurs out of necessity with a big contractor, but rarely to suit the needs of a design's function, maintainability, cost and long-term interest.

Finally, there is the issue of heavy equipment and how golf course features are created. To create the classic look that breeds genuine design character requires immense skill. To operate a backhoe or bulldozer requires hours and hours of training, and even then, an artistic sense is required. This project marked my first chance to get on a bulldozer and I became enamored with its potential. Initially, I was terrible, and by the end of construction, I was able to push around dirt without doing too much damage. I have a newfound appreciation for the work of golf course shapers, in particular, those who create features that do not look man-made. Still, many of the best features are shaped with a shovel or by some accidental shaping that no one had thought of.

Once all of the features are shaped out, the real trick of building a golf course is no different than any other project: finish work. The details. I would have thought this aspect of design would have been the least interesting, but nothing gave me more joy than the sometimes tedious work of finding and "chunking" native grasses, cactus, yuccas, coastal sage bushes and even old splintery fence posts to replace scarred areas or simply to inject the rustic look into our hazards. I learned a great deal from Jim Wagner on this and was careful to check with him before undertaking most of these little projects because I was often "embellishing" bunkers that Gil had shaped and Jim had done the primary finish work on.

If one of my "chunked" areas looked too odd, Jim would just throw down a fake-looking rock and announce in his own lighthearted way, "Gas station–island landscaping 101." Some areas did take on that look, but in time, weather, weeds and whatever else the soil sends up will soften the look of our "native" areas.

One of the more interesting touches that many golfers probably will not recognize initially at Rustic Canyon will be the bunker "lips." If you have played older courses you know that they often have thick top edges or lips that lend a certain aged character. Thick lips of bunkers make a bunker appear more intimidating, yet new courses rarely have such features because it takes time for a bunker to achieve a more rugged appearance. Jim and the bunker crew of four would in essence create a bunker lip on each bunker by hand-carving a small shelf along the top edge, then stack varying depths of sod around the top edge of each bunker. It's tedious work, but the result is that evolved look of a bunker "lip" that I thought only thirty years of weather and maintenance could create.

> *The ability to create is to consider all the problems of a golf course. The architect must visualize the effect his work will produce from all angles of the game.*
> —*George C. Thomas Jr.*

When the course is open and chugging along day to day, I will be particularly curious to watch golfers play the short par-4s. Each has its quirks and backdoor routes to low scoring, and I often wonder whether golfers will discover these avenues we created. In analyzing the holes, we often thought of Alister MacKenzie's quote about the old men who would play St. Andrews and who could barely slap the ball around but still outsmart the long hitting "lusty youth." The idea of a less-than-average golfer still being able to sneak their way around the course is fun to think about as you are designing, and certainly helps keep things in perspective. It's easy to visualize how a hole will play for good players, but weaker golfers are often forgotten.

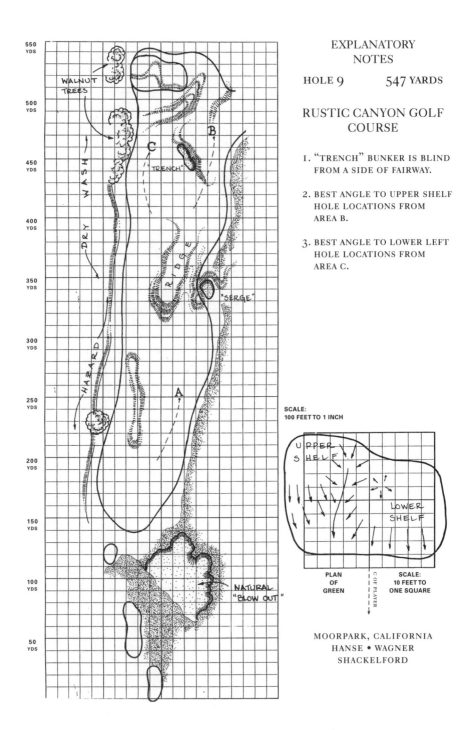

EXPLANATORY NOTES

HOLE 9   547 YARDS

RUSTIC CANYON GOLF COURSE

1. "TRENCH" BUNKER IS BLIND FROM A SIDE OF FAIRWAY.

2. BEST ANGLE TO UPPER SHELF HOLE LOCATIONS FROM AREA B.

3. BEST ANGLE TO LOWER LEFT HOLE LOCATIONS FROM AREA C.

SCALE:
100 FEET TO 1 INCH

| PLAN OF GREEN | | SCALE: 10 FEET TO ONE SQUARE |

MOORPARK, CALIFORNIA
HANSE • WAGNER
SHACKELFORD

(Labels within figure: 550 YDS, 500 YDS, 450 YDS, 400 YDS, 350 YDS, 300 YDS, 250 YDS, 200 YDS, 150 YDS, 100 YDS, 50 YDS; WALNUT TREES, DRY WASH, HAZARD, "TRENCH", RIDGE, "SERGE", NATURAL "BLOW OUT", C, B, A; UPPER SHELF, LOWER SHELF, C OF PLAYER)

Depiction of the 530-yard par-5 ninth hole, Rustic Canyon Golf Course. (GIL HANSE)

The 215-yard par-3 sixth hole, Rustic Canyon. There is more fairway on the other side of the scalebroom-filled wash than it may initially appear. A natural swale fronts the green and makes for interesting run-up shots. (GEOFF SHACKELFORD)

The 125-yard par-3 eighth hole, Rustic Canyon. A short pitch shot over native grass and sand to an elevated green, dubbed "peninsula." (GEOFF SHACKELFORD)

The second-shot view on the 425-yard par-4 eleventh at Rustic Canyon. (GEOFF SHACK-ELFORD)

The bunkers short of the par-4 eleventh at Rustic Canyon. (GEOFF SHACKELFORD)

View from the rear of the 330-yard par-4 twelfth at Rustic Canyon. The small elevated green is best approached from the middle of the fairway, where the player has a more forgiving shot. Drives close to the green and near the bunkers will be facing a crowned surface sloping slightly away from them. (GEOFF SHACKELFORD)

Rustic Canyon's 565-yard par-5 thirteenth. The pot bunker in the foreground is 245 yards from the back tee. The boomerang-shaped green sits in the distance. The lay-up area is over 100 yards wide, but players are rewarded for placing their shots on certain sides of the fairway depending on the day's hole location. (GEOFF SHACKELFORD)

View from above the 440-yard par-4 fourteenth at Rustic Canyon. The back tee faces a 175-yard carry over the scrub and wash seen here on the left. Middle and forward tees are in the foreground, where the hole plays 350 yards. (GEOFF SHACKELFORD)

The par-3 seventeenth viewed from above the 165-yard tee. The hole favors a left-to-right shot carrying the sand and native scrub area. (GEOFF SHACKELFORD)

Many of the strategic choices at Rustic Canyon deal with placing a tee shot or lay-up shot so that you give yourself the best *view* of the hole. Safer plays off the tee leave an obstructed view of a hazard, obstructions caused by the contours or slopes of the land, or by the height of hazards. I can already hear the complaints! But in time, such a hole requiring thought and a good memory will become fun for those with local knowledge.

In my initial playing of certain shots on the course while it was growing in, I found out several things that even two years on the site never really revealed. The holes playing down the canyon played shorter and the holes playing up the canyon were surprising long. Some of the carries we envisioned worked perfectly for strategic purposes, but others may need tweaking or may just take on a different meaning than we planned. With grass growing, you also see things that months of staring at dirt just can't reveal—primarily the size of greens or the scale of bunkers. Most things came out better than I imagined, but a few things, like the size of greens, surprised me. Some look too big, others look too small.

Such results are to be expected. We tried to emulate and re-establish some of the design ideas created by the region's greatest architect, George Thomas. His work served as my inspiration during the planning process for this course. Thomas was a strong believer in creating the same design dilemmas for public courses and private lay-outs. So in particular, the short par-4s, the boomerang-shaped thir-teenth green and some of the more subtle strategies were inspired by Captain Thomas, while the look of bunkers and use of drainage swales was definitely an ode to Thomas's design associate, Billy Bell, a master design engineer and builder.

Hopefully the many satisfying days we spent planning and con-structing Rustic Canyon will be apparent to golfers. In time, we'll know.

The Fifteenth Hole

Armchair Design

An Opportunity to Create Your Own Design Ideas

Every golfer is an architect at heart, mentally building his own layout just the way he thinks a course should play. —John Low, 1903

Now that you have played fourteen holes (well, read fourteen chapters), you are better prepared than most golfers to create interesting hole designs. Actually, you know as much as some practicing architects when it comes to the basic ingredients of enjoyable, interesting golf architecture. Therefore, let's use this knowledge to stretch you creatively. This is a chance to design holes you would like to play or see built, all in the privacy of your own home. That means you can try whatever you want without worrying what golfers will think or say.

We are providing "canvases" here so that you can play armchair architect. Each includes a brief description of the hole site and its characteristics. Some are imaginary places, a few might be real properties and a couple might be from famous golf course sites. There are, however, a few ideas to consider if you decide to tackle some of these sample canvases for design or, if you are an avid computer user, employ one of the interesting course design software programs that are included with various golf-computer games.

General Concepts to Keep in Mind

The difficulties that make a hole really interesting are usually those in which a great advantage can be gained in successfully accomplishing heroic carries over hazards of an impressive appearance, or in taking great risks to place a shot so as to gain a big advantage for the next.

—*Alister MacKenzie*

Before starting, your best bet would be to head down to the local printing store to make photocopies of the samples provided. You will find that you wish to erase, add, subtract and, in general, try different ideas out before you finalize your designs. Also, make sure that if you enlarge these samples on the copy machine, that you keep scale in mind. You should keep photocopies at 100 percent but if you prefer to work on a grander scale, enlarge these pages using workable numbers such as 150 or 200 percent. I also suggest marking up a ruler in pencil with different yardages, say, 25 yards, 50, 100, 200, 250, etc. This will help you save time and erasers and will ensure that your design functions properly. There is nothing more frustrating than coming up with something that looks out of scale, and proper scale is usually the first thing architects suggest improving when students send them design drawings.

You are more than welcome to come up with your own drawing style, though the style employed by Gil Hanse throughout this book should give you the best place to start for how to clearly delineate bunkers, greens and other features. One of the joys of armchair architecture contests over the years has been to witness the different types of renderings people present. Though the format here is limited, by no means do you have to stick to the sample canvases presented. Transferring the features to a different canvas is simple, again—just don't forget to keep scale in mind.

There are many computer-design software programs included these days with the leading golf games, so if you are computer savvy you may find these to be the easiest for opening your armchair-architecture practice. You create your own canvas on the screen by recreating these concept properties, and then designing however you please. And if you are familiar with these programs, you know that you can import actual properties that you find online by going to various map and government sites, and simply uploading digital elevation maps. So if there is a stretch of dunes nearby that you've always wanted to build a golf course on, there's a good chance you can actually pull it off.

One last practical note: If you have a scanner and e-mail address, you can log onto the website listed in the back of this book and submit drawings you think are worth sharing. Some will be posted online so that you can compare your ideas with other readers for the hole sites presented here. And in the spirit of modern golf, awards will be presented!

> *Hazards should not be built solely with the idea of penalizing bad play,*
> *but with the object of encouraging thoughtful golf and of rewarding the*
> *player who possesses the ability to play a variety of strokes with each club.*
> —*William Langford*

On the creative side, the goal is to have fun. Think bold. Put down ideas that you feel would excite all golfers, not just yourself. Take a few chances and present some quirky strategic scenarios. The canvases here should allow you to try just about anything you'd like.

Many armchair architects were annoyed with a recent magazine contest because the design opportunity tried so desperately to show readers the obstacles architects face that creativity was stifled. Charismatic design possibilities were encouraged but restricted. The sample canvas contained so many environmentally sensitive areas and logistical sticking points that the effort was focused on coming up with a design that merely functioned. We can only assume the goal was to let readers know how difficult it is to be a modern-day architect.

This is not to disagree with the notion that golf course design is complicated. The planning and construction process provides numerous obstacles that render sites less ideal than when the design process starts. Environmental issues, housing development priorities and other issues do consistently cause problems for architects. However, the point of this chapter and these doodling opportunities is to have fun, to encourage ideas that elevate the art of golf course design to a new level.

In these sample canvases you will find a few obstacles that might hinder a design idea, such as existing trees or contours or abandoned man-made structures. You can simply order their removal, however; you are the architect. The same features you may remove or ignore are features other readers will find interesting and worth incorporating into their design.

If you are designing with a computer-simulation program, you can still stick to the principles and ideas laid out here. Because most of those games are played using a system where the player clicks the mouse on a swing meter, players tend to hit shots in a small radius with low scoring commonplace. The tendency is to stick to penal design concepts to maintain some challenge. (There is a more realistic form of golf simulation, where the player swings the club by using their mouse only, and not a swing meter. This leads to more inconsistency and a more difficult version of the game, but perhaps one that would be open to classic design concepts.)

So just like actual golf played in three dimensions, you can take the interest level of the various PC games to another level by incorporating elements preached throughout this book: strategy, naturalness and playability. Anyone can load up their computer screen with bunkers, lakes and pencil-thin landing areas. It's another thing to create clever holes requiring decisions based on equally tempting options and local knowledge.

These philosophies and other principles have been covered throughout this book, but some are worth repeating as you sharpen your pencil or fire up the computer, and prepare to become an armchair architect.

I am beginning to think that the idea of flat greens or slightly falling greens is more truly scientific than the American plan of small greens targeted or banked to stop almost any shot that hits them. Only a real golf shot will hold those big, flat or slightly retreating greens; and you may have to exercise yourself between the ears in selecting the shot to play.

—*O. B. Keeler*

Start at the Green. When designing a course, most architects find areas with the best character for green sites and design from those points backwards. Here, some of the green site selecting has been done for you. Certain examples provide multiple green site opportunities while others will have few interesting features to work from, meaning you will have to do some creative work. Either way, the green site should be your starting point.

Lightly pencil in a green design, then think of the angle and style you want the putting surface to have. If you can't get past the idea of a circular green, try some potato chip–shaped greens to start with. Then consider how you want the green guarded by hazards (if any). From there, the possibilities should begin to unfold, and you can modify the hazards and the green's main characteristics as you proceed. Don't be afraid to add interesting "compartments" or "wing" hole locations after you see the design coming together. Such hole locations add interest and strategic possibilities.

Temptation. Thinking of how to tempt the player is the simplest way to create strategy. With every tee shot, bunker placement and green complex you sketch, ask yourself, "Is this going to tempt the player to try an aggressive shot? Am I allowing for a reasonable chance to pull off a bold shot while also providing enough room to play a safe shot? Will this design cause the player to think about options and fret between the lay-up shot or a riskier play?"

Comic Relief. Some of the armchair design scenarios presented may not lend themselves to an offbeat, quirky hole, but others will. Try to preserve or inject features that you think would add a little humor to the golf while remaining stylish. And even if you end up erasing existing features, just considering offbeat ideas may lead to other interesting possibilities. In computer-simulated designs, the comedy often revolves around who can build the tightest, most outrageously difficult hole. But like the recent wave of summer "gross-out" movies, the ultradifficult comedic hole can only entertain so long. Timeless design comedy is inspired by more subtle and thought-provoking humor.

Function and Playability. Put yourself in the shoes of golfers of all levels. Just because you play the game a certain way does not guarantee you will find it easy to visualize how others would play your design. Ask yourself how beginners or short hitters would tackle the hole. Think about John Daly. Also consider the everyday, average slicer. And after allowing for all other styles of play, then ask whether you would want to play the design. If you approach architecture with only your own game in mind, you may find that some will suggest your design is lacking in interest for a variety of players. If you only think of your game, however, at least you might have something in common with one famous player-architect who is often criticized (sometimes unfairly) for building holes only for his own game: Jack Nicklaus!

Maintenance. It is important to consider whether your contours can be mown or your bunkers maintained (in other words, try not to pencil in forty-two bunkers on a single hole, like a certain design team actually built on a course in Myrtle Beach). Keeping the basics of maintenance in mind will help keep your design looking simple in a distinguished and tasteful manner.

The Paper Effect. The greatest courses are created using ground features found by the architect while routing the course. The two-dimensional format here limits some possibilities, especially after you've learned that the best features are often "found" already sitting in the ground, simply awaiting an irrigation system and a mower.

Because of the limitations presented by paper drawings or software, the focus for these canvases should be on interesting strategic holes instead of the creation of elaborate, visually beautiful designs. Most strategic ideas should translate well to paper or computer. After all, Alister MacKenzie made a name for himself by winning a 1914 *Country Life* magazine contest, and his winning hole design was later built by C.B. Macdonald and Seth Raynor at Long Island's now extinct Lido course.

So remember, have fun and think bold!

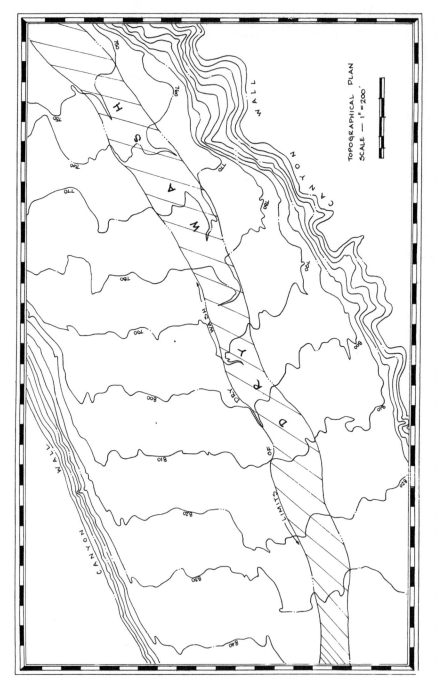

A site similar to the terrain at Rustic Canyon. Tee location should be somewhere on the right, while the teeing ground for the next hole is somewhere on the far left. Thus, a hole may be designed anywhere in between and should be a par-4 or par-5. Or, you can create two shorter holes. The "Dry Wash" can be kept or removed or altered, it's up to you. Note that the elevation rises gently from the right side of this site to the left.

(GIL HANSE)

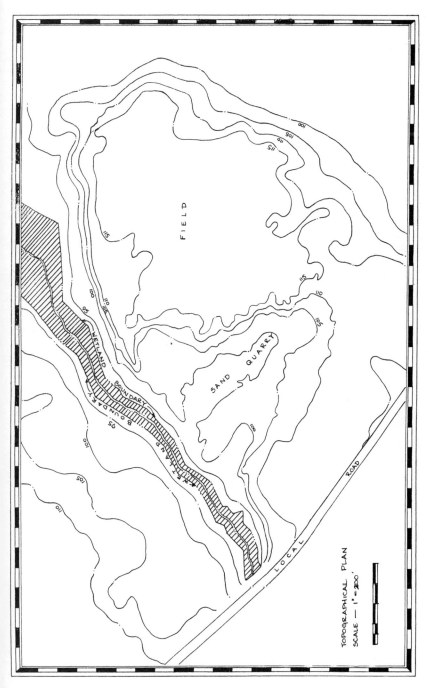

TOPOGRAPHICAL PLAN
SCALE — 1" = 30'

FIELD

SAND QUARRY

WETLAND BOUNDARY

WETLAND BOUNDARY

LOCAL ROAD

Another site where you can place one hole or as many as three. You can dictate where the preceding green is and where the next tee will be, allowing the freedom for many possibilities. In this case, the "Wetland Boundary" is the only area you cannot alter, nor can irrigated turf come within 25 feet of the shaded area. All other areas can be used however you please. Note the elevations here, as they are subtle. The "field" sits at the highest point while the "sand quarry" is at the lowest. (GIL HANSE)

The Sixteenth Hole

Random Thoughts

The Character of Golf and Other Elements That Make It Interesting

I have no wish to criticize anything, or anyone unfairly, but I believe that the only way to promote the interests of golf as a competitive sport is to discuss openly and fairly the problems which arise in playing the game.

—Bobby Jones

Golf architecture requires a delicate balance of elements coming together, assuming a design hopes to entertain and function. If any aspect is out of order, the balance crumbles and the architecture will fail to shine. Perhaps a course is overmaintained to the point its hazards lose the ability to intimidate. Or maybe the turf is so soft that the design is unable to present a variety of options and decision-making situations.

Golf has constantly witnessed the introduction of advanced technology, but only in the last twenty years has it become so pervasive that architecture's integrity is consistently undermined due to the game's emphasis on power. Shot-shaping and long-iron play has been eliminated from the professional game, unless you consider players using long irons off the tee as an interesting test.

The old architects warned of the technology dilemma in the twenties and recently we have witnessed the effect a power-driven environment can have on the entire game of golf. Some see technology as wonderful progress, others see the problems that arise from the imbalance created when you have courses designed for certain distance or "slope" standards. Tennis saw a similar shift from shotmaking to power. For years, tennis aficionados warned that too much power would render the professional sport less interesting. They argued that less interest in the pro game ultimately undermines the popularity of the recreational version of the sport. They were right, and golf took notice, with several figures saying that golf would never take such a turn toward the power game. So far, golf has not learned from the example set by tennis of the late 1980s and early '90s.

Technology in the construction business was supposed to speed up the building process, but somehow new courses cost more than ever to build and seem to have less character despite the additional time and resources architects have to fine-tune design features. Many new courses lack a certain soft, settled character that modern earth-moving machinery is either unable to create during construction, or which those doing the work have been unable to create using the new equipment. Handwork, care and time are still required to give a course that final bit of design character that makes certain places so appealing.

Various playing formats that lend more interest to golf and permit interesting design to shine have disappeared from the modern game. The "stymie" was a favorite of Bobby Jones. He longed for its return to the occasional competition. Even basic match play has flirted with extinction on the professional level, kept alive by the Ryder Cup, contested every two years. Television has a bizarre influence on the modern game, as does the massive amount of money driving the business side of golf.

Thanks to improved communication systems, we have more information than ever before, particularly swing instruction. Yet the major golf publications are held hostage by manufacturers, meaning very little in the way of honest reporting appears in print anymore. Other important topics deemed too minute for discussion in golf magazines will instead be discussed here. They range from whether money buys great design, the classic course restoration movement and the art of setting up a course to take advantage of its architecture.

Does Spending Millions = Greatness?

I would suggest, however, that no money be lent for constructing an elaborate clubhouse. The first club of which I was a member had only a hundred dollar hut as a clubhouse and beer and sandwich luncheons, yet we got as much health and happiness out of it as any other.

—*Alister MacKenzie*

In modern golf, sound architecture and a unique atmosphere are seen as achievable only by spending large sums of money. Greatness can only be purchased by those with vast resources. Most developers or those operating existing layouts often fail to enhance a facility with a charming, low-profile design because they believe that only expensive-looking features will create a successful golf course. Blinding white crushed-marble bunker sand, cascading waterfalls, protective mounding and, of course, a massive clubhouse (heavy on the cherry wood) all supposedly equal greatness.

Overdone features that photograph nicely may create a "wow" effect and instantly gratify the senses, but just because a hole stands out in a magazine does not mean it provides long-term playing satisfaction. Flashy elements work for marketing but lasting enjoyment is found in more subtle, even quaint courses. To create layouts with a certain timeless, natural impression, the required investment comes in the form of a caring architect, not through swift, expensive construction.

I'm always fascinated by the modern developer who states that he wants to create a "Top 100 course." He will spend lavishly on amenities: dazzling entrance road, plenty of earth rearranging for "bowl-effect" fairways, two million dollars on one "signature" hole and private jet trips around the world to study the great courses. When it's all done, the developer can't figure out why the lavish new course isn't deemed to be the second coming of Augusta National.

The overspending approach is even more mystifying when you learn that many of those developing these wannabe "great" courses have played the world's best. They observe that the amenities at the Pine Valleys and Cypress Points and Sand Hills of the world are understated. The atmosphere is low-key, not pompous. The décor or dress of the caddies would be considered tacky anywhere else. When the design has integrity, however, those tacky or quirky elements become a symbol of character and tradition!

The best facilities also earn rave reviews because golf is the focus and flashy touches are absent. There is a settled feeling to the ground, with a look of naturalness and simplicity. Greens and tees are close together. The courses contain integrity and charm unlike anything else you'll find in the game.

The great golf courses feel like the Boston Gardens or Fenway Parks or Wrigley Fields. They might be a bit odd for some people's taste and certainly lack modern amenities, but they still have character that money cannot buy. And most of the greatest designs—old or new—were created by spending surprisingly little. Yes, sometimes this was due to the presence of fine soils and land features that did not require expensive amendments, but the savings can be traced to the architects' willingness to maximize the existing land features and minimize wasteful spending on elements that look silly in a short time.

Ambiance, character and sound design take time and care to create. Not millions upon millions of dollars.

Is Temptation Dead in Championship Golf?

How am I supposed to hit and think at the same time? —Yogi Berra

The emergence of high-tech equipment and longer-flying golf balls threatens the character of the game because it eliminates the tempting qualities of many great holes, or in some cases, eliminates any kind of thought altogether.

During the 1996 Masters, Greg Norman and Nick Faldo analyzed the approach to Augusta National's par-5 thirteenth green for almost ten minutes. They were teased and tempted by the architecture. Faldo was debating whether to hit a soft 4-wood or 2-iron into the green. The professional game was in balance for one last time before technology would soon strip such temptation away.

Jump a whopping five years later. During the 2001 Masters, Tiger Woods and Phil Mickelson were battling for the lead. Both players hit an 8-iron into the thirteenth green. Woods used a 3-wood off the tee. Their ability to hit such bold and long tee shots under pressure is impressive, but the thirteenth hole's ability to tempt and tease was gone, a victim of technology. The green was within easy reach for both players, the hole location an afterthought. The opponent's strategy, the trickling creek, the lie, the shape of shot and the number of holes remaining in the round—all elements normally contributing to the hole's challenge—had become insignificant factors. Technology eliminated the alluring qualities of the most tempting hole in the world.

Only a regulated tournament ball or a distance rollback can preserve our existing courses. Trying to adjust the courses is an expensive and lost cause. The need for a permanent distance standard for all of golf has been insisted upon by many golfing greats. In 1927 Bobby Jones advocated such a ball, and Jack Nicklaus has been pleading for one since the late 1970s. If it does not happen, architects will have a hard time figuring out how to create tempting 500-yard par-4s, because after all, they too will soon become outdated.

The Stymie

I have never experienced so many chills and thrills in so short a time.
          —Bobby Jones, referring to a memorable stymie situation

Few golfers realize that the most heated debate in golf history was not over square grooves, springlike effect or superhot golf balls. Instead, it was a twenty-year argument over the "stymie." What is a stymie? Or, rather, what *was* a stymie and what does it have to do with golf architecture?

Prior to 1952, a ball could not be marked and picked up on the green in order to allow your match-play opponent an unobstructed putt to the hole. Players could position their putt to prevent their opponent from getting a straight putt at the cup. But there were many risks involved in the strategy to stymie your opponent.

Bobby Jones wrote a lengthy chapter in his 1959 biography, *Golf is*

My Game, entitled, "The Stymie—Let's Have it Back." Jones explained exactly how the stymie worked and presented a strong argument for the stymie returning to some match-play events. The stymie would add excitement to match play and another element of strategy. It could become an exciting format in golf again, opening the door to a return to more imaginative and provocative match-play design ideas.

No, the stymie should not be a part of everyday golf, because it might lead to divots on greens, and maybe even fistfights over incidents that broke up someone's string of pars. But imagine the stymie as just one more interesting format, one more twist on this great sport.

Perhaps the stymie could come back to spice up the local match-play tournament, or perhaps in a "silly-season" match-play event on the PGA, LPGA, or Senior PGA Tour? Imagine a better-ball of partners match play with the stymie in effect. It certainly would be more entertaining than another seventy-two holes of stroke play. And regardless of technology's influence, the stymie and more match play would be one way to return some strategy to golf.

The Influence of Television

There has always been a good deal of evidence that when it comes to announcing golf on television, it pays to be uninformed. Note that I am too nice a fellow to have said 'stupid.'　　　　　　　*—Dan Jenkins*

As exciting as match play is or as the occasional stymie could be, television does not want any part of either. They want control, first and foremost. The chance for entertaining, maybe even thrilling, play is less important because the most important entities in television—the local affiliates—want to know that a telecast will sign off on time.

Stroke play, for the most part, can be controlled. Sure, you have playoffs and rainouts, but in general television knows when and where a seventy-two-hole stroke-play event will end. A sixty-four-player match-play event is too unpredictable and difficult to cover, even if played on an interesting design where it could be downright thrilling. The first day of a match play event is messy, because there are thirty-two contests with many intriguing matchups. Fast forward to the final day, which only has one match—meaning television has only two players to show. Surely, a creative solution to these issues could be created if television really wanted to put forth the effort, but television and the PGA Tour would first have to realize that an interesting format and a compelling design leads to exciting golf.

Television has also changed golfers' expectations when it comes to the look and character of courses. Big, sometimes garish features translate well to blimp shots and camera angles. Subtle, satisfying features that would make year-round golf more fun do not look as good for television or other media. And because most new courses aspire to be seen on television or in print, architects create features that emphasize catching the eye, instead of stimulating the senses.

Maintenance has also changed because of television. We all know green looks better on television, but many golfers hold unrealistic expectations for green at their home courses. In fact, many superintendents master the art of growing green grass, even though it is not necessarily the best playing condition they could provide. Most course operators and clubs will take green over good fairway lies, unfortunately.

Television's final effect on golf comes from the announcers. Very few have any sense for architecture or what makes a hole special, and therefore rarely say anything of substance about design. So do not take the announcers too seriously; they are mostly former pros who think like players, not like architects. There are exceptions—usually the older British announcers who have studied the game and understand its history.

The Art of Course Setup

The course is playing the players instead of the players playing the course.
—Walter Hagen, on the 1951 U.S. Open setup at Oakland Hills

Whether it is by the superintendent, a committee or a member of one of golf's governing bodies, the architecture of a course can be enhanced or rendered useless depending on how a layout is set up. Course preparation entails the selection of tees to be used, hole locations, fairway widths, green speeds, grass-mowing heights, and how hazards and boundaries are marked. All of this seemingly subtle groundwork can make or break how a design is received.

There is an art to setting up a course to reward great play while also penalizing poor planning and execution. Such a balanced setup is rarely seen in modern times because those setting up courses are focused on either preventing low winning scores or masking the role of improved technology. In other words, egos are setting up courses, not common sense.

The model for setup was created by the Masters committee preparing Augusta National from 1960 to 1997. Consider the remarkable stretch of golf the Masters produced during that time. There were triumphs and tragedies, with sound all-around golf consistently rewarded. There were some low winning scores and some very high ones. Most years, however, the leaders separated themselves from the rest of the field. When it was a tightly-bunched leader board, there was still a feeling that a player could mount a final-nine charge to separate himself from the rest. Solid play and well-timed risk taking was rewarded by the design, while lesser play was punished. It is a fallacy that the Masters only rewarded the best putter each year, as its diverse group of champions proves. The setup rewarded a combination of placing drives, precise iron play, deft chipping touch and the ability to putt.

Rarely does excellent course setup get noticed anymore because there have been so many modern blunders to consider. The various setup debacles occur when the committee pushes green speeds or hole locations to the limit, all out of fear of low scores. Or they narrow fairways and grow rough to the point that luck is emphasized, when the opposite should be their goal. Others believe that setting up a course is a scientific process, not an art. Viewed in a formulaic manner, those in charge fail to properly weigh the influence of weather conditions, green speeds, faster tournament conditions or the basic principles that reward sound play. The real artisans of course setup will study the possibilities the design presents. They can set their egos aside when making decisions about tee and hole locations. They recognize their job is simple: Take weather into account, present a variety of day-to-day dilemmas by altering tee or hole locations, and make play difficult for those who practice careless course management. Such a basic approach will identify the best player and reward excellent play.

The Modern Bunker

If I had my way there would be a troupe of cavalry horses running though every trap and bunker on the course before a tournament started, where only a niblick could get the ball out and then but only after a few years. I have seen a number of traps and bunkers that afforded better lies and easier strokes than the fairway. This, of course, is ridiculous.

—*C. B. Macdonald*

There is no need to run a "troupe of cavalry horses" through bunkers, but wouldn't it be nice if just one tournament course eliminated the severity of the tall rough and, instead, made the bunkers real hazards? If there is sufficient fairway to play away from bunkers, then

The par-4 eighth at Sand Hills, with its green wrapping around a fronting bunker. These are true hazards. (GEOFF SHACKELFORD)

The short par-3 seventeenth at Sand Hills, viewed from the 100-yard member tee. (GEOFF SHACKELFORD)

no golfer can cry foul when he or she hits into a nasty bunker and is left with a bad lie. But as modern golf emphasizes growing nasty rough, bunkers will have to remain an oasis for players unwilling or unable to play to the target. And golf will remain in a backward state where bunkers are often better places to be than the surrounding grass.

How about just one week on the PGA Tour, we prohibit raking of bunkers after Wednesday's Pro-Am? Players (excuse me, their caddies) can rake with their foot or whatever means they devise. But let the bunkers get a little unpredictable. Just one week?

The Restoration Movement

I'm going to start an organization called the "Classic Golf Course Preservation Society." Members get to carry loaded guns in case they see anybody touching a Donald Ross course.
> —*Tom Weiskopf, 1980, upon seeing George and Tom Fazio's changes to Oak Hill*

After the disastrous late-seventies redesign work at Oak Hill and Inverness, a new attitude soon emerged toward older golf courses. Pre–U.S. Open changes made at these two classics were so out of character with the original Donald Ross designs that clubs began to take their original architecture seriously.

Not until the early 1990s did restoration become a buzzword, and not until the late 1990s did it become popular. Some architects now specialize in the process of restoring older layouts. Many courses recognize the value of preservation and are rushing to care for what is left of their layouts. When the restoration projects go well, the prices of memberships and green fees have risen and the quality of golf has drastically improved.

In some cases, architects arrive and claim that restoration is not the best way to go. These same architects proceed to leave their own design mark on a few holes with the hope that the golfers will want the new design style throughout the rest of the course (meaning more work for the architect in the future). Or the architect and his shapers simply have no eye for matching new features with the old. Either way, there have been far too many of these not so memorable, ego-driven projects, where in short time they are viewed as unsuccessful by the golfers.

Be wary of the architect who says he is doing "what (fill in master architect's name) would do if he were here today." This is your first tip that the architect is going to deviate from the original design in an attempt to "modernize," or simply does not know how ridiculous it sounds to make such a sweeping, presumptuous statement!

Like any movement the restoration trend has other pitfalls. Interesting restorations are often held back by golfers who've grown up in the stroke-play mindset, who refuse to let well-intentioned architects bring back old-style or quirky features. As stated earlier, many clubs have held off on major restoration projects because some members are worried the rating or slope will go up and affect their handicap. Others are worried the slope will go down when greens are enlarged to their original sizes, and the course will not be the test it is now. Most of the time though, golfers fight the restoration of certain bunkers that they think will only penalize their own game, when in all likelihood, the bunkers were created by the original architect to make their round of golf more *interesting*.

Still, the increased enjoyment found in restored courses along with the added respect given to properly renovated layouts is one of the great triumphs for classic architecture as well as for modern golf.

More Bethpage Blacks?

I can't go back to the public courses, now. I can't. I won't. I mean, you know what that's like? It's crowded, the grass has big brown patches in it, they don't rake the sand traps. Not to mention the caliber of people you have to play with!
                                                 —Kramer, on Seinfeld

Bethpage State Park on Long Island has one of this country's finest public golf facilities. Four of the five courses there were designed or redesigned by famed architect A.W. Tillinghast in the mid-1930s, while the Green course was created by the fascinating Devereux Emmet. Over the years, the facility was neglected and underappreciated by local government just like so many other municipal golf complexes.

The par-4 eighteenth at Bethpage State Park, Black Course. Despite this over-the-top renovation on the finishing hole, the project was a great success and should be the model for more public course restorations if golf hopes to grow and prosper in the United States. (GEOFF SHACKELFORD)

In 1997, after awarding the 2002 U.S. Open to Bethpage Park's Black Course, the United States Golf Association funded a $2.7 million renovation. The Black's tees, greens, fairway grasses, bunker sand and irrigation system were replaced at the deteriorated but still architecturally sound design. Rees Jones donated his architectural services to the project, and after its opening in 1998, the Bethpage restoration has proven to be a major success, successfully hosting the U.S. Open in 2002.

If golf is going to grow and prosper, the public-golf situation in this country must be returned to respectability. Most of our big-city public courses are in a sad state of decay despite ample budgets and equipment. They are often run by well-intentioned people who don't have any experience operating and maintaining golf courses. Most have maintained parks and don't understand the differences between a golf course and the average park, nor do public officials understand the potential that classic architecture has to satisfy customers and keep new players in the game. Or they are moved around to facilities so often, they don't have time to get to know the nuances of a particular course and its specific maintenance needs.

Classic design has the potential to inspire new and old golfers while creating civic pride. There are hundreds of older facilities merely waiting to be restored and taken care of. The technology to maintain turf and the new, hardier grasses make it almost inexcusable to see the conditions that some of our once great public courses are in. Furthermore, it is discouraging when cities spend huge sums on stadium facilities for professional teams, but neglect to properly maintain publicly supported recreational facilities that are used year-round.

Perhaps the USGA will look into loaning some of its stockpiled millions for more projects like the Bethpage Black renaissance. Such restorations would give numerous golfers across the country a special design to experience, while helping the USGA eliminate much of the elitist stigma that it constantly tries and fails to rid itself of with symbolic but ineffective programs.

Restoring sound design to everyday golf will go much farther than well-intentioned programs that look wonderful on paper but which only inspire young golfers for so long before they are ready to graduate to designs with more challenge. Restoring old public layouts is the best way to keep golf and its traditions alive for future generations.

More Beginner and Fun Courses

As a diverting pastime the little courses are fine, and as a kindergarten for the real game, and as a means of stimulating interest in legitimate golf, I think they are things which a person in popularizing the sport would like to see fostered. And likewise they can serve a useful end if they will show to our city officials, mayors, aldermen, councilmen and commissioners, that a lot of people would like to play golf if they had proper facilities at a low enough cost.   —Bobby Jones

Golf is in desperate need of more par-3, executive and short courses, not only to provide a place for beginners and to ensure prosperity in the sport, but also to lend variety to our golfing options. For some reason we've come to think that only a full-length, eighteen-hole course constitutes "real" golf. Anything else constitutes insignificant golf. Yet many scratch golfers enjoy the experience of a good short course just as much as they would a "championship" design.

Through 1997, there were 14,208 regulation-length layouts in America, but only 1,825 par-3 and executive-length courses. Yet in the British Isles, where golf has thrived consistently for several hundred years, courses come in all shapes, sizes and pars. The layouts were rarely built with standards in mind; they were constructed to fit the existing piece of property. The variety of courses is appreciated, but most golfers are just happy to be outdoors enjoying nature, perhaps contesting a friendly match. They don't care what others think of the type of course they play or the total length or even the number of holes.

The majority of American golf clubs are in the red, gore of the steam shovel, blood drawn by mound builders. We have learned nothing from Scotland and England where the ancient and honorable game can be enjoyed on marvelous links at one-tenth the admission fees, dues, green fees, etc. that prevail in the land of the free.   —Perry Maxwell, golf architect, 1935

American developers, architects and municipalities shy away from building par-3 and executive layouts because they aren't as prestigious, and the profit potential is not as great as in the $150 upscale daily-fee course.

I wonder what's going to happen when baby boomers start retiring and realizing that the corporate office isn't going to pick up those expensive green fees. Or when Generation Xers start having families of their own and realize that spending $150 to do something with their sons and daughters is easier, more rewarding, and more sensible than paying the same amount for six hours of golf?

When these inevitable cyclical changes occur, what will happen to the business model for all of these "prestige" courses? Will they turn private? Will they fold? They certainly seem to have an aversion to the easiest solution: lowering their green fees.

Meanwhile a well-run, interesting par-3 course and driving range can provide a small but steady profit on a piece of property that is not suitable for a full-length eighteen-hole course. Short courses are more affordable and there will always be beginners looking for affordable and less intimidating places to begin the game.

Not only do we need short courses for beginners, but also for the rest of us. Most golfers today have poor short games. You put a wedge in any but the very best hands, and the golfer does not know how to create shots. They are unable to relax their hands and hit big "scoop" shots like Phil Mickelson can, or those wristly little bump-and-run shots like Bobby Jones once played. Creative touch shots are self-taught. And most golfers have no place to learn or experiment with such shotmaking. Par-3 courses are the best places that players can genuinely learn to be comfortable with such shots, or with golf in general.

Downsizing

Do not let certain standards become an obsession. Quality, not length; interest, not the number of holes; distinction, not the size in the greens— these things are worth striving for. A well-designed short course kept up to a high standard will often be more popular than many long, tiresome, unkempt courses which boast of championship length. —Robert Hunter

Golf courses need to get shorter, quainter and quirkier, not longer, larger and more dull.

The game needs to find ways to offer faster rounds while making nine-hole courses more attractive. There are a few fifteen-hole layouts that people love to play because they take three and a half hours to get around in, which is more than enough time to spend with friends, get some much needed fresh air and a little exercise. However, non-eighteen-hole courses are considered poor and golf associations will rarely give them a rating, so golfers who need to establish a handicap stay away.

The old architects warned of the dangers of excessive technology forcing courses to get longer. In 1927 Bobby Jones advocated a regulated ball to keep most golf courses around the 6,300 yard average. We are not far from seeing 8,000-yard courses with even less character than the many dull layouts we have now. The game already takes many hours to play and scares millions away because the challenges are too difficult to overcome. Much of this has to do with the length of courses and the lack of fun most golfers have in playing them. No matter how many equipment advances come along, lengthy courses still fail to bring much joy or improvement to the average golfer's game.

Golf is like a rubber band, in that it can only stretch so far before snapping. There are fractures in the band beginning to appear, and one wonders how much longer golf can withstand this stretching before long courses, technology and the time it takes to play all conspire to fracture the game.

The Seventeenth Hole

The Future

Revolutions, X Golf, Liability, Popularity and Other Prospects for Golf Design

You cannot have progress without change, but not all change is progress.
—John Wooden

Do you ever wonder where golf is headed? —Ben Crenshaw

Golf's evolution will continue to be shaped by strange twists, fads and the influence of money (or lack of capital). Changes in technology, the stock market, the climate and the overall cost of golf are factors that will determine where the game heads. But sometimes the simplest prevailing tastes, or the latest trends found in "Top 100" lists can transform the way courses are designed and why people play (or don't play) golf. Therefore, the future is impossible to predict, but no rule says that hypothesizing is forbidden.

The Character of the Game

All architects will be a lot more comfortable when the powers that be in golf finally solve the ball problem. A great deal of experimentation is now going on and it is to be hoped that before long a solution will be found to control the distance of the elusive pill. If, as in the past, the distance to be gotten with the ball continues to increase, it will be necessary to go to

7,500-and even 8,000-yard courses and more yards mean more acres to
buy, more course to construct, more fairway to maintain and more money
for the golfer to fork out. —William Flynn, golf architect, 1927

Will new courses soon average 7,500 yards, with tournament layouts pushing the 8,500-yard envelope? Is this unreasonable to consider
when Bobby Jones hoped a competition ball would be introduced in
1927 to keep courses around 6,300 yards? We are obviously well past
that plateau and it is hard to imagine golf going that far backwards.
Winged Foot will have par-4s over 500 yards when it hosts the 2006
U.S. Open; Augusta National pushed the par-4 tenth hole over that
barrier in 2002.

Will maintenance in the future become so refined that every course
is immaculate, or will technology develop artificial surfaces that eliminate any need for grass? Maybe golf courses will only hire staff to over-
see the sweeping of the artificial turf and rake the bunkers. Or will
someone even develop a self-cleaning turf and self-raking sand? You
would hope that such money would be spent on providing better edu-
cation for our children or curing deadly diseases.

The next thirty years will depend on how the game deals with
technology, in particular the golf ball. At some point, enough people
will realize the beauty of having a unified sport playing by one set of
rules for competitions and regular golf alike. Playing courses of a reasonable length that take less time and more thought to play should be
the emphasis.

In the foreseeable future, golf professionals will play a power game
and resist change, so that they can make millions on endorsement
deals and their ball companies can keep creating new balls that travel
ridiculous distances. Eventually, television ratings will drop just like
they have in other sports where power overtook the exciting, strategic
elements that were more fun to watch. And how often can consumers
afford upgrading to the latest wave of expensive new equipment? In
golf, the past has proven that instead of resorting to less expensive pur-
chases, most golfers who find the game too costly simply give it up.

Recreational golfers may lose the ability to relate to the long-
hitting robotic professional who appears to have it too easy (even

though we know that hitting a 340-yard drive under pressure is no small feat). As with tennis, golf will suffer because it is one of the last sports where the recreational player can relate to the predicaments of the professional. Once that connection is lost, popularity will suffer.

But because the classic courses can only be changed so much and many golfers want to play their home course the way it was designed, the game may have to split into two versions.

Some golfers—let's call their version Old Golf—will abide by USGA rules and play a version of the sport using a special regulated ball. Others will take to a new consumer-driven version, let's call it X Golf. A game without rules, played with the latest technology, on courses designed to accommodate 400-yard drives. The X version will ignore the values of tradition, history and rules—the very principles that draw so many people to play and talk about golf.

History has shown us that unchecked, overpriced fads like X Golf self-destruct because it becomes too expensive to stay current with the latest technology. X Golf will take too long to play and ultimately will become boring because the player is not faced with strategic dilemmas. Nor will they learn the joys of shaping shots or feel they have a fighting chance against long hitters. X Golf will be a series of eighteen long-drive contests.

After popularity suffers a bit, some will figure out how grand the game once was and how charming it could be again, and they will jump on the tradition bandwagon. There will be the inevitable "retro" movement that takes hold after a plunge in the golf business. Or the retro phase will catch on because society moves to yet another chapter celebrating a version of golf that almost disappeared but was kept alive by a few. Just like retro clothes, retro ballparks and retro films, it'll happen in golf too.

As in baseball, tennis, basketball and other sports, there may eventually be a backlash against the excessive, power-obsessed version of golf, spurred on by a movement to reintroduce shorter, quirkier courses. A regulated ball would allow for shotmaking and architecture to play a role in golf again. Shorter courses that are cheaper and take less time to play could become popular, even hip.

Perhaps a wise operator of public courses will sell golfers on the joys of facing strategic design, and doing it in shorter time, at less cost. After all, there are several major course operators who make much more money off of green fees than they do pro shop sales. Maybe they will look for ways to maintain a popular version of golf with the hope of fostering repeat players who enjoy the value they receive from the golf course operator, and who reject the marketing ploys of an equipment company looking to boost third-quarter earnings. Perhaps it will be the course operators who ultimately stick up for the integrity and good of the game. It's a task that the governing bodies have felt obligated to ignore for quite some time.

Will Liability Affect Golf Architecture?

Does it seem to you that anyone can bring a claim for practically anything? They can. When justice turns on a value judgment, all anyone has to do is make up a theory. Nothing could be easier. Someone always could have done something differently. . . . Literally any harmful event can be a lawsuit, even being struck by lightning, as the city of Denver recently learned when sued by a golfer. —Phillip Howard, author

Golf architects are getting sued all the time and will continue to be blamed for incidents that impact a golfer's rights. Even though we all know a golf ball can hit us from just about any place on a golf course and such an incident may have little to do with a design defect, the number of claims filed against architects and course operators increases each year.

In the future, liability claims may go a step further than just the safety issue. We may see the elimination of interesting golf architecture on the competitive level. It is only a matter of time before a professional golfer who loses a major tournament because of a setup disaster or extreme design element sues an architect or governing body. Maybe a hole location on a too-severe portion of a green or bad maintenance negatively influenced a shot. Someone will lose a tournament in such a way, and with that loss, millions of dollars in bonuses or potential endorsements will be lost. Somewhere, a judge who remembers a similar situation on the links and believes that in theory the golfer's troubles could have been prevented, will sympathize and let the case at least be heard by a jury, which would be enough to effect how architects approach courses hoping to host big-time tournaments.

With the amount of money at stake, a player will feel compelled to turn to the judgments interpreted from the law. After all, if being struck by the most random of all natural occurrences, lightning, constitutes grounds for a lawsuit, then anything is possible.

What Types of Facilities Will Be Popular?

The architects have done nobly; they have fought the good fight, but it ought not to be a fight. The fact that it threatens to become so is the fault of the ball. Whether or not the ball can ever be brought back to its proper limits is another story, but unless it can, the architects will be forever fighting an uphill battle. —*Bernard Darwin, 1936*

No matter what direction the character of the game takes it seems inevitable that country clubs, golf clubs or any kind of place where "everyone knows your name" will regain their popularity in the future. The pain of handing over $150 per round will grow tiresome as Baby Boomers grow older and more frugal, and look to enjoy the simplicities that membership in a club can provide—as long as the club is affordable and a place that fits someone's needs.

When you consider that three million people a year are quitting the game, the question must be asked, "What is driving them away?" We know pace of play, cost and difficulty are the obvious reasons most people quit. However, there are those who stay with golf despite their frustrations because they find a routine that is comforting. They discover that playing with a group of friends whose company they enjoy is comforting. Or maybe just hitting a bucket of balls once a week is all they need, while some day their children will have the time and energy to take up the game at the same club. And when all of this happens at the same facility, the "upscale daily-fee" experience looks like a poor value.

Joining a club, seeing familiar faces, having a place for a family to meet, used to be an enjoyable and affordable pursuit. Clubs in Scotland helped the game prosper because they were less formal and materialistic than in America. They charge far less for membership and dues, and make up the difference with guest green fees. This semi-private model is rarely considered in the United States today, though it was part of the game at one time (you could actually get on Pine Valley as a guest up until the 1960s). Shifting to more semiprivate courses may be the best solution for financially strapped facilities, and certainly would give people the opportunity to experience designs they might otherwise never consider seeing.

Clubs drew many golfers to the game when they were children, either through work as a caddy or tagging along with parents, and clubs develop a long-term loyalty to golf. But in our current "instant gratification" mind-set, the upscale daily-fee course serves a certain purpose for those who can't afford some of the ridiculous initiation fees that modern clubs ask for. These are the same clubs that discourage family golf, particularly junior play or occasional access provided to high school and college teams.

In the long run, however, it is doubtful that the upscale daily-fee model for golf will survive, and it is also doubtful that clubs can keep asking for high initiation fees except in certain neighborhoods. There will soon be many older golfers. Most will be looking for a reasonable place at a reasonable price—golf's version of *Cheers*, where everyone knows your name. Only in golf, they will seek out places where a family can come and socialize, play golf and feel like they are getting some value for their money. And if the design is interesting, a course to get to know and love.

There also figures to be a call for diversity in the types of golf facilities built. (Assuming those with the resources figure out that the majority of golf facilities today scare away beginners, juniors, seniors and women.) Marion Hollins developed a Long Island golf club only for women in the early 1920s, and some consider it remarkable that there has not been an effort to design and build a women's-only course since. Alice Dye has done wonders for designing better forward tees for women, but she has only scratched the surface. Courses designed specifically for women, seniors or kids will appear, as will a few men-only courses. Feathers are ruffled when the men-only courses seemingly "discriminate," but if there are alternatives, few will notice them.

The key to a successful golf course is creating a comfortable environment for those who find golf uncomfortable or awkward. The architecture can play a vital role in making prospective golfers comfortable, and the future may prove this. When golfers step onto the grass to play, they must be provided with designs that pose interesting problems to overcome in the form of attractive hazards, with room for error as well. Such courses will remain popular if they are faithful to these simple notions.

A late-twentieth-century improvement was seen in practice facilities and we can expect that architects and teachers will work together to make practice facilities more fun and functional. Many golfers, particularly in Japan, never set foot on a course or only rarely do, but they enjoy practice because it takes less time and affords enough exercise to relieve stress.

Perhaps the future will see practice facilities with improved surfaces to hit off and better target areas that inspire a golfer's imagination. There may be more computer simulated range stalls where players can envision different on-course scenarios or wear simulation goggles that allow them to play famous holes while standing on a driving-range tee. There are already several interesting indoor variations on this technology. Though it makes some traditionalists cringe, such technology does provide a version of golf that entertains and perhaps even prepares beginners for regular course play. It also involves creative thinking involving interesting architecture-induced decisions, which should spur discussion and interest in the art of design when players are ready to graduate to a real course.

The Revolution That Never Happened

We should revere the cradle of golf with its fine spirit and distinct atmosphere; but we may also be proud of our own development, and strive not only to keep up the standards of our past, but to go on and improve our newer productions, for the ultimate in golf and golf architecture is not yet attained. —*George C. Thomas Jr., 1927*

Architect George Thomas envisioned a time when golfers would long for strategic architecture and enjoy the challenges of a wildly different course setup from day to day. Thomas felt that architects could create multiple courses within an eighteen-hole design so that players would never grow tired of playing the same layout. One day the course might be a 5,900-yard par-69 test with tucked hole locations and a soft touch required to post a fine round. The next day the course could present a 7,100-yard par-73 monster where the player would have their long game tested and their patience rewarded.

Alister MacKenzie also believed that changes in the golfing mindset would occur, with the new forms of strategic design prospering that would outdate his own timeless designs. He also saw "natural" taking on a new meaning when golfers spoke of a course's look and feel. New features would include dramatic bunkers that golfers might assume were existing sand dunes. Or subtly shaped ground contours that looked authentic but were actually carefully crafted to pose interesting shotmaking decisions. Architect Bill Diddle built a bunkerless course in the late 1930s that relied solely on natural contours for interest and as a way to save maintenance dollars.

Clever strategy, intense variety and extreme naturalness. The old architects all believed that they had set the stage for such elements to take hold and transform golf. Such a design revolution would spur growth, led by golfers pursuing their love for experiencing interesting architecture. However, the Great Depression intervened. And after World War II, when golf became popular again, a new take on architecture became popular. In some cases architecture was not given much thought at all. The revolution never happened.

Assuming the Revolution Did Occur

The question of strategy is of the utmost importance to the golf architect and to the golfer, and such strategy will be developed more and more during the coming years. —*George C. Thomas Jr., 1927*

It's 2010 and the USGA has taken firm hold of the game again. A competition ball or reduced flight or weighted ball was introduced, and

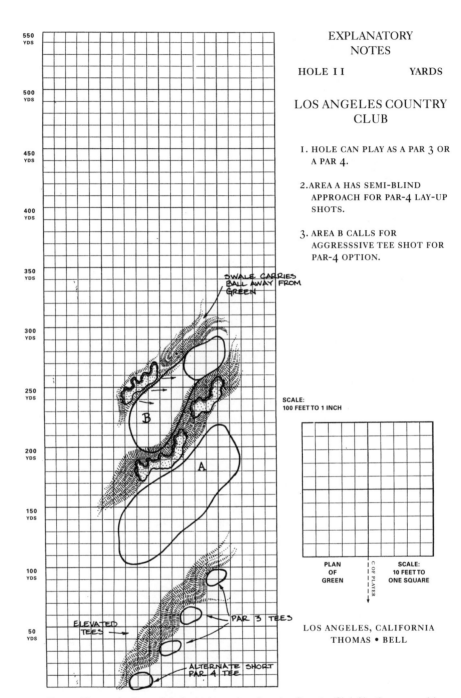

550
YDS

500
YDS

450
YDS

400
YDS

350
YDS

300
YDS

250
YDS

200
YDS

150
YDS

100
YDS

50
YDS

EXPLANATORY
NOTES

HOLE I I   YARDS

LOS ANGELES COUNTRY
CLUB

1. HOLE CAN PLAY AS A PAR 3 OR
A PAR 4.

2. AREA A HAS SEMI-BLIND
APPROACH FOR PAR-4 LAY-UP
SHOTS.

3. AREA B CALLS FOR
AGGRESSSIVE TEE SHOT FOR
PAR-4 OPTION.

SWALE CARRIES
BALL AWAY FROM
GREEN

B

A

SCALE:
100 FEET TO 1 INCH

PLAN   SCALE:
OF   10 FEET TO
GREEN   ONE SQUARE

C OF PLAYER

LOS ANGELES, CALIFORNIA
THOMAS • BELL

ELEVATED
TEES

PAR 3 TEES

ALTERNATE SHORT
PAR 4 TEE

George Thomas's eleventh-hole design at Los Angeles Country Club North was one idea
for the future of golf. The hole could alternate as a par-3 or a par-4 and play many different ways, creating the ultimate in day-to-day playing variety. Such surprises could make
playing the same course repeatedly more interesting and challenging. (GIL HANSE)

within a few years became the ball all golfers used again. Once-out-dated Cherry Hills will be hosting the 2018 U.S. Open. Golfers are clamoring to play dramatic strategic holes that test their minds and imaginations as much as the perfection of their swing planes. The retro revolution has begun; championship courses are averaging 6,700 yards. Alright, so I'm a dreamer. But assuming golf takes this dramatic turn, what kind of design ideas might we see?

The first trend would be toward variety within each hole design. George Thomas was well ahead of his time when he came up with different ways a hole could be presented from day to day. The Scottish game thrives on the ever-changing conditions that make each day a new adventure on the links. But golf in America does not have such dramatic shifts in conditions nor the interesting linksland to accentuate the conditions, thus variety has to be created by the architect.

Consider the George Thomas "multiple holes within a hole" concept, depicted in this chapter by Gil Hanse. Some might say Thomas's ideas require too much land or too much leniency from golfers trying to post a decent score, but the goal is always the same. Ask the player to consider tempting situations, present them with variety and lure them into taking risks. Golf with an intelligent purpose not only tells us who the best player is, but it also creates the most enjoyable golf.

The Last Putt

If I can supply a thought you may remember it and you may not. But if I can make you think a thought for yourself, I have indeed added to your stature.   —*Elbert Hubbard*

In this day where everything from the news to television shows to art apparently needs to be interactive to capture the attention span of the public, golf architecture is long overdue in achieving the popularity it deserves. Not only is there joy in studying and understanding golf course design, but it is one of the only genuine interactive art forms alive.

Golf course design will continue to inspire as long as the architects and players continue to adhere to the words of Bobby Jones: "We want our golf courses to make us think. However much we may enjoy whaling the life out of the little white ball, we soon grow tired of playing a golf course that does not give us problems in strategy as well as skill."

But even more important than the role of the architect is the responsibility of golfers everywhere, who should remember the words of Alister MacKenzie: "Golf is a game, and talk and discussion is all to the interests of the game. Anything that keeps the game alive and prevents us being bored with it is an advantage. Anything that makes us think about it, talk about it, and dream about it is all to the good and prevents the game from becoming dead."

Keep dreaming, thinking and talking about golf. The future of the game is in your hands.

The Eighteenth Hole

Appendix and Acknowledgments

List, List, O list —William Shakespeare

Above Any "Ranking"

The National Golf Links of America
   (NY)

The Old Course at St. Andrews
   (Scotland)

Masterpieces

Cypress Point (CA)

Merion GC—East (PA)

Pebble Beach (CA)

Pinehurst #2 (NC)

Pine Valley (NJ)

Riviera (CA)

Royal Dornoch (Scotland)

Royal Portrush (N. Ireland)

Sand Hills (NE)

Shinnecock Hills (NY)

Somerset Hills (NJ)

Classic Designs

Baltimore CC—East (MD)

Crystal Downs (MI)

Garden City Golf Club (NY)

Inverness GC (OH)

Oakmont (PA)

Pasatiempo (CA)

Plainfield GC (NJ)

Royal County Down (N. Ireland)

San Francisco Golf Club (CA)

Winged Foot—West (NY)

Special Places

Augusta National (GA)

Baltusrol (NJ)

Bethpage State Park—Black (NY)

Cherry Hills (CO)

The Creek Club (NY)

Cuscowilla (GA)

Friar's Head (NY)

Hidden Creek (NJ)

Lahinch (Ireland)

Los Angeles Country Club—North (CA)

Maidstone (NY)

Muirfield (Scotland)

Olympic Club (CA)

Prestwick (Scotland)

TPC Sawgrass (FL)

Valley Club of Montecito (CA)

Maybe Not Well-Known, but Courses with Special Character

Armand Hammer GC (CA)

Austin Golf Club (TX)

Brook Hollow (TX)

Crail GC (Scotland)

Delaware Springs GC (TX)

Detroit GC—South (MI)

Easthampton (NY)

Elie GC (Scotland)

Engineers (NY)

Franklin Hills (MI)

Huntington Country Club (NY)

Inniscrone GC (PA)

Legends GC—Heathland (SC)

Long Cove (SC)

Pacific Grove Muni (CA)

Southfork GC—Hanse Nine (NY)

Stonebridge (NY)

Talking Stick—North and South (AZ)

Tallgrass Golf Course (NY)

U. of Michigan GC (MI)

Whistling Straits (WI)

Designs I Have Yet to Experience

Royal Melbourne (Australia)

Kingston Heath (Australia)

Royal Adelaide (Australia)

Sunningdale (England)

Woodhall Spa (England)

Chicago Golf Club (IL)

Seminole (FL)

Newport CC (RI)

Myopia Hunt Club (MA)

The Country Club (MA)

Essex CC (MA)

Fisher's Island (NY)

Prairie Dunes (KS)

Wild Horse (NE)

Yale (CT)

Cape Breton Highlands (Canada)

Banff (Canada)

Courses I Would Most Like to Have Played in Their Early Days (Before Mother Nature or Someone Else Altered Them)

The Old Course at St. Andrews
(Scotland)

Cypress Point (CA)

Pasatiempo (CA)

Riviera (CA)

Riviera Par-3 (CA)

Bel-Air (CA)

Augusta National (GA)

Engineers GC (NY)

La Cumbre (CA)

Lido (NY)

Timber Point (NY)

Ojai Valley (CA)

Oakland Hills (MI)

Sharp Park GC (CA)

Best Match-Play Courses

The Old Course at St. Andrews
(Scotland)

The Country Club (MA)

PGA West—Stadium (CA)

Augusta National (GA)

Favorite Golf Books and Source Material

Hazards, Alec Bauer

The Way of Golf, Robert Brown

A Feel For the Game, Ben Crenshaw

Golf Course Architecture, H. S. Colt
and C. H. Alison

Golf Course Design, Geoffrey Cornish
and Robert Muir Graves

Links Golf, Paul Daley

Golf Between Two Wars, Bernard Darwin

The Golf Courses of the British Isles,
Bernard Darwin

The Greatest of Them All, Martin Davis

The Anatomy of a Golf Course, Tom
Doak

The Confidential Guide, Tom Doak

Bury Me in a Pot Bunker, Pete Dye

Aspects of Golf Course Architecture,
Fred Hawtree

The Art Spirit, Robert Henri

Pebble Beach Golf Links, Neal
Hotelling

The Links, Robert Hunter

Golf Course Architecture, Michael
Hurdzan

Golf is a Funny Game, Ken Janke

Fairways and Greens, Dan Jenkins

Rude Behavior, Dan Jenkins

Golf's Magnificent Challenge, Robert Trent Jones

Rough Meditations, Bradley S. Klein

The Golf Courses of Old Tom Morris, Robert Kroeger

Scotland's Gift—Golf, C. B. Macdonald

Golf Architecture, Alister MacKenzie

The Spirit of St. Andrews, Alister MacKenzie

Wry Stories on the Road Hole, Sid Matthew

My Story, Jack Nicklaus

The Making of the Masters, David Owen

Golfer at Large, Charles Price

The World Atlas of Golf, Price, Wind, et al.

Golf Has Never Failed Me, Donald Ross

Pine Valley: A Chronicle, Warner Shelley

The Art of Golf, Walter Simpson

The Book of the Links, Martin Sutton

Golf Architecture in America, George C. Thomas Jr.

The Course Beautiful, A. W. Tillinghast

Reminiscences of the Links, A. W. Tillinghast

The Story of American Golf, Herbert Warren Wind

Herbert Warren Winds Golf Book, Herbert Warren Wind

The Architectural Side of Golf, Wethered and Simpson

Missing Links, Daniel Wexler

The Architects of Golf, Ron Whitten and Geoffrey Cornish

The Quotable Golfer, Robert Windeler

Some of the Best Things Ever Said About Golf Course Design

Golf is a game and not a mathematical business, and . . . it is of vital importance to avoid anything that tends to make the game simple and stereotyped. On the contrary, every endeavor should be made to increase its strategy, variety, mystery, charm and elusiveness so that we shall never get bored with it, but continue to pursue it with increasing zest, as many of the old stalwarts of St. Andrews do, for the remainder of our lives.

—Dr. Alister MacKenzie

Hazards make golf dramatic; and the thrills that come to one who ventures wisely and succeeds are truly delectable. Without hazards golf would be but a dull sport, with the life and soul gone out of it. No longer would it attract the lusty and the adventurous, but would be left to those who favor some form of insipid perambulation, suited to the effeminate and senile. —Robert Hunter

Sinfully juggled. —A. W. Tillanghast on changes to a
                              Donald Ross design

When it is more generally realized that a truly fine round of golf represents the accurate fitting together of shots that bear a distinct relation to each other, with the greens opening up to the best advantage after placed drives, then the game will be a truer test of all the mighty ones than so many courses now present. —A. W. Tillinghast

Golf at its best is a perpetual adventure, that it consists in investing not in gilt-edged securites but in comparatively speculative stock; that it ought to be a risky business. —Bernard Darwin

Best Things Ever Said by Non-Golfers (but Easily Linked to Golf Design)

A man has got to know his limitations. —"Dirty" Harry Calahan

I can avoid anything but temptation —Oscar Wilde

The past is never dead. It's not even past. —William Faulkner

The masters must be copied over and over again . . . and it is only after proving yourself a good copyist that you should reasonably be permitted to draw a radish from nature. —Edgar Degas

Best Restorations

Baltimore CC (MD), by Brian Silva and Doug Petersan

Pasatiempo (CA) (in progress), by Tom Doak and Jim Urbina

Cypress Point (CA) (in progress), by Jeff Markow

Valley Club (CA) (in progress), by Tom Doak, Jim Urbina and Sean McCormick

Plainfield (NJ) (in progress), by Gil
Hanse and Jim Wagner

Huntington CC (NY) (in progress),
by Myles McLaughlin

Worst Tournament-Influenced Renovations to Great Courses That Should Have Been Left Alone

Inverness GC (OH), by George and
Tom Fazio

Oak Hill GC—East Course (NY), by
George and Tom Fazio

Merion GC—East (PA), by Tom
Fazio

Favorite Golf Landscape Paintings

The "Postage Stamp" Green at Troon,
by Harry Rountree

*Westward Ho! The Carry at the Fifth
Tee*, by Harry Rountree

St. Andrews, by Harry Rountree

Prestwick, by Harry Rountree

Portmarnock (Coming Home), by
Harry Rountree

Cassiobury Park, by Harry Rountree

Seventeenth at Cypress Point, circa 1929
by Mike Miller

Seventh at Sand Hills, by Mike Miller

Third at Fox Hills, by Mike Miller

Thirteenth at Augusta, circa 1932, by
Mike Miller

*Clubhouse Study, Cypress Point, circa
1930*, by Mike Miller

If I Had Control of the USGA's Millions, the Public Courses that I'd Invest in for a Design and Maintenance Restoration Designed to Spread the Gospel of Golf

Belmont Golf Course, Richmond,
Virginia (A. W. Tillinghast)

Bethpage Park, Farmington, New
York (the other courses)
(A. W. Tillinghast)

Biltmore Hotel, Miami, Florida
(Donald Ross)

Brackenridge Park, San Antonio,
Texas (A. W. Tillinghast)

Brookside #1 and #2 Golf Courses,
Pasadena, California (Billy
Bell/A. W. Tillinghast)

Cedar Crest, Dallas, Texas (A. W.
Tillinghast)

Cobbs Creek, Philadelphia, Pennsylvania (Hugh Wilson)

Eastmoreland, Portland, Oregon (H.
Chandler Egan)

Eisenhower Park—Red, East Meadow, New York (Devereux Emmet)

Francis Byrne Municipal, East Orange, New Jersey (Charles Banks)

George Wright Memorial, Boston, Massachusetts (Donald Ross)

Griffith Park Golf Courses, Los Angeles, California (George Thomas)

The Hill Course at the French Lick, Indiana (Donald Ross)

Keney Park, Hartford, Connecticut (Devereux Emmet)

Kebo Valley Course, Bar Harbor, Maine (Herbert Leeds)

Knoll Golf Course, Boonton, New Jersey (Charles Banks)

Lakewood Golf Course, Lakewood, New Jersey (Walter Travis)

Leatherstocking, Cooperstown, New York (Devereux Emmet)

Manikiki, Cleveland Metropark System, Ohio (Donald Ross)

Mark Twain Municipal, Elmira, New York (Donald Ross)

Memorial Park, Houston (John Bremedus)

Montauk Downs, Long Island, New York (Robert Trent Jones)

North Fulton, Atlanta, Georgia (H. Egan Chandler)

Norwich Municipal, Groton, Connecticut (Donald Ross)

Rackham Park, Detroit, Michigan (Donald Ross)

Seaview—Bay Course, Absecon, New Jersey (Donald Ross)

Shawnee On-the-Delaware, Shawnee, Pennsylvania (A. W. Tillinghast)

Sharp Park, San Mateo, California (Alister MacKenzie)

Shennecosset, Groton, Connecticut (Donald Ross)

Sleepy Hollow, Brecksville, Ohio (Stanley Thompson)

Tennison Park Municipal, Dallas, Texas (John Bredemus)

Timber Point, Long Island, New York (H. S. Colt and C .H. Alison)

Triggs Memorial, Providence, Rhode Island (Donald Ross)

Wachusett, West Boylston, Massachusetts (Donald Ross)

Wellshire Golf Course, Englewood, Colorado (Donald Ross)

Wilmington Municipal, Wilmington, North Carolina (Donald Ross)

Winnapaug, Westerly, Rhode Island (Donald Ross)

ACKNOWLEDGMENTS

The author wishes to thank the following for their loyal support: Gil Hanse for beautiful drawings and faith in the author's ability to make the leap from writer to design consultant; Ben Crenshaw and Bill Coore for building classic courses, sharing your insights and raising the bar for all of modern golf design; Dan Proctor and Dave Axland for your wisdom and efforts to build interesting courses; Sandra Sheffer and Marge Dewey for years of research help and for holding the Ralph Miller Golf Library together, and to Saundra for thinking of the book title.

Special thanks to those associated with Rustic Canyon Golf Course, a project that significantly influenced the information and views in this book: Jim Wagner for your common sense approach to design; Rodney and Carolyn Hine, Craig Price, Lisa Woodburn, Charlie Amos, Jeff Hicks, Mark Wipf and the hard working construction crew for all of your efforts.

Heartfelt gratitude to all of those who have helped shape the author's interest in golf course design and supported all efforts to write about it: my parents Lynn and Diane, my grandparents Ray, Louise and Etta, Mike Miller, Alex Galvan, Eric Shortz, Daniel Wexler, Ron Forse, Mike Riedel, Ron Papell, Tommy Naccarato, Todd Connelly, Jim Langley, Geoffrey Cornish, Jim Frank, Joe McNeely, Patty Moran, Doug Petersan, Tom Paul, Dick Youngscap, Brad Klein, Ran Morrisett, Bob William, George Bahto, Ken Bakst, Martha Reddington, Harrie Perkins and to three people I always wanted to meet but never got the chance: Ralph W. Miller, Bill Bryant and Jean Bryant. Several fine people inspired my interest in course management, the golf swing and golf psychology, and each has devoted their life and talent to the game: John Geiberger, Kurt Schuette, Jeff Gove, Maury DeMots, Jim Empey, Dr. Deborah Graham, Mac O'Grady, Fran Pirozzolo, Jim Petralia, Carl Welty and Jim Schaeffer. And I must credit Lee Harris for explaining the facets of design simulation software and the popularity of that fast-growing segment of the armchair-architect population.

Special thanks to all of the superintendents and golf professionals who have allowed me to visit their courses and ask questions. Most of all, this book would never have been possible if not for the faith and perseverance of Marilyn Allen and Bob Diforio.

The Nineteenth Hole

Index

Architectural Side of Golf, The (Wethered and Simpson), 13, 88
Art of Golf, The (Simpson), 5, 178
Augusta National Golf Club, 260–62, 275
 Amen Corner at, 77–81, 96
 architectural mastery and, 154–55, 157, 159
 course management and, 182–83
 eleventh hole at, 72, 77–79
 humor and, 72
 maintenance and, 215, 221–22
 Masters at, xiii–xiv, 79–81, 95, 182, 222, 261–62, 265
 and Old Course at St. Andrews, 22, 24, 101, 104
 strategic design of, 51
 temptations at, 76–81
 thirteenth hole at, xiii–xiv, 77–80, 87, 92–96, 101, 104, 182–83, 261–62
 twelfth hole at, 77–79, 182

Ballybunion's Old Course, 204, 215
Baltusrol Golf Club, 164–65
Bandon Dunes Golf Club, 56, 203–4
Banks, Charles, 41, 145–46
baseball, 189, 276
 comparisons between golf and, 3, 10–11, 20, 30–31, 49, 62, 87
 humor and, 60
 schools of design in, 29–31
beauty:
 architectural mastery and, 152, 161

classic course designs and, 114, 117, 120–22, 127–28, 135–36, 143–44
course management and, 177
daydreaming and, 197, 199
Behr, Max, 36
Bel–Air Country Club:
 humor and, 67–69
 twelfth hole at, 68–69
Bell, Billy, 147, 164, 176, 249, 282
 great holes and, 96–97
Bendelow, Tom, 147–48
Berra, Yogi, 261
Bethpage State Park, Black Course, 164, 269–70
 classic design of, 111, 113, 137–44
 eighteenth hole at, 269
 fifth hole at, 141–42
 fourth hole at, 140, 142
 seventeenth hole at, 144
 temptations at, 77, 139
 U.S. Open at, 139, 143, 270
Brown, Robert, 9, 228
bunkers, *see* hazards
Burbeck, Joe, 137, 141
Burke, Jackie, 77, 81

Caddyshack, 211–12
Campbell, Sir Guy, 202
championship golf, temptation in, 261–62
Chapin, Edwin, 73
chip shots, 265
 great holes and, 105

chip shots (*cont'd*)
  maintenance and, 216
  temptation and, 74
Colt, H. S., 147, 153–54
  classic course designs and, 115, 118
  strategic design and, 36, 38
Concerning Golf (Low), 7, 81, 87
Connelly, Michael, 188
Coore, Bill, 41, 151, 168, 181, 230
Cotton, Henry, 25
Country Club of Indianapolis, 168
Country Life, 255
course management, 5–7, 172–85, 266
  daydreaming and, 199
  great holes and, 89–90, 95, 98,
    101–103, 182–83
  master architects and, 169
  pars and, 179–80, 185
  pride and, 180
  principles of, 183–85
  and schools of design, 30, 38, 49,
    175–77, 184
  temptation and, 75–77, 80–81, 176,
    178, 182–83
  tricky issues in, 173
Crenshaw, Ben, xiv, 6, 41, 92, 150, 181,
  230, 274
Crump, George:
  classic course designs and, 114–18
  humor and, 70
Crystal Downs Country Club, 154, 158
Cypress Point Golf Club, 7, 154, 260–61
  humor and, 66
  sixteenth hole at, 87, 92, 105–10,
    182–83

Darwin, Bernard, 9, 14, 114, 187, 278
daydreaming, xviii, 186–87, 195–99
  about banal, boring holes, 197–98
  about overbuilt holes, 197–99
  rules for, 196
Demaret, Jimmy, 39
"Designers and Developers" (Jenkins),
  210
Diddle, Bill, 281
Doak, Tom, 41, 168, 175
  course management and, 180, 182
  maintenance and, 214
Dobereiner, Peter, 9, 15, 53
drives, 149, 262, 265, 282
  classic course designs and, 122, 125,
    127, 131–32, 142
  course management and, 176
  creating your own holes and, 254
  daydreaming and, 198
  in future, 276
  great holes and, 98–99, 101, 104, 108,
    110

maintenance and, 218, 221
master architects and, 166, 171
Rustic Canyon and, 247, 249
temptation and, 74
Duval, David, 71–72
Dye, Alice, 168–69, 171, 237–38, 279
Dye, Pete, xvi
  career summary of, 168
  course management and, 177
  humor and, 60–61, 72, 171
  maintenance and, 220–22
  mastery of, 145, 153, 168–71
  notable designs of, 168, 170
  and schools of design, 41–45, 53–54
  temptation and, 171

Easthampton Golf Club, 225
Egan, H. Chandler, 120–21, 123–26

fairways, 260, 264–67, 270
  classic course designs and, 117, 125,
    133
  contours of, 219–20
  course management and, 177, 181
  daydreaming and, 197
  great holes and, 92–98, 101–103,
    106–8
  humor and, 63, 66, 71–72
  maintenance and, 213–21, 225, 227
  master architects and, 170
  of Old Course at St. Andrews, 16–17,
    20–21, 23–24, 32
  Rustic Canyon and, 238–39, 242,
    244–45, 247
  and schools of design, 32, 35
  temptation and, 74–76, 81–83
  training your design eye and, 192
fairway woods, fairway woods shots,
  261–62
  great holes and, 99, 101
Faldo, Nick, xiii–xiv, 21, 261
Fazio, George, 267
Fazio, Jim, 71
Fazio, Tom, 204, 267
  on schools of design, 43, 55
featheries, 18
Feherty, David, 219
Fenway Golf Club, 164, 167
flag, flagstick, 205–6
Floyd, Raymond, 41, 200
flyer lies, 219
Flynn, William, 6–7, 38–39, 75, 147,
  275
framing school, 43–45, 55–57
  course management and, 175–77
freeway school, 41–43, 53–55
Furgol, Ed, 25

golf club, definition of, 206–7
Golf Course Architecture (Hurdzan), 41
golf course architecture and architects:
  appreciation and passion for, xv
  armchair, xvi–xvii, 195, 197, 199,
    250–57
  balance in, 258
  complexity of, 57
  elements of, xiv–xvi, 7–13
  finances in, 259–61
  injecting humor into, xvi–xviii, 59–73,
    129–30, 164, 171, 193, 254–55
  as interactive art form, xv–xvi, 1–6,
    13, 283–84
  language of, 200–210
  minimalism in, 32, 45
  misinterpretation of, 4–5
  mythological name status awarded to,
    145–46
  presenting tempting shots in, xvii, 59,
    73–86, 88–89, 91, 94, 96–98,
    100–101, 104–9, 139, 171, 176, 178,
    182–83, 193, 227, 254, 261–62, 283
  successful, 146–47
  suits against, 277–78
  types of, 147–53, 155
  uniqueness of, 6–7
golf courses:
  assembly–line approach to, 52, 57
  for beginners and fun, 271–72
  classic, 111–44
  downsizing of, 272–73
  future popularity of, 278–80
  naming of, 207–10
  rankings of, 10, 55, 57–58
  restoration of, 267–71
  setting up of, 264–66
Golfer at Large (Price), 29
Golf Illustrated, 164
Golf is My Game (Jones), 262–63
grain, 220–21
Grant, Douglas, 120–21, 123–24
grass, grasses, 258, 264–65, 267, 269–70
  classic course designs and, 135, 139,
    142
  cool–season, 212–14
  course management and, 177
  in future, 275
  great holes and, 87
  and language of architecture, 204
  long, 216–18
  maintenance and, 211–18, 220–24,
    227
  master architects and, 169
  and Old Course at St. Andrews, 15
  Rustic Canyon and, 234–35, 237–38,
    242–44, 249
  and schools of design, 54

short, 214–16, 218, 220–21
temptation and, 74, 80
warm–season, 212–14
great holes, 87–110, 280
  course management and, 89–90, 95,
    98, 101–103, 182–83
  elements of, 87–92
  examples of, 87, 92–110
  temptations of, 88–89, 91, 94, 96–98,
    100–101, 104–9, 182, 261–62
green fees, green committees, 206
greens, xiii–xiv, 4, 13, 149, 238–42,
    253–54, 261–66, 268, 270, 282
  Augusta National and, 182
  California, 223
  classic course designs and, 114,
    117–25, 127–28, 131–35, 140–41,
    143–44
  course management and, 174, 176–79,
    181–82, 184
  in creating your own holes, 254, 257
  daydreaming and, 196–99
  double, 15–16, 20
  drainage of, 228
  in future, 277
  grain on, 220–21
  great holes and, 88–90, 92–99,
    101–109, 182
  humor and, 59–61, 63–71
  maintenance and, 211–12, 214–24,
    227–28, 264
  master architects and, 155–58,
    161–62, 164–71
  and Old Course at St. Andrews,
    15–21, 23–24, 26–28
  Rustic Canyon and, 239–42, 244–47,
    249
  and schools of design, 30, 33, 37, 40,
    49, 54, 56, 92
  speeds of, 221–22, 227–28, 265
  stymie and, 262–63
  temptation and, 74–75, 77–82, 84–86,
    254
  training your design eye and, 187,
    189–94
  USGA, 223–24
ground features and scale, 189–91
gutta percha balls, 18

Hagen, Walter, 264
hands–on designers, 151–53, 155
Hannigan, Frank, 166
Hanse, Gil, 148, 174, 231, 251, 283
  Rustic Canyon and, 233, 236–41,
    243–44
Haultain, Arnold, 2
hazards, 4, 12–13, 149, 258, 260,
    266–70

hazards (*cont'd*)
  classic course designs and, 111, 114,
    117, 120–21, 123, 125–26, 130–35,
    137, 139–43
  course management and, 174, 177–84
  in creating your own holes, 251–55
  daydreaming and, 197–99
  definitions of, 202
  in future, 275, 281
  great holes and, 87–90, 92–100,
    102–3, 105–8, 182
  humor and, 60–61, 63, 65–72
  and language of architecture, 201–2
  maintenance and, 214–16, 224–28
  master architects and, 155–57, 165,
    167, 169–71
  modern, 266–67
  and Old Course at St. Andrews, 15,
    17, 19–21, 23–24, 31–32
  Rustic Canyon and, 235, 238–44,
    246–47, 249
  and schools of design, 30–32, 35,
    38–39, 41, 43, 49, 54, 56, 92
  temptation and, 75–77, 80–83, 85–86
  training your design eye and, 186–87,
    189–95
Henri, Robert, 57
heroic school, 39–41, 52–53, 117
Hine, Rodney, 174, 238–39
Hoch, Scott, 25
Hogan, Ben, 52, 67, 173, 183
hole variety, 114, 116–17, 121–25,
  127–30, 137–39
Hollins, Marion, 154, 279
  great holes and, 105–8
Hope, Bob, 171
Howard, Phillip, 277
Hubbard, Elbert, 112, 283
Hunter, Robert, 17, 154, 156, 192, 273
  great holes and, 90, 105–8
hunting, 3, 115, 143
Hurdzan, Michael, 41, 234
Hutchison, Horace, 17, 51

Inverness Golf Club, 160, 268
iron shots, 258, 261–62, 265
  course management and, 179
  great holes and, 95, 101, 104
  maintenance and, 219
  temptation and, 74, 78, 80
irregularity, 190–91

Jenkins, Dan, 9, 150, 183, 208, 210,
  263
Jones, Bobby, xiii, xv, xix, 1, 183,
  258–59, 271–73, 275, 283–84
  Augusta National and, 154–55, 157,
    159, 215

course management and, 179
great holes and, 92–93, 95–96, 105
humor and, 59, 66–67, 72
and language of architecture, 202
master architects and, 150–51,
  154–55, 157–59
and Old Course at St. Andrews, 22,
  105
and schools of design, 38, 47, 50–51
on stymie, 259, 262–63
on temptation, 79
Jones, Colonel Bob, 72
Jones, Rees, 143, 270
Jones, Robert Trent, Sr., 177, 205
  heroic design and, 39–41, 52
  humor and, 60–61

Keeler, O. B., 254
King's Course, Gleneagles, 201
Klein, Bradley, 30

Lahinch, 65, 218
land planners, 147–48
Langford, William, 38, 41, 168–69, 252
Lema, Tony, 14
lengths, 10–11, 272–76
  classic course designs and, 116, 134,
    138–39
  course management and, 178–79, 185
  in creating your own holes, 251
  in future, 274–76, 281–83
  great holes and, 101
  maintenance and, 228
  of Old Course at St. Andrews, 19
  temptation and, 76, 80
  training your design eye and, 187
links courses:
  definition of, 202–204, 208–9
  maintenance and, 214–15
Longhurst, Henry, 9, 100–101, 201
Los Angeles Country Club North, 282
Low, John, 7, 81, 87, 250

Macdonald, Charles Blair, 11, 13, 64–65,
  196, 209, 236, 255, 266
  classic course designs and, 128–35
  course management and, 180
  humor and, 65
  Redans and, 84–86
  and schools of design, 36, 38, 50
Mack, Connie, 115
MacKenzie, Alister, 1, 12, 38–39, 45,
  188, 251, 255, 260, 281, 284
  Augusta National and, 154–55, 157,
    159, 215
  career summary of, 154
  classic course designs and, 111,
    120, 124–25

daydreaming and, 196–97, 199
great holes and, 91–96, 105–10
humor and, 62–63, 66–67, 70, 72
maintenance and, 216
mastery of, 145, 147, 151–60, 163, 165
on match vs. stroke play, 62–63
on natural design, 31
notable designs of, 154, 158
and Old Course at St. Andrews, 21,
    31, 62–63, 154, 157, 243
strategic design and, 36, 38, 51
temptation and, 79
Maidstone Club, 217, 224
maintenance, 6, 211–29, 258, 270
architectural mastery and, 152
classic course designs and, 121
creating your own holes and, 255
daydreaming and, 197
fairways and, 213–21, 225, 227
flyer lies and, 219
in future, 275, 277, 281
greens and, 211–12, 214–24, 227–28,
    264
hazards and, 214–16, 224–28
humor and, 65
and Old Course at St. Andrews, 16,
    18–19
Rustic Canyon and, 239–40, 242–43
and schools of design, 29, 54–55
stimpmeters and, 221–22
and talking to superintendents,
    226–29
temptation and, 227
training your design eye and, 189, 194
match play, 178, 259, 262–64
humor and, 61–63
Maxwell, Perry, 38, 70, 154, 156, 158,
    271
Mayo, Joe, 126
memorability, 189, 193–94
Merion Golf Club, 115, 206, 231
Michigan, University of, 70
Mickelson, Phil, 262, 272
Morris, Old Tom, 17–19, 31–32, 47–48,
    50, 129, 159, 164, 206, 224
humor and, 66–67
Muirfield, 61, 71
Murray, Jim, 96
Mystery of Golf, The (Haultain), 2

National Golf Links of America, 204,
    209
classic design of, 111–13, 128–38
eighth hole at, 131
first hole at, 134
fourth hole (Redan) at, 84–85, 133
humor and, 64, 66, 129–30
second hole at, 64

seventeenth hole at, 132
Short Hole at, 66
sixth hole at, 134
water tower/windmill at, 135–36
naturalness, natural school, 31–33,
    35–36, 38, 47–50, 53, 57, 260–61
classic course designs and, 125, 133
in creating your own holes, 253
daydreaming and, 198
in future, 281
great holes and, 88–91, 95–96,
    99–101, 104–8
humor and, 65–66
maintenance and, 220
master architects and, 163, 169
Rustic Canyon and, 239
training your design eye and, 190–91
Navarro, Tony, xiv
Neville, Jack, 120–21, 123–24
Nicklaus, Jack, 41, 150, 168, 183, 255,
    262
classic course designs and, 120, 122
daydreaming and, xviii, 186, 195
great holes and, 94, 96–98, 101
humor and, 61, 71
on Old Course at St. Andrews, 19, 22
and schools of design, 54–55
Norman, Greg, xiii–xiv, 261
North Berwick, 85–86, 133

Oak Hill, 160, 267–68
Oakland Hills, 160, 264
Oakley Golf Club, 159
Oakmont, 29, 225
Olmsted, Frederick Law, 51, 152, 157
Owen, David, 72

paper effect, 255
pars, 8–10
classic course designs and, 116, 139
course management and, 179–80, 185
in future, 281–82
great holes and, 88, 92–94, 96, 98,
    100–101, 105–8
and Old Course at St. Andrews, 24,
    179
Price on, 9–10
and schools of design, 31, 33–34, 37,
    40, 42
temptation and, 74, 77
Pebble Beach Golf Links, 51, 203
classic design of, 111, 113, 120–28
seventh hole at, 10, 126
sixteenth hole at, 127
third hole at, 123
thirteenth hole at, 124–25, 127
U.S. Opens at, 121
penal school, 34–39, 41, 43, 48–51, 56

penal school (*cont'd*)
  classic course designs and, 117
  course setups and, 265
  creating your own holes and, 252–53
  daydreaming and, 196–99
  great holes and, 91–92, 103, 106
  master architects and, 166
  temptation and, 76, 83–84
  training your design eye and, 190–91, 193
Pinehurst Resort, Pinehurst Resort #2, 55, 209, 215
  Ross's mastery and, 151–52, 159–63
Pine Valley Golf Club, 7, 29, 51, 166, 209, 260–61, 279
  classic design of, 111–20, 137–39, 143
  eighteenth hole at, 70
  fifth hole at, 10, 119
  humor and, 70
  seventh hole at, 118
  temptation at, 77
  tenth hole at, 119
pins, pin placement, 13, 205–6
pitch shots, 105, 107–8, 245
Plainfield Country Club, 162
playability:
  in creating your own holes, 253, 255
  great holes and, 88, 91–92, 95–96, 100, 105, 108–9
player–architects, 150–51
Prestwick, 17–18, 31
Price, Charles, 9–10, 29, 206–7

randomness, 190–91
Raynor, Seth, 38, 41, 85, 168–69, 255
Redans, 84–86, 133
Riviera Country Club, 238
  humor and, 67, 69
  eighth hole at, 176
  sixth hole at, 67, 69
  tenth hole at, 87, 92, 96–100, 182–83
Robertson, Allan, 16–19, 31, 47, 206
  great holes and, 100, 102, 105
Robertson, R. C., 60
Ross, Donald, 53, 267–68
  career summary of, 159
  humor and, 67
  mastery of, 145, 147, 151–53, 159–65
  notable designs of, 159–63
  and Old Course at St. Andrews, 50, 159
  strategic design and, 36, 38, 50
Rough Meditations (Klein), 30
roughs, 265–67
  course management and, 179
  maintenance and, 216–19
  temptation and, 76
routing, 7–8

classic course designs and, 113–14, 116–17, 121–25, 129–30, 138–39, 143
creating your own holes and, 255
master architects and, 156, 160–61, 165
of Old Course at St. Andrews, 23–24, 31, 130
Rustic Canyon and, 236–37, 239
and schools of design, 31
Royal County Down, 227
Royal Dornoch, 159, 163
Royce, Josiah, xv
Rude Behavior (Jenkins), 208
Russell, Alex, 154, 156
Rustic Canyon Golf Club, 230–49, 256
  approval process for, 234–36
  construction of, 239–49
  design process of, 236–37
  design style and theme of, 237–39
  eighth hole at, 245
  eleventh hole at, 246
  environmental obstacles to, 231–35
  fourteenth hole at, 239, 248
  ninth hole at, 239, 244
  prior to construction, 232–35
  seventeenth hole at, 248
  sixth hole at, 245
  tenth hole at, 239–41
  thirteenth hole at, 247, 249
  twelfth hole at, 247

St. Andrews, Old Course at, xvi, 14–29, 62–63, 206, 243
  British Opens at, 14–15, 21–22, 25, 101
  and classic course designs, 128–30
  eighteenth hole at, 15, 19–20, 24, 32
  eleventh (Eden) hole at, 24, 26, 63
  evolution of, 16–19, 22, 31–32, 101
  and humor, 63, 66, 72
  and master architects, 154, 157, 159, 161
  routing of, 23–24, 31, 130
  and schools of design, 31–32, 36, 47, 50, 103
  seventeenth (Road) hole at, 15–16, 24, 63, 66, 87, 92, 100–105, 179, 182–83
  sixteenth hole at, 28
  twelfth hole at, 27
  unpredictability and irregularity of, 25
  Valley of Sin at, 19–20, 24
Sand Hills, 55–56, 204, 260–61
  eighth hole at, 265
  hazards at, 266–67
  seventeenth hole at, 267
San Francisco Golf Club, 164–65

schools of design, 29–59
  and classic course designs, 117, 125,
    133
  and course management, 30, 38, 49,
    175–77, 184
  evolution of, 46–58
  framing, *see* framing school
  freeway, 41–43, 53–55
  in future, 45, 58
  and great holes, 91–92, 103, 106
  heroic, 39–41, 52–53, 117
  and humor, 59, 66
  natural, *see* naturalness, natural school
  penal, *see* penal school
  strategic, 36–39, 41, 43, 50–52, 57, 92
  and temptation, 76, 83–84
Scioto, 160, 195
scores, xiv, 5
  classic course designs and, 114, 122,
    139
  course management and, 173–75,
    178–80
  course setups and, 265
  future and, 283
  great holes and, 104–6
  humor and, 61–63, 66
  maintenance and, 216
  and schools of design, 52–53
  temptation and, 76
  training your design eye and, 189
  see also pars; stroke play
Seinfeld, 269
Shawnee Country Club, 164
Sherwood Country Club, 61, 71–72
Shinnecock Hills, 39, 204
signature designs, definitiion of, 205
signature holes, definition of, 204–5
Simpson, Sir Walter, 5, 178, 186–87
Simpson, Tom, 1, 13, 88, 147, 172, 195
  and schools of design, 38, 46, 48
Snead, Sam, 15, 52, 62, 67
Somerset Hills Golf Club, 164–66
Soul of Golf, The (Vaille), xix, 186
Spirit of St. Andrews, The (MacKenzie),
    62–63, 154, 157
stimpmeters, 221–22
strategic school, 36–39, 41, 43, 50–52,
    57, 92
strategies, 4–6, 11–13, 258
  classic course designs and, 114, 117,
    120–21, 125, 127, 130–33, 139–43
  course management and, 173, 176–78,
    183, 185
  in creating your own holes, 252–55
  daydreaming and, 197, 199
  in future, 276–77, 281–84
  great holes and, 88–89, 92–98,
    100–104, 106–8

humor and, 64–65, 67–69
  maintenance and, 215–16, 220, 227
  master architects and, 163, 169, 171
  and Old Course at St. Andrews,
    19–21
  Rustic Canyon and, 237, 239, 249
  stymie and, 262–63
  temptation and, 82
  training your design eye and, 189,
    191–94
stroke play, 263, 268
  humor and, 61–63
  see also scores
stymie, 259, 262–63

Talking Stick North, 181
Tallgrass Golf Club, 174
Taylor, J. H., 35, 48, 100
tees, tee locations, tee markers, 261,
    264–67, 270
  course setups and, 264–66
  in creating your own holes, 256–57
  in future, 282
  maintenance and, 228
  Rustic Canyon and, 240–42, 247–48
Thomas, George C., Jr., 11, 38, 115,
    147, 190, 193, 239, 243, 249
  course management and, 173–76
  future and, 280–83
  great holes and, 96–97, 100
  humor and, 61, 67–69
  temptation and, 176
Thompson, Stanley, 38–39
Thomson, Peter, 22
Tillinghast, Albert Warren, 10, 18, 38,
    53, 115, 198, 269
  career summary of, 163–64
  classic course designs and, 137,
    139–41, 143–44
  on great holes, 89
  humor and, 70, 164, 171
  maintenance and, 219
  mastery of, 145, 147, 153, 163–67,
    171
  notable designs of, 164–66
  and schools of design, 50
  on temptation, 76
TPC at Sawgrass, 43, 54, 168
  fourteenth hole at, 170
  Players Championship at, 177
  seventeenth hole at, xvi
training your design eye, 186–96
  areas of focus for, 189–94
Travis, Walter, 115
Trevino, Lee, 41, 223

Vaille, P. A., xix, 186
vitality, 195

Wagner, Jim, 236–40, 242–44
Watson, Tom, 21, 41
Way of Golf, The (Brown), 9, 228
weather:
  course management and, 183–84
  course setups and, 265–66
  maintenance and, 212–14
  Rustic Canyon and, 243
  training your design eye and, 187, 192
  see also wind
wedge shots, 74, 216
  great holes and, 98–99, 101
Weiskopf, Tom, 41, 150, 197, 267
Wethered, H. N., 13, 88, 172
Whigham, H. J., 85, 128
Wilson, Dick, 39–41, 52
Wilson, Hugh, 115

wind, 228
  Augusta National and, 182
  course management and, 182–83
  great holes and, 98, 106, 109, 182
  at Old Course at St. Andrews, 21, 24
  Rustic Canyon and, 232
  temptation and, 77
  training your design eye and, 187
Wind, Herbert Warren, 9, 77–78
Winged Foot Golf Club, 164–65, 275
Wooden, John, 274
Woods, Tiger, 262
  course management of, 172, 183
  great holes and, 98
  on Old Course at St. Andrews, 22
world– or regional–traveler architects,
    148–52